AF583687

THE NEW
PLATFORM PAPERS

The Arts and Soft Diplomacy

Discovering How to be Australian

VOLUME 3
December 2023

Julian Meyrick
GENERAL EDITOR

CURRENCY
HOUSE

A snail may put his horns out

THOMAS SPENCE (1750–1814) was an English radical who campaigned against private ownership of land. He argued instead for a system of democratic parishes. He was also a passionate believer in equality between the sexes. He was particularly active in the 1790s when he produced a radical magazine, *Pig Meat, or Lessons for the Swinish Multitude* from his book shop in High Holborn, London. He also produced a series of tokens, many of which carry radical messages. Some of these were overt—one bore an image of William Pitt the Younger's head stuck on a maypole surrounded by dancing revellers. Others, however, were more subtle. He was fond of combining animals with political slogans. 'A Snail May Put His Horns Out' was a reminder that even the most powerless have the ability to effect change through resistance.

Contents

Illustrations

plates section

Julian Meyrick , General Editor

Julian Meyrick is a leading Australian theatre director and Professor of Creative Arts at Griffith University. His research focuses on the problem of value and evaluation processes in arts and culture.

Harriet Parsons, Director

Harriet Parsons took over the directorship of Currency House from her mother, Katharine Brisbane, in 2021. She is a contemporary artist and independent researcher specialising in the intellectual history of artistic practice.

Katharine Brisbane, Patron

Katharine Brisbane was the national theatre critic of the *Australian* from 1967 to 1974, a time of radical change. In 1971 she co-founded Currency Press, Australia's leading performing arts publisher, with her late husband, Dr Philip Parsons. Upon her retirement in 2001, she founded Currency House Inc., a not-for-profit association for promoting the value of the performing arts and expanding its discourse in public life.

Stephen Sewell, Authors Group

Stephen Sewell is the founding convenor of the Currency House Authors Group, a discussion group for the authors of Platform Papers, their associates and friends of Currency House. He is one of Australia's most celebrated writers for theatre and film, a former chair of the Australian National Playwrights Centre and was the Head of Writing for Performance at NIDA for eight years.

*

The history of Thomas Spence was kindly provided by Professor Hamish Maxwell-Stewart.

Thanks

As ever, we are grateful to our donors for their continuing support:

Major Donor

Currency Press

Annual Donors (3 years)

Katharine Brisbane, AM
Elizabeth Butcher, AM
Penny Chapman
Sally Crawford
Wayne Harrison, AM
Margaret Leask
Harriet Parsons
Maisy Stapleton
Caroline Verge
Rachel Ward, AM and
Bryan Brown, AM
Kim Williams, AM

2023 Donors

Gil Appleton
Marilyn Christiansen

And the many small donors who have supported our work throughout the year.

Special thanks to Bryan Brown and Alison Carroll for donating their work. We also thank Currency Press and the many friends who have kindly shared their advice and expertise.

Foreword

Harriet Parsons
Wurundgeri country

This year is quite a special one for me, because it is the last in a three-year plan I envisaged at the beginning of my tenure as the Director of Currency House, to review our work over the past two decades and shape a plan for the future.

My mother, Katharine Brisbane, started Currency House in 2001 as a not-for-profit organisation to promote debate in the performing arts. Her contribution over her long lifetime has transformed the industry in Australia. As a theatre critic in the 1960s, she championed the New Wave of Australian playwriting. In 1971 she founded Currency Press with my father, Philip Parsons, and put those plays into print. As a result, Australian drama is now on the curriculum of every high school in Australia.

She retired from Currency Press in 2000, and, as the publisher of the not-for-profit Currency House, created Platform Papers. Platform Papers is the only publication where practitioners in the performing arts speak as the experts on their industry—and speak beyond their industry, about the wider interests of our national culture. She published 63 issues, including some of the most influential writing produced by the performing arts in this country. Currency House got the industry talking about what it does and why it matters.

In 2019 she retired for the second time. I took over as the Director of Currency House and launched the New Platform Papers. This year I want to thank all of you for the confidence you have shown in me over the past three years, by your continuing support. What you have contributed, whether it is by donating to our cause or volunteering or simply by contributing your ideas, has helped us to renew our mission in the most challenging of times. I especially want to thank the Editorial Committee, who carry the burden of our administration, including Martin Portus, who has been a stalwart supporter since our first meeting in 2001. He has tirelessly promoted the Papers, bringing these important issues to the attention of the public.

Julian Meyrick has also been a mainstay of our organisation, and he gallantly took on the role of General Editor of the New Platform Papers in 2021. In Volume 3 we are publishing more authors than ever before, and this collection bears his stamp. Julian unexpectedly had to leave us in 2023, before we could complete the three-year plan which we had hoped to see out together. I am enormously grateful to him. He has backed my vision for Currency House all the way—that includes supporting the new format for the New Platform Papers and the ideas behind them and establishing the annual Authors Convention.

The General Editor is a kind of mentoring role and the main relationship our authors have with us. It requires a certain personality—it needs vision, tact and sensitivity. These are all qualities that Julian possesses in spades.

Julian is succeeded in this role by Associate Professor Ian Maxwell from the Discipline of Theatre and Performance Studies at Sydney University. He has been on the editorial committee since I became Director and he has welcomed many of you at our events. He has been an endless source of support and good advice and I am delighted that he has accepted our invitation.

In 2024 we embark on our new program of publications that will draw on the lessons of the past three years to guide the editorial vision into the future. I urge you to continue your support, because there's nothing else like us for performing arts practitioners in Australia.

Season's Greetings

Dear Friends,

Last year ended on a high, with big ideas and widespread reforms promised by a brand-new government. Pre-eminent among them was the referendum on an Aboriginal Voice to Parliament, and, for us in the arts, a new national cultural policy. In 2023 the government has set about delivering on these promises.

For some, the national cultural policy, *Revive*, has been a disappointment, hurriedly put together with little to offer that is new, but for others, the jury is still out. At the time of writing, the referendum is still two weeks away and that too is uncertain. The clarity of the Uluru Statement From the Heart's simple message has become confused in a fractious campaign and from an early majority in the polls, it now seems likely that the 'no' campaign will carry the day. And there are other practical challenges to contend with as well: rising interest rates and energy prices, a labour shortage and a housing crisis—and now we are about to enter the bushfire season.

The honeymoon is over, but this government is facing challenges unlike any before it. Others may have dealt with financial crisis, natural disaster, pandemic and war, but never at the same time. Against this backdrop of looming disaster, progress may seem slow, but public attitudes are transformed from what they were even five years ago. It is no longer a question of whether change is coming, but if it is coming fast enough.

Government and the community, business and industry, are all on a steep learning curve: we take the bushfire season seriously now; we understand the local impacts of global wars; and we are starting to recognise how the human decisions made by governments around the world, including our own, shape the future for us all.

Our most daunting challenge is resisting the temptation to become a divided society. The past decade has seen the social norms of Western countries transformed by impassioned movements that started with a hashtag: MeToo. These movements have brought about outstanding reforms, but they have also taken their toll on the complainants; and as the causes have multiplied, from Extinction Rebellion to the anti-vaxxers, their objectives have become less clear.

Protest is cathartic, but forced reform causes a rift in society that has to be healed. At present, the mechanism for coming together again is missing from our debate. As you read this, the referendum has either succeeded or failed, but the message of the Uluru Statement from the Heart remains, and there are lessons to be learned from Makarrata: 'coming together after a struggle'. Our greatest challenge at present is neither political nor economic or technological. If we are to meet the challenges ahead, we must learn to work together despite our differences.

Wishing you all a peaceful holiday season and every good prospect for 2024 from Gadigal country,

The Editorial Committee:

Ian Maxwell, General Editor
Katharine Brisbane
Thomas De Angelis
Amanda Morris
Brian Obiri-Asare
Harriet Parsons
Martin Portus
Stephen Sewell and
Linden Wilkinson.

Note to the reader

Since the talks and essays in this volume were commissioned the Australia Council for the Arts has changed its name to Creative Australia.

Introduction: Acting Australian

Harriet Parsons
Wurundjeri country

Over twenty-two years, Currency House has established itself as the voice of practitioners in the performing arts and the home of debate on Australian culture. This debate has never been more important. We are living through extraordinary times, and extraordinary times are an opportunity for extraordinary change but if we are to seize this opportunity, we need to up our game.

Since I was a child, discussion in the arts community has been about two things: how to get more funding versus how to sell more tickets. These arguments—and they are arguments now, no longer debates—have become so deeply entrenched that, like the frog in the well, we have forgotten there is a world beyond. The conversation needs to be wider and creative practitioners and arts workers need to think more broadly about their role in society; but first we need to develop a much better understanding of what it is the arts contribute.

The Currency House Authors Convention was created in 2021, to help bring about this change, by putting creative practitioners in conversation with other thinkers to talk about the major issues that affect not just the arts but the character of our culture as a whole. The Convention has become an annual event and for the last three years it has set the theme for each volume of the New Platform Papers. These first three volumes in the series will become our future central point of reference.

2021: *What Future for the Arts in a post-Pandemic World?*

The theme of our first Convention was 'imagination in economics'. In 2021, the pandemic was at its height and we were all in lockdown. The global crisis was turning economics on its head and, probably for the first time since the Second World War, economists were wondering if we needed government more than business.

Those who advocated for dumping the 'deficit myth' and pouring money into social security were far from radicals. Some were former government advisers. Ross Garnaut's book, *Reset*, even called for the unthinkable: a universal basic income. But they were having a hard time persuading the politicians to give up on austerity. The metaphor that had served them so well—the national household that 'has to live within its means'—had gained such a strong hold on the public imagination that even those who were persuaded were at a loss as to how to change it.

The Convention was about this rhetoric: the metaphor that can be instantly pictured, the smart phrase that trips off the tongue, and makes a bad idea seem irresistibly attractive. As a discipline, modern economics started life, not in mathematics or accounting, but satire. Economic theories are simply the speculations of economists about how people behave, and we invited satirist Jonathan Biggins and economist John Quiggin to discuss the poem where it all began: Bernard Mandeville's *The Fable of the Bees*, first published in 1705.

The Fable of the Bees is the story of a beehive in which all the bees pursue their own self-interest. Their economy flourishes, but as the rich get richer and the poor get poorer their society falls into moral decay. The world has been seriously experimenting with Mandeville's scenario since Milton Friedman won the Nobel Prize for Economics in 1976. He and his peers turned 'the pursuit of self-interest' into a mantra and Mandeville's prediction proved uncannily accurate: you may recall the royal commission into the banking industry in 2019, which revealed that AMP was selling life insurance to the dead. Not even Mandeville thought of that one.[1]

It was Adam Smith who developed Mandeville's principle into the most powerful metaphor of modern economics—the 'invisible hand of the market'—but even he had warned against the seductive power of such 'imaginary machines'.[2] What Friedman failed to take into account when he proposed throwing off the regulating hand of government was the countervailing forces of reputation and self-respect in Smith's moral philosophy, which prevent society from degenerating by prompting the self-interested individual to ask, What will people think of me? and Will I be able to sleep at night?

The lockdowns in 2021 produced something that economists could hardly have dared imagine: a natural experiment that shut down the market economy. The temptation for governments around the world was to cut their liabilities and allow the weak to fail. In Australia, the weak were the itinerant workers of the 'gig economy': artists, international students and others whose jobs had been casualised. Unexpectedly, it turned out, they were the ones who were 'essential'. The Latin root of 'liability', *ligo*, means 'to bind or tie' and it was the security guards, cleaners, food delivery riders and aged care workers, and the artists who kept us entertained, that held society together through the crisis. Instead of a battle for survival of the fittest, the pandemic showed what people are capable of when they are allowed to act like a society. Panic over the national debt has since ebbed away and, in time, a new truism may succeed in supplanting the national household in our daily rhetoric: 'When the government is in surplus, the community is in deficit.'[3]

2022: *From the Heart: The Voice, the Arts and Australian Identity*

Australian culture suffers from a dilemma that no amount of economic development can resolve. It relates to land ownership, but not the ownership of private property. National cultures are not generated by commercial transactions, they are produced by history: the relationships that grow up between people and places over time, and most importantly, the story that is told of why they are entitled to be there.

The right of the first discoverers to absolute possession of their country as their property, was set down in law by Hugo Grotius in 1609:

> Equally shameless is it to claim for oneself by right of discovery what is held by another, even though the occupant may be wicked, may hold wrong views about God, or may be dull of wit. For discovery applies to those things which belong to no one.[4]

Interestingly enough, James Cook, who must have been well aware of this founding principle of modern international law, claimed first *European* discovery when he took possession of New South Wales in 1770—but that's another story.

These original property rights as defined by Grotius are the source of the heritable power of sovereignty in Western culture. The creation of 'settler sovereignty' in the nineteenth-century, a 'uniquely destructive' legal innovation that violated its own founding principle, has produced a crisis in national confidence in Australia that has never entirely dissipated.[5] We no longer speak of 'the cultural cringe', which was replaced by a brash nationalism in the bicentennial year of 1988, but that has been tempered by a more thoughtful appreciation of the moral complexity of our position as Aboriginal culture has come to occupy an increasingly central place in Australian identity.

Traditionally, the sovereign has only three explicit rights with respect to the parliament. These rights are not defined in our constitution, but became part of the unwritten constitution of England when they were put into words by Walter Bagehot in 1865:

> The Sovereign has, under a constitutional monarchy such as ours, three rights—
>
> the right to be consulted,
> the right to encourage,
> the right to warn.[6]

In other words, the sovereign has the right to a voice to parliament. In his victory speech at the last election, the prime minister, Anthony Albanese, promised Australians a referendum on an Aboriginal Voice to Parliament and, in a second promise to the arts community, a national cultural policy. Presciently Jo Caust, the author of our first commissioned long essay, had already connected these two ideas in her Paper, *Arts, Culture and Country*. She asks whether it would be possible to follow the example set by First Nations, and replace productivity with the values of cultural custodianship as the measure of artistic success in Australian arts policy. Our First Nations keynote speakers at the July Convention—constitutional lawyer Eddie Synot, artist Sally Scales and actor and director Rachael Maza—discussed how the Voice would change Australian culture, and what it would mean for the arts; and in two additional contributions, Tyson Yunkaporta and Noel Pearson explored other dimensions of the national implications in detail.

Key to the question was what the Voice would look like in practice. In Britain, it takes the form of a private meeting. The late Queen famously met with every British prime minister from Winston Churchill to Liz Truss, in a weekly private audience. Harold Macmillan's recollection of these meetings has been echoed by many others. The Queen was a great support to him as prime minister, he explained, 'because she is the one person you can talk to'.[7]

These regular meetings with the Queen have been valued by British prime ministers for her discretion and long experience. In Australia, the Queen, and now the King, is widely regarded as an anachronism and the role receives little attention—until things go wrong. The sacking of the Whitlam government by the Queen's representative in 1975 caused a constitutional crisis. A similar crisis erupted last year on a smaller scale, when it emerged that during the pandemic the prime minister, Scott Morrison, had been secretly sworn into five ministries. The Governor-General, David Hurley, had no choice but to sign the 'administrative instrument', but, as one expert on constitutional law noted, 'the governor-general does have the ability to ask for further information, or give advice to the government'.[8] On this occasion, rather than over-reaching, the governor-general was accused of failing to exert his authority and advise the prime minister against such action.

As a mechanism of democratic government, the Voice to Parliament works in Britain because it is tightly bound by protocols. It is this dimension of government that has been neglected here. As Eddie Synot explained to the Convention, in crises such as the one caused by Morrison, it is these informal standards and practices that protect democracy as much as the law. 'Our Westminster parliamentary system has conventions of transparency and ministerial responsibility that protect its integrity and by ignoring them and acting on his own authority, he has undermined our democracy.'[9]

At the time of writing, the referendum on an Aboriginal Voice to the Australian Parliament is still weeks away. As an expression of sovereignty, this Voice has the potential to carry enormous weight. Its advisory power may seem amorphous and insubstantial, and in this case, it would be limited to issues affecting Aboriginal people only, but its influence would likely carry much further. Sovereignty has the responsibility of cultural custodianship: maintaining languages, customs, history and heritage. As Australians, every time we listen to the Welcome to Country, we are implicitly acknowledging the importance of Aboriginal custodianship, not just to Aboriginal people, but for maintaining the integrity of Australian culture as a whole.

In Britain, the sovereign receives the Sovereign Grant, much of which devolves to the arts. It is used for ceremonies and protocols that employ traditional trades and skills as well as for commissioning new works. Whatever the result of the referendum in Australia, it is imperative that we, as a colonial nation without a treaty, start taking Australian sovereignty seriously. If the referendum on the Voice to Parliament succeeds, it could produce a uniquely Australian form of democracy.

2023: *The Arts and Soft Diplomacy: Discovering How to be Australian*

In the current volume we ask how to apply these conclusions to the way we conduct ourselves on the international stage. Sandy George's Paper, *Nobody Talks About Australianness on Our Screens*, was commissioned in 2022 and held over for this volume. The writing coincided with an industrial dispute over the tax offset for offshore film production. The proposal to reduce the offset for Australian production, while simultaneously raising it for offshore producers, was, as Bryan Brown told his audience at the National Press Club in July 'Robbing *Crocodile Dundee* to pay for *Forest Gump*'. Brown's address is published here alongside George's essay.

The problem of 'Australianness' on our screens is, however, more complex than the rate of the offset. As George explains, Australian production doesn't have to look Australian to be eligible for government subsidy. Sometimes being made by Australians is enough:

> Australia regularly creates outstanding film and television drama that deeply connects with Australians who recognise it as *their* film and television. Stories are thrashed out in writers' rooms and brought to life on set, as they've always been, but changes to the viewing environment, business pressures and growing weaknesses in the legislative scaffolding, that ensure Australian stories exist on our screens at all, are having a negative impact. Less Australian drama is being made than in the past, it's less accessible, uncertainty is swirling around its future, and some of it feels a lot less Australian.

But what does 'Australianness' look like these days anyway? For the next issue, *Diversity and Inclusion: Building the Good Life in Australia*, performance maker Jeremy Neideck and arts consultant Morwenna Collett approached the question from a different direction, by looking at 'the good life'.

For the first essay in this issue, 'Queer(y)ing the Australian Way of Life', Jeremy Neideck takes as his point of departure a speech that was delivered by the former prime minister, Tony Abbott, at the opening of the Centre for the Australian Way of Life in 2003. Neideck argues that Abbott has manufactured nostalgia for a non-existent past in order to create a cis-straight fantasy in the present of what it means to be Australian. Confronted with this narrow fantasy, queer artists are embarking upon a process of 'nationhood as creative practice', to construct their own ideal of 'the good life' in Australia, through the practices of their daily lives as parents, friends, lovers and creative practitioners.

In 'More Risk, More Play: Creating an Inclusive Culture', Morwenna Collett asks what Australia would look like if we genuinely embraced diversity 'in all its glory'. Whether through illness, accident, old age or the social barriers that say we just don't belong, all of us will have 'accessibility issues' some time. Access is the key to living the 'the good life' in Australia because it is the embodiment of social belonging.

The speakers at the Convention addressed the role of artistic practice as a tool of soft diplomacy in international relations. Soft diplomacy is a regular remit of the arts. Peter Cooke, as one of our most distinguished theatre designers, a teacher and former administrative head at both NIDA and the Carnegie Mellon University's School of Drama, and a visiting professor at the National School of Drama in India since 2004, has nurtured countless international relationships between artists and institutions, through the creative process of producing drama together. However, the support from government that would allow Australia to build on these relationships is regularly swept away with a change of policy or politics.

Such close ties that transcend the interests of trade are badly needed in our region right now. Last year the Foreign Minister, Penny Wong, flew to the Solomon Islands on an urgent mission after the Prime Minister, Manasseh Sogavare, signed a security pact with China. Australia has been a major player in Pacific security since 2003. We led the Regional Assistance Mission to Solomon Islands known as RAMSI until 2017, and continue to provide training to police across the Pacific, support for their military forces through the Defence Cooperation Program, and patrol boats to Pacific Island Forum countries through the Pacific Maritime Security Program. However, Australian's colonial past does not recommend us in the region, and others, unencumbered by such history, are able to compete with our muscle and charity. In recent years, Beijing, intent on extending its Belt and Road initiative into the Pacific, has also started providing security-related training and equipment to countries such as Vanuatu, Samoa, Cook Islands and Papua New Guinea, albeit at a much lower level.[10]

Closer ties created through cultural exchange could produce the depth of mutual understanding that Australia needs to justify its place as the preferred partner of Pacific nations.[11] The infrastructure to support such exchanges could be provided by an international cultural agency—an 'Australian Goethe-Institut'. In 2012, two veterans of arts advocacy in Asia, Alison Carroll and Carrillo Gantner, proposed a plan which was published in Platform Papers. *Finding a Place on the Asian Stage* is reprinted in this volume, and Carroll revisited it in her keynote speech to the Convention while Gantner offered further comments in the closing discussion.

First Nations diplomacy has a much longer history in our region than the diplomacy of the Australian Government. Last year we published 'The Trouble with this Canoe' by Tyson Yunkaporta in which he describes how, in First Nations diplomacy, sovereignty and trade come together to produce growth in a give-and-give economy:

> international trade between us and the lands to the north of our continent was different. Ours was a give-and-give economy, not give-and-take, as those who believe in ancient free-market instincts of reciprocity like to tell us. There was no invisible hand entity guiding us, only the Law of the land. In embassy and trade, we shared

> this give-and-give relation across the sea to the north. This relation enriched us, not with growth, but with increase. Our increase-based economy measured wealth in the multiplication of connections rather than the hoarding of resources and credit.[12]

A First Nations diplomat, Tupaia, was also present on Captain Cook's *Endeavour*. Tupaia was perhaps the most powerful political figure of the eighteenth-century South Pacific and he joined Cook's ship in Tahiti. In her keynote speech to the Convention, internationally renowned Māori artist, Lisa Reihana, discussed her large-scale video, *in Pursuit of Venus [infected]* which reimagines the meeting between Cook and Tupaia. *Tupaia's Sketchbook* has given us the iconic images of first European contact and Reihana sees herself, as a contemporary artist travelling the world, as following in his footsteps.

An Indigenous Foreign Policy was another promise of the Labor Party's election campaign. James Blackwell, an expert in Indigenous diplomacy at the Australian National University, wrote about the potential he saw:

> First Nations peoples have so much to offer the world of foreign policy, diplomacy, and international relations. Here on this continent we have been engaged in our own forms of inter-polity relations for tens of thousands of years, including with peoples beyond Australia; all based on our own unique law, culture, history. We operate from a fundamentally different place on political ordering and the role of individuals versus the state, and have our own unique ways of knowing and being.
>
> These approaches can, and do, co-exist with traditional Western understandings of foreign policy and international relations, and

> the advantages of our relational, interconnected ways of being are manifold. On issues of climate, human rights, land use, and our engagement with our allies, First Nations peoples and perspectives have the potential to provide great insight.[13]

The arts have the potential to create broad networks and long-term relationships in our region, but at present, the relationship with government is at a low ebb. Create Australia (previously the Australia Council), has just gone through its seventh international director in seven years; and the Department of Foreign Affairs and Trade (DFAT) is reluctant to engage. In Gantner's view, the turning point came when the Department of Foreign Affairs became the Department of Foreign Affairs and Trade:

> The downside is that DFAT has become a transactional department and, in my observation, what we have lost are the great thinkers and analysts. Foreign Affairs used to be full of thinkers. You look at them now and these people are mostly dead or retired: people like John McCarthy and the senior and serious Australian diplomats, who reflected on relationships and understood the cultures of the countries with which they were dealing. Now they are told to go forth and sell things and that has been, I think, a source of national weakness. It might be good for the economy to have trade dominate our international relations, but it has not strengthened our understanding or appreciation of the countries around us or the world in which we must make our home.

From 2024 the discussions we have initiated between practitioners and other thinkers over the past three years, on economic value, culture and diplomacy in our region, will begin to inform our future policies and activities. With this body of work as our reference, we aspire to support new writers who will take debate in the arts beyond the stale arguments of the past, to nurture those ties that will enrich our country by their increase in a give-and-give economy, as we set about discovering how to be Australian in a rapidly unfolding new world.

Endnotes

1. *Royal Commission into Misconduct in the Banking, Superannuation and Financial Services Industry, Final Report.* Commonwealth of Australia, 2019. Vol. 1 p. 148. royalcommission.gov.au.
2. Adam Smith, 'The Principles which Lead and Direct Philosophical Enquiries; Illustrated by the History of Astronomy' in *Essays on Philosophical Subjects.* Edited by W. P. D. Wightman, J. C. Bryce and I. S. Ross. Oxford: Clarendon Press. 1980, p. 66. First published in 1795.
3. Unreferenced quotation by Jane Caro on *The Drum*, ABC TV, June 28, 2023 at 7mins 23 secs into the video. abc.net.au.
4. Hugo Grotius, *De Jure Belli ac Pacis Libri Tres.* Vol. 2, book 2, 1625, p. 187. Quoted in Merete Borch, 'Rethinking the Origins of Terra Nullius.' *Australian Historical Studies*, Vol. 32, no. 117, 2008, p. 233. doi: 10.1080 /10314610108596162.
5. Lisa Ford, *Settler Sovereignty: Jurisdiction and Indigenous People in America and Australia, 1788–1836.* Harvard University Press, 2011, p. 2.
6. Walter Bagehot, *The English Constitution.* Project Gutenberg, Ch. 3, 'The Monarchy', I. First serialised in the *Fortnightly Review* in 1865 and published in book form in 1867. gutenberg.org.
7. Alistair Horne, *Macmillan 1957–1986: volume 2 of the official biography.*

Macmillan, 1989, p. 4. Quoted in Michelle Clement, 'The Queen and her Prime Ministers', Gov.UK, History of government, blog. history.blog.gov.uk.

8. Josh Butler, 'Why didn't the governor general push back against Scott Morrison's secret ministries?' *Guardian*, August 18, 2022. theguardian.com.
9. Eddie Synot, 'The Meaningful Expression of Indigenous Sovereignty Through the Uluru Statement from the Heart', The New Platform Papers, Vol. 2, *From the Heart: The Voice, the Arts and Australian Identity.* Currency House, 2022, p. 98.
10. 'Unpacking the Solomon Islands' security pact with China'. Australian National University, 'News'. May 6, 2022. anu.edu.au.
11. Lice Movono and Kate Lyons, 'Solomon Islands PM rules out China military base and says Australia is "security partner of choice"'. *Guardian*, July 14, 2022. theguardian.com.
12. Tyson Yunkaporta, 'The Trouble with this Canoe'. The New Platform Papers, Vol. 2, *From the Heart: The Voice, the Arts and Australian Identity.* Currency House, 2022, p. 51.
13. James Blackwell, 'Labor's Indigenous foreign policy looks like real, substantive change'. *Canberra Times*, May 28, 2022. canberratimes.com.au.

Nobody Talks About Australianness on Our Screens

SANDY GEORGE

No. 4

First published online
June 2022

Acknowledgements

Thank you to Currency House for giving me the time to think long and hard about Australian film and television drama. Thank you too to Professor Julian Meyrick, who helped me through the research and writing with encouragement, patience and great guidance, and Harriet Parsons, for her suggestions and edits. Thanks also to Martin Portus, for his support and for getting the draft Paper out to the media, and to the Sydney Film Festival for hosting the launch and discussion.

Thanks to Glenda Ballantyne, Sue Brooks, Paul Bugeja, Fiona Cameron, Sally Caplan, Kim Dalton, Dorothy Ford, Julie Hoare, Mat Kesting, Sue Maslin, Nicki Roller, Lyndall Smythe and Alison Tilson, all of whom helped greatly from the outset. The New Platform Papers begin life as a public first draft with an open invitation to provide feedback, and then more pondering is done for the final version. Thanks to Su Armstrong, Helen Bowden, Antony Ginnane, Ben Grant, Lawrence Johnston, Patrick May, Morgan Richards, Brian Rosen, Craig Rossiter, Kelly Vincent and Alek Voninski, who all went above and beyond in the feedback phase.

Thanks to Colum McCann. The style of his fabulous book *Apeirogon* was inspiring when it seemed like it would be too hard to construct one long piece of prose about such a messy, complex industry. Thanks to Waleed Aly and Scott Stephens from the ABC Radio

National program *The Minefield.* That show helped in the quest to make the Paper understandable and entertaining.

Special thanks to Emile Sherman and Tony Ayres, two very successful practitioners, who took part in interviews for this Paper—see the Appendix. Both care about the industry in ways that go beyond self-interest and their involvement was a blessing. Three women were also invited to participate in this way but declined.

Abbreviations

ACMA	Australian Communications and Media Authority
ATO	Australian Taxation Office
AWG	Australian Writers' Guild
BVOD	Broadcast video on demand
FTA	Free to air
PDV Offset	Post, Digital and Visual Effects Offset
PO	Producer Offset
SAC test	Significant Australian Content test
SPA	Screen Producers Association
SVOD	Subscription video on demand. Also known as streamers

Introduction

The simple act of watching film and television equates to very big business for some. In 2019, prior to the pandemic blowing up life as we knew it, nearly $1.3 billion was spent on cinema tickets in Australia.[1] Revenue flowing from this country to subscription video on demand services (SVODs), also known as streamers, is estimated at $2.5 billion a year and it is predicted to rise to $3.6 billion in 2025.[2]

While the public is spending up big on the pleasure of watching, not much Australian content is available to them. The amount of content on SVODs ranges from less than 1% on Apple TV+, Britbox, Disney+ and Mubi, to 9.2% on Paramount+. In the case of Netflix, the most popular service in Australia, it is 3.3%.[3] Of the 754 films released in cinemas in 2019, 205 (27%) were from the US and 59 (8%) were Australian.[4]

SVODs closely guard their data on audience behaviour, including how much Australian content is being consumed, but the cinema business is transparent by comparison. The ten most popular Australian films in 2019, led by *Ride Like a Girl*, together attracted nearly $37 million in ticket sales,[5] compared with nearly $436 million taken by the ten most popular films overall, led by *Avengers: Endgame*.[6] The biggest hits were Hollywood films, although *Aquaman* was filmed mainly in Australia by director James Wan, who moved here from Malaysia when he was a boy.

In 2021 Hollywood films were held back around the world due to the COVID lockdowns because, with many cinemas closed, they couldn't do their commercial best. This helped features 'under Australian or shared creative control' attract 11.8% of all revenue from cinema tickets sold that year—the first double figures achieved since 1988.[7]

The actual making of film and television helps the economy tick along nicely, irrespective of whether the public watches the finished work or not. Looking at drama alone, a record $1.51 billion was spent on 97 Australian projects that went into production in the financial year 2021–22; alongside them, a further $777 million went into making 65 foreign projects.[8]

Drama, local and foreign (excluding online production), makes up about 30% of all of Australia's audio-visual expenditure. There are also reality programs, commercials, news and current affairs, and so on.[9]

All this is the context for this Paper, but I'm writing about something much more important than commercial value namely, the cultural value to local audiences of Australian long-form drama and how it's under threat. Australia regularly creates outstanding film and television drama that deeply connects with Australians who recognise it as *their* film and television. Stories are thrashed out in writers' rooms and brought to life on set, as they've always been, but changes to the viewing environment, business pressures and growing weaknesses in the legislative scaffolding that ensures Australian stories exist on our screens at all, are having a negative impact. Less Australian drama is made than in the past, it's less accessible, uncertainty is swirling around its future and some of it feels a lot less Australian. So, am I saying that cultural value is being eroded? Yes, slowly and surely and from many angles. That erosion is the elephant in the room. Ignoring it is especially disrespectful to the industry's key stakeholders: local viewers.

A tangle of reasons accounts for what's happening. Among them are the decades-long difficulties of getting Australian films into cinemas, difficulties hardly acknowledged, let alone addressed. Inside the home, Australians have turned away from free-to-air (FTA) television towards SVODs, which are unregulated, offer a vast array of choices and, in the main, are part of global conglomerates. The SVODs are fundamentally changing the nature of Australian drama and weakening the industry that makes it. Meanwhile, in Canberra, the policy objective behind the financial incentives to make Australian drama courtesy of the taxpayer, is no longer clear. All the while, the difference between Australian production with foreign elements and foreign production with Australian elements is getting harder to discern, and the evidence that economic value is taking precedence over cultural value grows. And on top of all this, the behaviour of the production industry itself is unhelpful.

While new technology now enables people to watch what they want, when they want, it is not being utilised to help Australians find home-grown drama, or share their love when they find stories that appeal to them. I get texts from shops where I've bought one item when they have a sale on. It's crazy that I can't sign up to a service that notifies me when a new Australian series premieres or a new local film opens.

Ultimately, I'm calling for Australian drama to be made more accessible; and on government, to be more transparent and take much more care to support productions that are meaningful to local audiences because they are imbued with the spirit of Australians and Australian life.

The industry and the new government that was elected on 21 May 2022 need to make a judgement call on whether the current system is delivering. While writing this Paper, I was bothered at first by how many questions it raises. Now I think that asking them is the point: it is a good thing in itself.

A short critical essay that engages with a field as wide as film and television drama, faces issues of scope as well as detail. Talking about the elephant in the room includes the additional challenge of getting the elephant to fit into the room in the first place. In what follows, I have adopted a style of making serial, multiple observations that throw light on different aspects of Australia's drama industry. Circling the elephant in this way has its hazards, but it affords the reader a holistic view and, hopefully, will help them understand the many pressures that are being exerted on cultural value—and the people who make film and television.

Early in the essay, I discuss what I mean by the term 'Australianness' and talk a little about the technological and viewing landscape of film and television production that has been significantly disrupted around the globe. It is a convoluted and rapidly changing narrative, and I aim only to give readers a sense of the issues involved, not to explain them in full.

Later I touch on financing and regulation. This is another complex story, and the same caveat applies. But some knowledge of costs, regulation, the different pots of money available, the number of partners involved in each production and how financing is changing, is necessary to appreciate why commerce and culture frequently clash in this business.

As part of the process of writing this essay, I asked practitioners Emile Sherman and Tony Ayres to think on a question and take part in an interview. The question was this: 'How can more and better film and TV with (on-screen) Australianness at its heart be made and seen?' They had not read my essay, so they couldn't comment on my views. Their edited responses are in the Appendix.

It is important to include the voice of practitioners because, without them, Australian drama wouldn't exist. As the quality and consistency of their work attests, Emile and Tony are among Australia's best. They have also got themselves into a position where they have more access to significant resources than your average Australian on-screen storyteller.

1

Let's talk about cultural value and 'Australianness'

Local cultural value = eat your vegetables

Nobody with Australian film and television drama in mind is enthusiastically shouting 'What do we want? Cultural value! When do we want it? NOW!' Especially not publicly. Not the people who pay for it, make it, or put it on screen. Remember being told as a child to 'eat your vegetables because they're good for you'? The term 'cultural value' has that tone. It's old-fashioned, uncool. It's also jingoistic and the production industry likes to think of itself as global. Taxpayer funding and government regulation underpin the creation of drama, and the previous government rarely used the term. They didn't put much thought into its meaning, nor into interrogating how it was best created or by whom. The way the production of film and TV is funded by the taxpayer in Australia is now fifteen years old. It's been changed and built upon, but not reviewed as a whole. The landscape has changed, and now there's even a national cultural policy, courtesy of the current government. It is time to step back and look at things afresh—but renovating that term could well be impossible.

Seeing ourselves on screen is part of life

As the title conveys, the 2016 report *Measuring the Cultural Value of Australia's Screen Sector* looked squarely at cultural value, putting it out of step with the norm. It was commissioned from the London-based consultancy Olsberg•SPI to provide a 'credible, comprehensive assessment' of the cultural value of predominantly, 'scripted fiction' in Australia, (the modern term for drama).[10] In the film and television production industry, a report on cultural value stands out in a sea of reports that focus on economic value.

Key to the report were 928 Australians who were asked to identify their three 'most culturally impactful' pieces of Australian content. The heavy hitters of the 271 productions mentioned were *Crocodile Dundee, Home and Away, Neighbours, The Castle, Mad Max, The Adventures of Priscilla, Queen of the Desert, Four Corners, Australia, Gallipoli, Q&A* and *Rabbit-Proof Fence.*[11] The list is diverse and all the dramas reek of Australia: accents, actors and the characters they play, behaviours, the setting and so on. Note how many are feature films and that none of them were then less than a dozen years old.

The 2020 options paper *Supporting Australian Stories on Our Screens* was put together by the Australian Communications and Media Authority (ACMA) in conjunction with Screen Australia at the request of the former Federal Government.

On the question of why Australian stories are necessary, the paper reads:

> Australian stories reflect who we are as a nation, to ourselves and to the world. These stories make sense of our past (*First Australians, Gallipoli, The Sapphires*), define ourselves in the present (*The Castle, Home and Away, Mystery Road, Offspring, Bluey*) and promote our people, our creativity and our country to the world (*Crocodile Dundee, Australia, Mad Max, Lion, Wentworth, McLeod's Daughters, Cleverman, Miss Fisher's Murder Mysteries*).[12]

It notes that cultural significance is not easily quantifiable but is highly recognisable.

Cinema operators always say that when an Australian film manages to tap into the zeitgeist it over-performs big time. When Australia is up on screen the sense of recognition and belonging sparks an intensity of feeling that drives this popularity, irrespective of whether the emotion that's being felt is a damn good belly laugh or a lump in the throat.

Some 'Australian stories' don't look and feel Australian

Australia's population is small, local drama is expensive to make and drama bought in from elsewhere is cheap. In essence, this is why Australia's long-form drama slate is dependent on regulation and taxpayer subsidies. All projects, except official international co-productions, must pass a significant Australian content (SAC) test to be eligible for these benefits. The test is spelled out in section 376–70 of the Income Tax Assessment Act 1997.[13] Subject matter, where the film is made, the nationality and place of residence of the people involved in the production, where production expenditure flows, and other criteria deemed relevant, are all taken into consideration.

What is never discussed is that Australian drama, as defined by industry and government under the SAC test, doesn't have to look or feel Australian. Some of it passes the test because Australians are making it and the money is being spent in Australia.

The director Baz Luhrmann's debut film *Strictly Ballroom* and the film he made about fifteen years later, *Australia*, radiate on-screen Australianness. But most of his films don't—think *Moulin Rouge!, Romeo + Juliet, The Great Gatsby* and the recently completed *Elvis*. All but *Romeo + Juliet* were filmed in Australia, with a long roll call of Australians on and off screen, buckets of international investment and a big slice of Australian taxpayer funding.

Three of the ten most popular Australian films shown in cinemas in 2021 had no on-screen Australianness, despite being classified as Australian by government: they were the action fantasy *Mortal Kombat* and two animations, *Maya the Bee: The Golden Orb* and *Peter Rabbit 2* (in the number one spot). The rest did: *The Dry, Penguin Bloom, High Ground, June Again, Buckley's Chance, Long Story Short* and the documentary *Girls Can't Surf*.[14]

Golden Orb was a co-production made under a formal arrangement between the Australian and German Governments, so it would not have had to pass the SAC test. Ditto the much heralded *The Power of the Dog*, a co-production with New Zealand. Official co-productions are eligible for local funds in both partner countries and benefit from regulation. Many don't have any on-screen Australianness. This is meant to even out across the co-production slate, but I've never heard of any formal check.

Some Australian movies are filmed entirely overseas without any Australian characters, including *Tanna*, which was nominated for an Oscar in 2017 for best foreign language film, and *You Won't Be Alone*, which was in competition at the 2022 Sydney Film Festival.

The eight-part Australian series *Clickbait*, a dark, fast-moving tale of kidnap, revenge and internet trickery set in Oakland in the US, was shot in Australia and had hardly a skerrick of Australianness on screen. Upon release in 2021, it hit the number one spot on Netflix in more than twenty countries.[15] This level of success from Australian creatives is exciting to see, as is their success in persuading Netflix to give them an eye-popping $52 million to make the show.[16]

Some filmmakers deliberately water down Australianness. The actor Anthony Hayes raised the budget for his second feature as a director, the dystopian *Gold*, on the strength of US actor Zac Efron. 'There are so many people after content, but at the same time you need to be a little less parochial in some aspects, hence the American accents and multilingual signs,' Hayes told the media.[17] Efron didn't have to adopt an accent but his Australian co-stars, Hayes and Susie Porter, did.

It's safe to assume that all the dramas just mentioned received federal funding from Australian taxpayers—all via tax legislation (which is subject to strict confidentiality rules), some with additional money from the agency Screen Australia. This Paper is not arguing that they shouldn't have been supported; it is arguing that there needs to be clarity about how and why certain Australian projects are backed and to what extent. Is it for industrial or cultural reasons? Is it for both? What is each pot of money there to achieve? Are certain projects supported because they make up shortfalls in the national slate? Most importantly, more regard needs to be given to dramas with on-screen 'Australianness'. The erosion of Australianness would be more noticeable if we had our own language or were more culturally dissimilar to the UK and the US.

Many filmmakers argue that stories made by Australian creators are inherently Australian, wherever they're set and whatever they're about. Australian documentary makers, in particular, often say this when working abroad. That's never washed with me.

An us-and-them mentality is always just below the surface when the issue of foreign production in Australia comes up—at least it's clear that taxpayer funding goes into this kind of production because it's good for the economy. In contrast, what's going on within the sphere of so-called Australian content is confusing and rarely seriously discussed, and it should be. To be clear, when I describe something as Australian, it's because the Federal Government and its agencies deem it to be. My view is that the guidelines around what's Australian and what's not, needs to be stricter for the sake of audiences.

Drama is never true to real life

Real life has a lot of boring bits. Usually these are cut out of drama and more emotion, action and confrontation is added in. It makes it more compelling. It's why so much drama revolves around crime and the police. Most viewers will have seen hundreds of people die on screen, and possibly none in real life, before they die themselves.

Only 'Australianness' can generate cultural value

As already mentioned, feedback is sought on New Platform Papers before the final version is published. In the first public version of this essay, I was adamant that if Australia is not recognisable on the screen, drama is not delivering national cultural value. 'Australianness' doesn't guarantee cultural value, because drama also needs to connect with its audience, but it delivers the *potential* for it. I am still adamant on this point.

'Australianness' takes on endless forms because Australia itself is so diverse. The nature of a country flows from the nature of its people. And the tropes of genre—horror, thriller, sci-fi—don't have to affect whether something is loaded up with Australianness. Australian characters might be riding the highs and lows of a life grounded in realism in *Home and Away, The Dry, Deadloch* or *Mr Inbetween*; or hunting vampires in the eight-part series on AMC+, a US streaming service, *Firebite*, where Australia is baked into every frame: the leading characters, a father and daughter, and the gorgeousness of the desert at sunrise and sunset.

It's simple really, it just has to be *recognisable* and *authentic.*

Or is it so simple?

A shortcoming of the first version of this Paper was that it didn't consider how Australianness and cultural value could be measured, and it prompted academic Anna Potter to point me towards a paper she co-wrote with Amanda D Lotz.[18] They measure cultural specificity by locating individual dramas on a spectrum that has 'placeless' and 'place based' at either end, and 'placed' somewhere in the middle. In simple terms, a placeless drama has a generic setting, a placed drama might be set in a recognisable city but without much in the way of local nuance, and a place-based drama couldn't take place anywhere other than where it is set.

Imagine a series set on a boat with three characters of different nationalities. In Potter and Lotz's classification system, it's 'placeless'—as is the aforementioned *Gold*. *The Twelve*, a courtroom drama that won the miniseries category at the 2022 Australian Academy Cinema Television Arts (AACTA) Awards, would go in the 'placed' category: the characters are all clearly Australian but it was adapted from a Belgian show and could have been set anywhere. Australianness drips from every frame of the 2022 winner of the series category, *Mystery Road: Origin*, and it is 'place based'.

Can characters be classified as placeless, placed or place based as well? Maybe.

Many, of course, would recoil at the thought of governments defining cultural value, but someone has to set the rules around spending taxpayer money, right?

Including the word 'Australianness' in the title of this Paper helped attract attention and prompt discussion but, surprisingly, some read a very parochial meaning into the word, as though it expressed a yearning for 'the good old days' of red dirt and shearing sheds, and, as one reader said, battlers and unlikely heroes—*Muriel's Wedding* and *Strictly Ballroom*. Some referred to the 2021 Census results as a measure of Australia's rich diversity and railed against how this is not reflected in our storytelling. Agreed. Australian production is subject to mandates on diversity and inclusion, but they are applied very literally, and often only to the characters. They could be used to encourage stories that explore what's particularly interesting, funny, profound and unique about living in every pocket of Australian society—and if creatures as peculiar as kangaroos live in Australia, why not flaunt them, but be prepared for some eye-rolling.

Great work, full of Australianness, is being made. *Here Out West*, which opened the 2021 Sydney Film Festival, immediately springs to mind. The characters and what they go through in its overlapping stories, attest to the western suburbs of Sydney as one of the most culturally diverse regions of the nation. Many terrific Australian films have hardly been seen by the wider public, and this is one of them. The bone-dry antipodean humour of the Prime Video series *Deadloch*, and its depiction of a modern-day enclave of gay women taking over a country town, gladdens my heart with its Australianness. As does *Mr Inbetween*.

I'm naming the recent drama I love most. Its Australianness is entwined with the passion I feel for it. I hasten to add that other material will appeal more to others. It's why making a decent amount of drama of all shapes and sizes is a necessity.

For the record, one highly experienced veteran producer I won't name, fervently disagrees that cultural value is the primary reason the government supports the production of drama, saying there's always been a delicate balance between commerce and culture. It is true that the two are glued together because only a healthy industry can deliver drama. We agree, however, that cultural value is important—and it requires cultural specificity.

Australianness promotes tourism and enables soft diplomacy

Australianness is as crucial to the indirect economic value of Australian content as it is to its cultural value. In 2016, Deloitte Access Economics found that 144,000 visits by international tourists to Australia per year were prompted by Australian films and television. This translates into $704 million in expenditure. An estimated 85,000 additional people stayed an extra 1.7 nights on average in order to visit the locations where Australian films or television had been shot, adding $21 million.[19]

Governments often mention that local film and television serves as a tool of soft diplomacy internationally. Without Australianness this would not be possible.

Advocating for Australian content is not pushing it down throats

The 2020 options paper mentioned above states that the vast majority (76%) of surveyed Australians are in favour of government support to the sector.[20] Twelve per cent were opposed, the rest didn't know what they thought.[21] A 2021 survey for Telsyte found that about half of SVOD customers believed it was important to see SVOD content that had 'Australian stories, voices, culture and values'.[22] Deloitte's 2020 Media Consumer Survey noted that about a third of its respondents said that it was important to be able to access Australian movie content and Australian TV drama.[23] Screen Audience Research Australia found that 77% of Australian women aged 55+ were 'most likely to prefer to watch' Australian films at cinemas, compared with a third of 16 to 24-year-olds. However, it should be noted that the 13,729 people surveyed were patronising independent cinemas and were therefore more likely to be fans of Australian films than mainstream cinema types.[24] Frankly, there's no clear picture of how strong the Australian desire is to see its own drama, and it varies wildly between individuals anyway. That said, advocating for Australian content to be made more widely available is *not* about pushing it down people's throats; it's about making it available to those who are interested.

Perhaps international casting undermines Australianness, perhaps not

Convincing a well-known actor to sign onto a drama has a big impact on whether it gets the green light. Actors, including Australians, are like butterflies, flitting around the world, opting to work on projects, often in the US with big budgets, big audience-reach and big potential for exposure. There is also a long history of non-Australian actors in Australian drama. When I casually asked producer Sue Maslin whether casting the UK actor, Kate Winslet, in the hit feature *The Dressmaker* had undermined its Australianness, she was stumped; but later, she more or less said that it hadn't, because the actor 'nailed the accent'. Indeed, in 2022, an article in the *Guardian* described Winslet as 'the queen of Australian accents'.[25] The line between US and Australian drama is blurring. A good example of this is the Stan series *Wolf Like Me*, in which Australian Isla Fisher plays a North American, opposite a real American actor, Josh Gad. The series is classified as Australian, but the script calls for their characters to declare that they're in Australia—so clearly that one can only assume that the creative team thought that otherwise viewers would not know where it was set! North American themes and characters seem to be more prevalent right now in Australian drama.

2

Uncertainty reigns as the ground shifts under Aussie drama

The drama mother lode is no longer on the free-to-air channels

Television drama has always been subject to market failure because making it is expensive compared with other types of Australian programming, and it's cheaper to buy in drama from elsewhere.

For decades, the Australian drama mother lode was on the FTA channels—along with Australian eyeballs. The ABC met the obligations of its public service charter with drama, and successive federal governments, under the influence of lobbying, forced the commercial networks—Seven, Nine and Ten—to show it. It wasn't all bad for the networks though: drama rated well, attracted advertising dollars, and the taxpayer part-paid for it.

My, how times have changed. Explaining why drama has

waned on the FTAs is a long and complex story that encompasses changes associated with the arrival of digital technology and competition, rising production costs, shifts in viewer behaviour, and the relaxation of regulation. Some argue that the commercial FTAs brought it on themselves when they launched their digital channels (7plus, 9now, etc.)—or that they even orchestrated it.

According to the latest research by the Australian Bureau of Statistics (ABS), in 2021–22, Australian drama cost on average $1.28 million per hour to make—an increase of nearly one hundred per cent on the 2015–16 figure.[26] According to Screen Australia's *Drama Report* for 2021–22, the average cost per hour for a series or serial was $300,000. A miniseries is defined as 13 hours or less and the average cost per episode was $1.9 million.[27] Eight episodes is common for drama: that's a price tag of more than $15 million. ABS research into 2015–16 indicated that drama cost $645,700 per hour to make, compared with $91,900 per hour for light entertainment and $11,900 for news and current affairs.[28] More recent figures don't appear to be available, but the general point is that drama is a very expensive format—it takes a long time to finesse drama scripts, and a small army is needed on set to shoot it. It's no wonder that the amount of first-release Australian drama being broadcast is way less than for other genres.

Bridget Fair, CEO of Free TV Australia, said in 2021:

> Over the past decade, the cost per hour of producing drama has more than doubled. Audiences have increasingly demanded higher quality production across all viewing platforms and this has in some cases resulted in series with fewer hours but higher production values being commissioned.[29]

Australian drama remains dirt cheap to make compared to US drama. But, with a population of more than 330 million, the US can cover the cost of production, then sell the drama around the world at a fraction of what it cost to produce. The options paper *Supporting Australian Stories on Our Screens* reads:

> An Australian network can generally import a high-quality program for $100,000 to 300,000 per hour, while commissioning an equivalent Australian program may cost a broadcaster anywhere from $500,000 to more than $1 million per hour. Older foreign content can be imported for as little as $1,000 per hour.[30]

Note that an Australian network buys the right to show a drama for several years, and this helps producers raise the finance to make it. The full cost of production is met from a variety of sources.

In late 2020, the Coalition Government relaxed the points-based drama rules for commercial FTAs, and in 2021 the Australian Writers' Guild (AWG), drawing on the work of Screen Producers Australia (SPA), predicted:

> The number of hours of Australian drama on Seven, Nine and Ten will be halved. Seven and Ten will now be able to satisfy their obligations by producing *Home and Away* and *Neighbours* alone. Nine, without a serial, can reduce its current annual drama production by 50% from 84 hours to 40 hours.[31]

Development on several dramas ceased as soon as the regulations were loosened. *Neighbours* subsequently died. Clearly, regulation has a decisive impact. Because the SVODs were not regulated, the commercial FTAs were able to argue, hand on heart, that the playing field was not level and the previous government proposed a vague plan to regulate the SVODs in early 2022. The current Labor Government says it will apply regulation, but as of August 2023 it hadn't happened.

The rule that 55% of all the programming broadcast on commercial FTA primary channels between 6am and midnight must be Australian, is still in place, as are the transmission rules for digital channels, but this doesn't help drama, because any type of programming qualifies.

Audiences have fragmented and traditional linear viewing has plunged in the US[32] and Australia.[33] People are going elsewhere for drama in particular. Of the 105 FTA shows that were seen by more than one million metropolitan overnight viewers in 2021—these figures exclude news programs—62 were sport or sport related, 41 were episodes of so called reality, with *Married at First Sight* (20 episodes) and *The Voice* (14) the most popular, and two were specials, *Oprah with Meghan and Harry* and *Hey Hey We're 50*.[34] Not one drama was among them.

How lucky for sport that it gets time at the end of most 'news' bulletins: it's great promotion. Sport and reality—and news and current affairs too—all deliver Australianness, and they have their fans, but they are not made with the same deliberation or attention to meaning as long-form drama. Drama is a unique on-screen experience. When it is compelling, it sucks you in for the long haul, like a great novel. The characters can seem real. Other types of programming aren't as widely recommended or binged as drama; and they are less likely to be sought out again for a second viewing.

On consolidated 28-day figures, and with regional viewers

added, *Fisk* and *RFDS* did manage to exceed one million viewers each in the calendar year of 2021, and *Home and Away* nearly did.[35] The prequel series *Mystery Road: Origin* also did exceptional business when it premiered in mid-2022. But, ten years ago, some Australian dramas, including *Underbelly: Razor* and *Packed to the Rafters*, attracted more than two million people to the FTAs.[36] Now viewers appear to be bewitched by ad-free drama from across the world on the SVODs.

In 2021–22, cameras rolled on 24 dramas for FTA television and its sister digital channels and online platforms—as with most of the figures given in this Paper, this excludes children's drama. These dramas represented 278 hours of drama; the five-year-average was 31 dramas and 358 hours. For those who have no wish to pay directly for television, that's less than one hour per day of new drama across all channels.[37] For the SVODs and Foxtel and its associated channels, 29 dramas went into production, representing 135 hours, considerably up on the five-year average of 13 programs and 61 hours.[38] A limited amount of Australian drama is also made for social media sites and YouTube.

Looking back over the past twenty years, the *Screen Australia Drama Report* concluded in 2020–21, 'Notwithstanding yearly fluctuations, the number of hours [of drama] produced has been in steady decline since 2000–2001, when 715 hours of content was produced'.[39] As flagged above, a decline in long-running series in favour of shorter run shows with higher production values, is one reason for this decline.

The less Australian drama is made, and the more it is scattered across multiple platforms and hidden behind paywalls, the harder it is going to be to find—and the fewer opportunities there will be for practitioners to practise their craft and create gems. Oh, and since 1998, as the result of a trade agreement, New Zealand drama can count towards Australian quotas. Weird hey?

Young fans are consuming local drama in new ways

A growing amount of Australian drama and comedy, much of it limited in length compared to FTA and SVOD series, is being shown on social media sites such as YouTube, TikTok and Facebook; and broadcast video on demand (BVOD) sites such as ABC iview and SBS on Demand. Some is finding millions of young fans, RackaRacka's work and *Superwog* are both examples. That's excellent, because these fans aren't seeking out local drama in traditional places. (And it's also excellent that the twins behind RackaRacka, Danny and Michael Philippou, are having such global success with their debut feature film *Talk To Me.*) Predicting what will happen in these spaces, including the prospects for long-form drama, takes a lot of thought and imagination. In mid-2022, US academic Professor Scott Galloway argued that TikTok's success as a streaming service was not being properly recognised. It had 1.6 billion active monthly users, was the world's most visited site in 2021, and was paying only US$200 million per year for content—via its top content creators—compared with Netflix's expected US$17 billion in 2022.[40] Could someone *please* give TikTok's top Australian creators $500,000 each, and tell them that they have to make long-form drama or comedy with it? Thanks.

Maybe long form will lose its appeal?

Nah.

Not all Australian drama is or can be fabulous

There will always be people who say Australians don't watch local drama because it's not good enough. This is maddening because, time and again, it is insinuated that a drama is disappointing *because* it is Australian. No, that's got nothing to do with it. It just didn't turn out as well as hoped. And so, the cultural cringe intensifies. It's why some think it's marketing suicide to tout a show's Australian credentials to Australian viewers. Every country has failures, including the US. We see everything that is made here—maybe it would be better if we didn't, because it sits alongside the best from around the world.

London-based Australian Cathy Payne is chief executive of Banijay Rights, the largest television production and distribution group outside the Hollywood studios. It has a catalogue of 120,000 hours and owns 120 production companies in 22 territories. She says Australians have good ideas but they lack the money and time to make scripts as good as they can be.[41] Many people have told me they are concerned about Australian development practices, and that they affect the quality of the finished product. So too does pushing projects into production before they are ready, but that's a whole other story.

Getting films into cinemas has long been neglected

The average number of Australian features produced annually throughout the 1970s was fourteen. In the 2000s it was 31, and in the 2010s, 37.[42] The current five-year average is still 37.[43] All are released in cinemas, but the majority are shown on a limited number of screens with little fanfare, and disappear without a trace within a week or two. This issue has been left unaddressed for decades. It really is crazy given that governments and other investors pump millions of dollars into films. Imagine building schools and not flinging open the doors to all. Frankly, the lack of action is devastating for anyone who cares.

It is not an even playing field. Marvel, Disney, Warner Bros and other US blockbusters, take up multiple sessions, on multiple screens per day, at the insistence of their distributors, and they take a bigger and bigger slice of the revenue each year. The films come tried and tested, accompanied by slick marketing materials, enormous promotional budgets and brand awareness. Cinemas want to show a range of product but they also want to pay the bills from the foot traffic these movies bring in.

You might say that audiences want to see these blockbusters. Yes, of course they do. But their taste and habits are shaped by a system which, in effect, blocks them from seeing the whole gamut of films made worldwide, including local films. Again, my taste is not everyone's, but it breaks my heart that the vast majority of Australians don't know that recent films such as *Babyteeth* and *Of An Age* even exist.

Cinema operators in the Republic of Korea have had to show local films since the 1960s. In fact, from 1996 to 2006 they had to show them for at least 146 days of the year. Then, in 2006, it was reduced to 73 days. It is understood that this was due to pressure from the US. A percentage of the revenue from each and every ticket is directed into local film production. For many years now, these regulations have motivated cinema operators to give local films a better chance of success by directly investing in them. Their thinking was, to put it coarsely, 'there's no point showing crap films, we can help to make them suit our audiences, and budget has a big impact on potential'. Korean films' share of admissions was 51% in 2019, 68% in 2020, 30% in 2021, and 56% in 2022.[44] If Australia took this kind of action, it would no longer be a miracle if the Australian share reached double figures.

In 2021–22, exhibitors, distributors, producers and investors came together three times for the Australian Feature Film Summit, and Australia's challenges were thoroughly examined.[45] Upping marketing budgets, allowing more time for word-of-mouth to build, providing data to filmmakers about audience preferences, enabling producers to take a cut of cinema revenues in addition to the fees they earn from production, other changes to the terms of trade, and encouraging more cinemas to focus on Australian films, were among the ideas discussed. Such cooperation is rare in such a siloed industry, and every little bit helps, but it looks like the summit will bring incremental rather than significant change.

The SVOD sector is disrupting cinemas as well as FTA television, although not as much as was initially feared. Cinemas do sometimes have to fight to prevent films being made available in homes via the SVODs, too quickly after they have been released on the big screen. The SVODs argue in response, that *they* are the ones filling in the financing gaps—cinemas don't contribute to production budgets—and that they are adding to the marketing noise around a film, which helps cinemas. Stan provided a significant slice of the budget for *Nitram*, a film about the perpetrator of Australia's biggest mass murder. The story about the events that led up to it was a microscopic study of Australian society, but Screen Australia declined to support it (more about this government agency soon).

Film and staying home breeds definitive voices and culture

The renowned film producer Tim Bevan (*Love Actually, Bridget Jones's Diary, Elizabeth, Atonement, Billy Elliot, Les Misérables*) of Working Title Films, is one of the most successful in the world. In late 2021/early 2022, he was producing *Ticket to Paradise* in Australia and I had an opportunity to quiz him on the subject of this essay.

He said that film is a director's medium, and its cultural value is mostly found in the work of great, local film directors. If Danny Boyle (*Trainspotting*) and Steve McQueen (*Hunger*) had come up through television, they wouldn't have developed such definitive voices, because television is a medium driven by producers and writers. The Britishness of their work, he said, 'literally happens by osmosis'. It did in his own case, as it did when director Richard Curtis decided to stay in London and tell stories there (*Four Weddings and a Funeral, Love Actually*), rather than telling them in America.[46]

Two thoughts emerged from this conversation. Firstly, many Australian practitioners seem to have given up on making features, and that is having terrible consequences for cultural value; and secondly, many talented Australian filmmakers have made the US their primary home. It used to be that filmmakers would make something here first, but now, given the opportunities over there, they often don't bother—and this weakens their desire to tell the stories of their birthplace.

The taxpayer funding of Australian production is often presented as an incentive for Australians who have gone abroad, to return and make projects on home soil. It may have added to the reasons US-based Phillip Noyce returned to direct the very influential *Rabbit-Proof Fence*. But it doesn't always lead to on-screen Australianness. In 2021, the Australian director Michael Gracey (*The Greatest Showman*), also US-based, filmed *Better Man*, about the English singer Robbie Williams, in Melbourne. It's not an Australian story, but it was an Australian production eligible for taxpayer funding.

Australian producer Bruna Papandrea got extensive media attention when she returned from LA during the pandemic to make *Nine Perfect Strangers* and *Pieces of Her* with the help of the taxpayer funding reserved for foreign production. It seems that the tall poppy syndrome doesn't apply to people who leave the country! The first film she produced was the earthy, funny feature, *Better Than Sex*, which opened the Sydney Film Festival in 2000. The difference in Australian cultural value between this and these two more recent productions, is clear as day.

The impact of SVODs on viewing habits is fundamental

So, it has come to pass that people can watch what they want, when they want—if they're prepared to pay.

As of June 2021, Australians had 19.1 million SVOD subscriptions and 57% of this group regarded them as 'an essential service'. The average number of subscriptions in a subscribing household was 3.1. Netflix (six million subscriptions), Amazon Prime Video (2.9 million), Disney+ (2.6 million) and Stan (2.4 million) were most popular. There are now more than 30 SVODs available.[47] That's replicated across the planet. When Disney+ launched in three countries on 12 November 2019, it took just 24 hours for the service to pick up ten million subscribers.[48]

That said, Australia's ThinkTV says that during the second half of 2022, only 15.3% of in-home viewing on all devices was SVOD viewing, compared to 62.5% on live linear television. About 10% was BVOD viewing and time-shifted programs, and the rest was on YouTube and other social media sites.[49] (ThinkTV promotes the value of advertising on television to marketers on behalf of Seven, Nine, Ten and Foxtel.)

Putting all this aside, Australian drama is now available in many more places. That's if it can be found amongst the vast array of viewing choices. (Interesting isn't it that taxpayers part-fund it but have to pay to access it on SVODs and Foxtel?)

In December 2020, the then Minister for Communications, Paul Fletcher, asked the most popular SVOD services to keep ACMA abreast of what they spent on all Australian programming annually. The SVODs, unlike the commercial FTAs, are unregulated and the implication was that he might force them to acquire a certain level of Australian content if they didn't spend enough. In 2021–22, five SVODs spent nearly $200 million on Australian drama, but ACMA's report, *Spending by Subscription Video on Demand Providers*, doesn't break that down into commissioned (new) and acquired (existing) material. The commissioned material comprised *Deadloch, Five Blind Dates, The Lost Flowers of Alice Hart* (Prime Video), *Last Days of the Space Age, The Clearing* (Disney), *Heartbreak High, Irreverent, True Spirit, Why Are You Like This* (Netflix), *Appleton Ladies Potato Race, Five Bedrooms, Last King of the Cross, More Than This, North Shore, Spreadsheet*, New Zealand show *The Far North, The Secrets She Keeps, 6 Festivals* (Paramount+), *Bump, Christmas on the Farm, Gold, Nitram, The Tourist, Wolf Like Me* (Stan).[50] Other projects are not mentioned for reasons of confidentiality. It's a lot of drama and a lot of opportunities for makers and audiences. ACMA notes in the same report that SVODs spent an additional $333.4 million on acquiring, producing or investing in sixteen 'Australian-related' programs made in Australia. This kind of material includes the aforementioned *Pieces of Her* and *Nine Perfect Strangers*. That is, foreign productions with well-known Australians in leading roles and a global/US look and feel. This report is an example of how agencies muddy the waters in terms of what's genuinely Australian and what's not.

The SVODs are resistant to government regulation guaranteeing local content, but these mostly global businesses—Stan and Binge are Australian—are raking in Australian revenue while there's no sign of local cultural value in their KPIs; and just because they are actively commissioning Australian drama now doesn't mean they will be in five years' time. In fact, if and when things get tight, they will certainly reduce production if they can. Local content guarantees are being put in place in other countries across the world. It should have happened here before the FTA rules were relaxed.

The national broadcasters play a key role in drama

When the former director of ABC TV, Kim Dalton, was interviewed for this Paper, he said that the scaffolding that supports Australian film and television has four pillars: regulation, direct funding, indirect funding and the national broadcasters.[51]

The ABC, and to a lesser extent SBS, which has fewer resources, are vital to the quantity and quality of Australian drama. Eleven of the 24 dramas that went into production in 2021–22 were made for the ABC. I've already noted that at the most recent AACTA Awards, *Mystery Road: Origin*, which was made for the ABC, won best series. In the previous year, *The Newsreader* won this category and *Fires* won the miniseries/telefeature category.[52] Both were made for the ABC. Six of the ten most popular FTA dramas in 2021 were ABC commissions.[53]

A recent report from Queensland University of Technology (QUT), authored by Anna Potter, Amanda Lotz and others, found that the ABC had been the most reliable source of Australian drama since 2009,

> despite the significant decrease in drama and children's funding it faced following the 2009–12 triennial budget that supported its digital expansion. The ABC's charter mandate leads it to priorities other than maximising viewership, which has led to its continued ambition in drama despite facing the same multichannel expenses. The ABC's commitment to Australian drama and its success making it available suggest that a more robustly funded ABC is an efficient and effective tool for modernising cultural policy aims for 21st century dynamics.[54]

However, if only one type of player is left commissioning Australian drama, it risks becoming ghettoised.

The SVODs are shaking the foundations of everything everywhere, including the public broadcasters. Respected UK producer Jane Featherstone (*Chernobyl, Broadchurch, Spooks*) says, 'BBC and public service [broadcaster] shows will find it harder to compete, both from a budget point of view [with the streamers] and also for talent'.[55]

It is theoretically possible for the ABC and SBS to decide to stop showing drama all together. This is unacceptable. There should be cast-iron guarantees—either imposed from outside or self-imposed—with the resources to match. And given that the ABC and SBS have a direct connection to their audiences, isn't it needlessly convoluted to channel their funding for drama through Screen Australia?

3

So many factors and moving parts impact the financing of drama

It is a relentless slog to finance local drama

Something needs to be made very clear: raising the money for a major drama requires entrepreneurialism that draws on every scrap of experience, exploits every contact and deploys considerable *chutzpah*. Oh, and it also requires a beautifully developed story, a team with an impeccable track record and probably a star or two, depending on the size of the budget.

So far I have been referring to drama made 'for the ABC', 'for SVODs' and so on, but it's actually made by independent production houses. Under this model, these entities have to cobble their budgets together from contributions made by these local screening platforms, international sales agents/distributors, federal and state governments and private investors. Some partners will only pay upon delivery, which means that bankers and lenders can become involved too.

It is a painful process and a juggle to meet the needs of

different stakeholders. Tensions may arise between those who want to please local audiences and those who are focused on global sales. Screen Australia might deem it necessary to boost on-screen diversity or the number of women behind the camera across its slate.

With so many factors and moving parts, and with costs rising, it is impossible to overestimate the difficulty of securing finance for television drama. The same applies to feature films. Seventeen of the 42 features that went into production in 2020–21 cost more than $5 million.[56] (Twenty-four went into production the following year, but their budgets were not available at the time of writing.) Anyone inexperienced or unconnected has trouble getting in the door.

Neighbours was cancelled because of a UK decision

New episodes of Australia's longest-running drama, *Neighbours*, disappeared from sight mid-2022, after 37 years on air and almost 9,000 episodes, because their UK broadcast partner, Channel 5, wanted to divert money to UK dramas. It is a crushing example of how a financing partner, on the other side of the world, can make a decision with monumental consequences for Australia. Thousands have learned their craft on *Neighbours*. Increasingly, global taste is impacting what Australian shows are made. Sally Riley, head of drama, entertainment and Indigenous up until mid-2022 at ABC TV, cared about how well the drama she commissioned performed internationally: 'I really do care. Because if it's a show I love I want to make more of it and if partners can sell the show, then we are going to make more.'[57]

The most exciting thing about attending the Screen Producers Australia conference in March 2021 was hearing the SVOD executives who dominated the speaker line-up discuss their interest in new Australian drama. (It certainly wasn't catching COVID, like I and so many others did.) These executives pondered out loud what 'authentic' Australian content might look like in the future. Netflix's first director of originals in Australia, Que Minh Luu, commented, 'we are all in the business of trying to work out what Australian shows are going to evolve into'.

Drama is being commissioned at a frenzied rate across the world in the race for subscribers. A couple of top producers, who were delighted to be making masses of drama for the SVODs, asked me why I wanted to draw attention to Australianness now. I told them it's because delivering authentic and recognisable Australian stories shouldn't be left to chance, especially if taxpayers are meeting some of the costs, and because quantity doesn't necessarily deliver the desired outcome.

The FTAs have always needed to please local audiences, but, whatever they say, most Australian SVOD executives know that they'll please their overseas bosses most if their commissions pop both locally and globally.

While writing this Paper I watched dozens of hours of Australian drama. Much of what I saw on the commercial FTAs was very Australian, but too middle-of-the-road for my taste. Who knows how these much-loved shows will fare in this brave new world. Australian drama with a global feel is mostly found on the SVODs, but not all the drama they show is like that. SVODs are currently free to commission whatever they like. If and when local content regulation comes in let's hope there has been very serious discussion about the pros and cons of supporting local production activity vs genuine Australianness on screen.

The 2022 European report, *Public Film Funding at a Crossroads*, is based on interviews with 700 screen industry leaders and they consulted a further 3,500 additional industry participants. Here's what it says about SVODs in general:

> Creative and artistic freedom is sometimes as great as it is in the old world, but it is more often curbed and restricted. Local content is attractive, but the majority of the 'originals orders' strive for generic expression and storytelling.[58]

The only thing about drama that is not in flux at the moment is its potential to speak to our hearts and get under our skin. Fingers crossed that, over time, the SVODs will make a very real contribution to drama, with the kind of Australianness that thrills Australians.

Here's a thought: maybe Australia needs a noir

The term 'film noir', first used by French critics in the 1940s, carries connotations of bleakness and darkness. Scandi or Nordic noir is associated with serious, compelling crime fiction from that part of the world. There is no identifiable Australian noir globally, but it's fun to think about the possibilities. When *Muriel's Wedding*, *Strictly Ballroom* and *Priscilla* hit the big time in the early 1990s, Australia could have adopted the term 'underdog blanc'. The ABC recently used 'outback noir' in relation to *Mystery Road: Origin*. Recent shows *Darby & Joan, Upright* and *The Tourist* fit into this category. Together, *Bump, The Let Down, Amazing Grace* and *The Commons* say 'baby noir'. *Deadloch* has been called 'feminist noir' as well as, like *The Kettering Incident*, 'Tassie noir'.

Remakes: a lesson in universality

Hamish Lewis, head of scripted at Warner Bros International Television Production Australia, happened upon the Swedish show *Älska mig* via his corporate network and decided it would suit Australia. (More will be said shortly about how companies owned by overseas interests can and do make plenty of drama classified as Australian.) Binge concurred and *Love Me* (the English translation) became the Australian SVOD's first original production. A friend who gushed over *Love Me* felt deflated when I told her that the show wasn't Australian born and bred: pride was mixed with her admiration. *Love Me*'s 'Australianness' comes from the actors and the way director, Emma Freeman, framed it as a love letter to Melbourne.

Älska mig didn't sell into the lucrative US market, but Australia's version did: it was acquired by US streamer Hulu. There are advantages to speaking and making drama in English. Storytelling is full of universal themes and one of *Love Me*'s—how love and grief can co-exist—made it perfect for crossing national boundaries. Binge is part of The Foxtel Group, which also commissioned the adaptation of *The Twelve*, originally made in Belgium. Foxtel's two other recent local drama commissions are *Colin From Accounts* and the second series of *Upright*.

The global business works both ways. Ten per cent of the

dramas that Screen Australia has invested in over the past five years have been remade by non-Australian companies.[59] The original acts as a proof of concept and there's less work for a new group of writers elsewhere to do on character and script, which helps alleviate budget and time constraints. *Love Me*, filmed in Easter, was available in December and that's mighty quick. And so, business once again has a very big influence on what's made. But Australianness, Swedishness, any sort of 'ness', can still resonate well. It's a question of degree.

Producers need a business environment that works for them

Screen Producers Australia consistently and wisely lobbies for fair terms of trade, a healthy commercial environment, and the retention of intellectual property rights by its producer members. If those who make the product don't have a strong business foundation, the long-term security of Australian drama is threatened.

Let's tease that out using a situation that's growing increasingly common. SVODs are regularly financing drama now and they own it outright. Without going into too much detail, in this scenario the company that makes the show is akin to a service provider. Getting a decent producer fee without having to struggle for production finance might seem like an attractive option, but it undermines the producer's capacity to build up a revenue stream from the intellectual property they have created, and this means less resources in the future to develop new shows. Australian companies and foreign-owned Australian companies, controlled by Australians, both make Australian drama, but this is a bigger problem for the Australian companies, because they are less able to defend themselves against the SVODs. Especially if Screen Australia isn't one of the financiers and can't act as police officer.

SPA represents businesses of all types, including foreign-owned companies. Many one-time Australian-owned companies have been bought out by or merged with foreign-owned companies, including Fremantle Australia, Curio Pictures (formerly Playmaker Media), Southern Star Entertainment, Matchbox Pictures, Lingo Pictures, Screentime and Endemol Shine Australia.

The QUT report already mentioned found there are now more production companies producing less drama than in the past, and those producing sizable quantities are more likely to be foreign owned:

> The concern about Australian ownership is less a matter of fear of foreign influence and more a recognition of the sizable advantages that companies enjoy once they have structural connections to multinational conglomerates with capital and international distribution capability. The increased internationalisation of the television industry makes stories that are specific to the Australian experience—a key objective of Australian content regulations—more difficult to produce. The scale at which Australian drama producers have been absorbed into foreign conglomerates raises complicated questions about the extent to which Australian stories continue to feature in their productions, although they continue to access significant sums of Australian support.[60]

These are complicated questions all right. In a nutshell, there are more foreign-owned companies making local drama and more foreign-owned entities commissioning it.

Undoubtedly the current government is more attuned to cultural value than the previous one. This statement, delivered at a Make It Australian campaign function in mid-2022 by the then, very new Minister for the Arts, Tony Burke, and now featured on the home page of the campaign website, would have turned heads if it had come out of Fletcher's mouth:

> If a film made in Australia has extraordinary success overseas, makes a heap of money, that is wonderful, but that is a bonus. That is not the first objective of Australian production. The first objective is to make sure our stories are told so that we know better ourselves; we know better each other and the world has a better way of knowing us.[61]

SPA is one of the organisations behind this campaign, but, above all, its job is to look out for its members. Right now, it makes sense for SPA to use the cultural argument, instead of the economic one, to protect those members, and that's good for local viewers. But there's some sleight of hand going on: the first line on the home page says 'We want Australian stories told on Australian screens by us, to us, about us', but producers also want drama made by Australians to be classified as Australian, whether it is about us or not. It is also understandable that they want that flexibility.

Producers have the loudest voice, but writers and directors and actors—those actually creating stories—might be the ones better suited to putting forward cultural arguments.

4

The federal government offers financial incentives for both local and foreign drama

Two types of taxpayer funding are available for locals

There have been many references in this essay to taxpayer funding and it is time to look at this crucial part of the federal scaffolding more closely. Public funding has been part of the landscape, in various forms, since the 1970s. There are two kinds available now for long-form Australian drama: an indirect tax rebate, officially called the Producer Offset (PO), and direct funding from Screen Australia.

Think of claiming the PO as sending a shoebox full of receipts to the Australian Taxation Office to prove what's been spent on a production, accompanied by a claim for a proportion of that expenditure. Spend, say, $3 million making a (low-budget) feature film or a two-part mini-series and when the project is finished, get back up to 40% if it's a film for cinemas or 30% if it's for the home screen. At least $500,000 has to be spent for a feature film to be eligible. For television it's either $500,000 or $1 million, depending on the format, and $500,000 per hour for series. The producer has to complete the project and secure a certificate confirming eligibility—which includes a commitment from a distributor in the case of the 40%—before submitting the claim to the ATO. In 2020–21, 118 certificates were issued for the PO, representing $175 million of rebates.[62] Not all of these were for drama.

Think of the direct funding, in contrast, as a briefcase full of money—like in a heist movie. Applications have to come with a tick of approval from a home screen viewing platform or, again in the case of features, a distributor, but the cash is given out at the discretion of the staff of Screen Australia and its board members. For both TV and film, a deal must be in place with a company that is committed to selling the production abroad.

Screen Australia contributed more than $60 million to production in 2021–22. The biggest slice, nearly $24 million, went to television drama, about $14.5 million to feature films, $13 million to online production, including games, $6.2 million to First Nations stories, and $6 million or so to children's drama. About another $6 million went to development.[63] The agency also puts finance into documentary, talent development, distribution, international marketing, festivals, and assistance to the guilds. The agency part-funded 37.5% of all the Australian features that went into production, 71% of all FTA and BVOD drama, and 40% of all SVOD and subscription television drama. (There are rules against continually backing new seasons of existing series.) The maximum amount the agency will put into any project is $2 million.

It is common for independent producers to access both kinds of funding at once: the PO, which is unlimited and available to any project that qualifies, and Screen Australia's finite, capped and discretionary briefcase of money. This is not the case for the most expensive form of Australian drama: films such as *Elvis* and George Miller's newer *Mad Max* films. They have US studio backing but only the PO acts as a sweetener. Most drama receives investment and/or grants from state governments too.

Big foreign projects also get taxpayer funding

When I voice my concerns about on-screen Australianness slipping away, many Australian practitioners assume, because of their own antipathy, that I'm whinging about the government putting money into foreign productions as well, as indeed it does. Providing funding from Australian taxpayers does seem a bit at odds with the scale and inevitable success of what rolls onto our shores from abroad, but these mega-budget Hollywood series and features are good for the economy and they're critical to the development of Australian industry infrastructure and keep its service companies thriving. Here's a recent sample of visitors: the feature *Thor: Love and Thunder*, made at Fox Studios Australia in Sydney in 2021; two series of *La Brea*, the second of which went into production at Docklands Studios, Melbourne, in early 2022; and the UK film *Ticket to Paradise*, starring George Clooney and Julia Roberts, filmed from late 2021 at Queensland's Village Roadshow Studios.

Big-budget productions need controlled environments, and the Sydney, Melbourne and Queensland studios are a big part of Australia's attraction as a location, as are its diverse natural environments and skilled cast and crew. But the bottom line is cost, and that's where the Location Offset comes into the equation. The Location Offset is for 'footloose' feature films that spend more than $20 million on filming in Australia and for television productions with an expenditure of more than $1.5 million per hour.

Australia received unprecedented interest from US studios during the COVID lockdowns because we had comparatively few cases and the industry was very efficient in its adoption of safe work practices. In contrast to live music, theatre and other art forms that were crushed by the lockdowns in Melbourne and Sydney, COVID created a boomtime for screen production and consumption. Everyone was in work, businesses banked the offshore earnings and upgraded their equipment, and local directors and writers scored gigs on foreign television and became more bankable.

Foreign productions get a lot of taxpayer funding but arrive with bulging wallets, so it's good for the economy. The marketing body, Ausfilm, stated in its 2021 submission to government that the Location and PDV Offsets had attracted approximately $4.2 billion of international spending in Australia over the last two decades.[64]

It has been said, however, that Australia is increasingly being perceived in Europe as a stalking horse for US content and studio interests, and this is limiting its capacity to develop broad relationships and co-production arrangements. Foreign production can also make life very difficult for homegrown drama by hiring the best facilities and services and, at inflated wages, the best personnel. One producer told me that some crew members openly say they're only willing to do one Australian 'charity' job per year, a reference to the lower wages paid.

Australia is also a global hub for visual effects and the other incentive that attracts foreign production is the 30% Post, Digital and Visual Effects (PDV) Offset. Australian expenditure must be $500,000 or more and the movie may be filmed anywhere in the world.

More studios are being planned for Australia. It is a bit concerning that nobody—nobody!—seems to remember when the value of the Australian dollar peaked against the US greenback in July 2008, with the result that not one US feature went into production here in 2008–09.[65] Foreign productions are a valuable source of revenue, but exchange rates sit well outside the industry's control. The brawl between US studios/streamers and actors and writers is now having ugly ramifications for the Australian industry: another example of Hollywood's insidious influence.

Let's clone Baz and George and fill the studios with Australian filmmakers making mega-budget productions financed from abroad. This would increase the likelihood of such productions telling Australian stories, and big-budget stories are more likely to find big audiences. For the record, unmistakeably Australian projects kicked off the careers of both these directors.

A brain teaser: is local production chicken or egg?

I was gobsmacked when a US producer said to me in an interview that Australian local production only exists thanks to the quantity of US productions made here. For me, it is the reverse: the US gets to use Australia because we have a local production industry. A diplomat, splitting the difference, might say that one feeds the other.

Confusion reigns over what's foreign and what's domestic

It is commonly speculated that foreign production receives a higher level of taxpayer support than Australian production. This is untrue, but only a mathematical genius of the likes of Isaac Newton could wade through the anomalies and detail and provide an accurate comparison.

For a start, although the Location and PDV Offsets are associated with foreign production, they are heavily utilised for creating Australian content. This often surprises even practitioners—as an aside, the industry would be much better off if there was greater understanding of all aspects of the business. In 2020–21, 45 certificates, representing $101 million in rebates, were issued for foreign productions, and 95 certificates, representing $62 million, for domestic.[66] The Department of Infrastructure, Transport, Regional Development and Communications won't separate these figures into Location and PDV Offset projects in case, it says, it inadvertently reveals confidential information.

Many Australian reality shows claim the PDV Offset, although this was never the intention. It is a big loophole. Government funding is meant to address the market failure of drama, children's television and documentary, not reality television, which has no trouble getting financing. Information on which productions are drawing on which pots of taxpayer funding is often unclear. Transparency is merely good governance.

Nevertheless, between the Location and PDV Offsets, the PO rebates, Screen Australia's direct funding and contributions from the ABC and SBS, Australian production gets way more support than foreign. It's probably ahead on drama too, even if it's not all recognisably Australian.

Governments around the world support their film and television. Disbursement methods vary enormously, so comparing levels of support is highly challenging. In decades of reporting on the industry, I've never heard any discussion on an appropriate per capita contribution, or the degree to which foreign production should be supported for its economic value, compared to local storytelling.

At 30%, the PO for Australian television drama is the same level as the Location Offset for foreign drama, although, as already explained, Australian drama might also attract Screen Australia money.

Nobody's perfect, not governments, not industry

When federal governments use a big, shiny, financial carrot to secure a big foreign production in Australia, there is often a press conference, a media release and smiley photo ops. The news hits the media and is amplified by the fuss made at a state level. Thus does Australia add to the glory of US content.

By contrast, when local production is in the news, the focus is often the battle of wills between the government and practitioners over the policy issue behind it. The same arguments are on repeat, sucking out the oxygen and leaving little room for big-picture thinking. No wonder the public perception is that federal governments support the local industry grudgingly, and the industry is an ungrateful and disorderly rabble with its hand always held out for more money.

Government and industry have a habit of lurching from one issue to another, without a strategic vision. The issue has been the lack of SVOD regulation for a while now. Before that, it was the proposed reduction of the PO for features from 40% to 30%. Many get involved in lobbying, but actor Bryan Brown got a lot of credit for preventing the fragile backbone of feature film financing from breaking altogether. Celebrity always helps in Canberra.[67] More than two years later, at an address to the

National Press Club in July 2023, he argued for the regulation of the streamers—after talking about how he came to acting, and the importance of the arts' ability to reveal the national spirit.[68]

'If our ability to present ourselves on film is taken away, we will become unsure of ourselves, in awe of others and less of a people,' he said. It is disappointing that this is not the starting point for all policy discussions. Inviting input from all stakeholders is how the political process works, but, in film and television, submissions to government reviews are so mired in self-interest that it is difficult not to become cynical. Governments shouldn't just provide a boxing ring. They need to lead. And all parts of the production community need to come together and build a coherent plan that *puts local viewers first*. The industry, complaining about its health and each other or lobbying on single issues, is ineffective. It needs to believe in what it does before anyone else will.

5

Ideas for going forward and cultivating Australianness

The new government needs to look hard at the sector and act

Long may the bipartisan political support that local drama production has enjoyed for decades continue. It is nerve wracking to be so dependent on regulation and taxpayer funding, but this is the reality and it is no different from what happens in most other countries with a film industry. The support only makes sense, however, if it delivers cultural benefits to viewers first and foremost.

When the former government abrogated its responsibility to protect Australian content for children—I won't provide the details, but it did—it was a stark indication of how incapable it was of applying vision and enthusiasm to the creation of local content in general.

It was heartening to see the government that replaced it release the *Revive* national cultural policy in January 2023, eight months after it was elected. Prime Minister Anthony Albanese's foreword was a salve for a film and television industry that was increasingly leaning into the global and the commercial.

> (The arts) bring us together, adding to life's great highs and helping us get through the lows. Our artists help us celebrate what makes us different, and rejoice in what we share... It is through our many and varied forms of artistic expression that we build our identity as a nation and a people—and that we project our culture to the world.[69]

Five pillars underpin the five-year plan, spelled out in 116 pages: the primacy of First Nations arts and culture; Australia's breadth of stories and the contribution of all Australians as the creators of culture; the need to support and celebrate the artist; strong cultural infrastructure; and audience engagement. We live in trying times and the new government has a lot on its plate, but it feels like it genuinely understands that the creative industries foster unity, pride and a sense of belonging, and also that the arts need to be embedded into every aspect of society.

That said, there is not yet any evidence of serious engagement with the subset of film and television beyond the SVOD issue. As the previous pages make clear, there are a lot of complexities behind the business, and significant push and pull between commerce and culture. There are no easy answers but here are some specific priorities to get the ball rolling:

- Instruct industry to embrace the term 'cultural value', despite its eat-your-vegetables feel, and accept it as the number-one driver behind the government's support for Australian production and make all its decisions accordingly.
- Take the administration of the PO away from Screen Australia and give it to the Department of Infrastructure, Transport, Regional Development, Communications and the Arts. The PO is non-discretionary, indirect taxpayer funding, available to all who qualify, and it distracts the agency from concentrating on getting cultural bang-for-buck with its suitcase of discretionary cash.
- Clarify the policy objectives of the Producer, Location and PDV Offsets and institute the changes that will make them fit for purpose, including closing loopholes.
- Examine how Australian production is faring in the wake of the big shifts in the home screen environment and act accordingly: look afresh at the commercial FTA quotas; appropriately regulate the SVODS; plan a strategy for online platforms; and assess the role of the ABC and SBS in delivering drama.
- In line with the fifth pillar of the national cultural policy, audience engagement, acknowledge the central role that the big-screen experience plays in delivering culture and investigate the options for introducing cinema quotas and diverting a cut of all film revenue to the local industry.
- When foreign productions come to town they should

be expected to agree to hosting internships and other training opportunities for locals that are often paid for by state film agencies. Suggest to industry that it thinks carefully about *all* the flow-on effects and be much bolder about designing and demanding initiatives that will fundamentally strengthen the local industry.

- Point Screen Australia and the production community to the third paragraph of the speech that the Minister for the Arts gave at the launch of the national cultural policy: 'The success of *Revive*, doesn't actually rest with government; it rests with you—our artists, creators, painters, poets and provocateurs. What you do with the cultural policy will determine the look, feel and soundtrack to life in Australia.'[70] The supremacy of producers must not be upheld if it undermines the survival of creators.

Once government has made clear its priorities specifically for film and television, it would be a perfect time for the industry to put together a broad plan that lays out the fundamentals, goals and targets for the future. Having a common purpose always brings positive results.

Fans ought to be able to exercise their love of Aussie content

'Where do I find these films that you're always talking about?' I've been asked that question all my adult life. Australians get no help finding out when and where new local drama in general is showing. They only hear about individual dramas if they're in the path of a publicity and marketing campaign or via word of mouth. In the digital age, this is madness. I get texts when shops where I've bought one item, have a sale. It's crazy that I can't sign up to a service that notifies me whenever a new Australian series premieres or a new local film opens.

Film and television is sexy. It sparks curiosity. Harness that for Australian work, just as Hollywood has done for years. With local television drama scattered across multiple platforms and local films disadvantaged in the cinemas, fans must be given the ability to exercise their love of homegrown fare by making it easy to find. Great things could come from systematically fostering a community of supporters. They would automatically share their love on social media networks, for example, and could act as a thunderclap at the time of release, especially if spurred on by privileged access. Screen Australia's *The Screen Guide* and the worldwide service *JustWatch* provide guidance on where to find shows, but not what's about to hit the screen, the moment at which there is the greatest anticipation—and the biggest potential for a ripple effect. Picture the marketing value of fan-led events being held across the country on the night of release. Act on the lessons learned from the remarkable popularity of Australian films at festivals. The overall impact could be phenomenal.

There's political value in all this too. Viewers sticking up for Australian content is more powerful than when practitioners do it, and viewers are voters and politicians take notice of voters.

Perhaps distributors and platforms could help meet some of the ongoing costs of such a community. Perhaps a big corporate player—a bank, insurance company or health fund with clients/customers/members across the country—might see the value of helping to drive this initiative.

Screen Australia *needs* to shout 'What do we want? Cultural value! When do we want it? NOW!' Senior executives say that local cultural value is a plank in their decision making, and it is. But the world has changed and big forces are crushing the local industry. It is time for Screen Australia to hold up a flag, like tourist guides, and say 'come over here, because we will support you to make compelling, entertaining film and television—but only if it digs down deep into who we are as a nation and a people'.

Screen Australia must seriously assess *all* programs, initiatives and actions through the lens of *exceptional* cultural value. What this means is tricky, no doubt about it, and skirmishes will break out. Maybe doubtful projects simply shouldn't qualify for this limited funding. And maybe this new Screen Australia needs a new SAC test that makes it obligatory for what's on screen to be, at the very least, clearly Australian. I acknowledge that this will make me unpopular with the big end of the production industry.

Here are three examples of misguided thinking. Firstly, there is a common notion that each SVOD and FTA platform deserves to receive a share of Screen Australia funding via their production partners. No. Australianness should trump even-handedness. Secondly, in mid-2022, $4 million in grants went to games developers under the Expansion Pack initiative, with absolutely no requirement for the games to have 'Australian themes'. Australianness should trump the growth of new businesses—especially now there's a federal games rebate. Thirdly, Screen Australia constantly talks to industry through newsletters and podcasts. This is absurd. It should be using those precious resources to reach out beyond the bubble, to interest potential audiences in Australian content.

Content makers can and should make what they like, but that doesn't give them the right to be eligible for every form of funding. The priority for Screen Australia investment must be the kind of on-screen Australianness that shines a light on our society, whether its via comedy, drama, horror or whatever. The PO is there to keep things on the boil. It serves the industrial model. There is no cap on what individual projects can claim nor on the total annual ask. It is available to all eligible projects without anyone exercising granular discretion, and it has been increased to 30% for television and held at 40% for features. Plus, unlike the funding available via Screen Australia, the PO keeps pace with rising costs and rising production levels.

The report, *Public Film Funding at a Crossroads*, mentioned earlier, lists the values that public film agencies in Europe aim to safeguard:

- cultural/artistic idiosyncrasies with specific territorial reference
- film as an art/culture form
- diversity in all its senses
- European ownership
- independent production companies that own underlying IP rights, and along with the filmmakers have artistic freedom and creative control
- rights handled territory by territory
- and cinemas as a central place for shared experiences.[71]

Note the leaning towards culture and the acknowledgement that the cinema experience is important. Everyone needs to work towards getting Australian films into cinemas, including Screen Australia. Yes, it's a high-cost, high-risk game, but developing a fan base will help, and maybe there are other opportunities as well, such as grouping and touring smaller films with lots of promotion attached.

What has constantly come to my mind during the writing of this Paper is how the current interest from non-Indigenous audiences in Indigenous-themed, Indigenous-made content has been built up from nothing over the past couple of decades. Quite deliberate decisions, to resource Indigenous practitioners to tell Indigenous stories, has been part of that, and the drama they have produced has changed society for the better. Audience taste is malleable.

Dare I say it, but I feel a bit sorry for the agency at times, because it is relied upon too heavily. Entitlement in the industry is rife, and Screen Australia is in a no-win situation because the funding supply doesn't meet demand. However, some of its problems are of its own making. It has its fingers in too many pies. It needs to stop thinking it can, and should, control everything and decide what it can do best in service of the Australian public.

In recent years, Screen Australia executives have been drinking the Kool-Aid of their old political bosses. This is demonstrated in the media release that announced the publication of the 2020–21 *Drama Report* (which its research department does an exemplary job of producing each year). It trumpeted: 'Aussie drama production reaches record-breaking $1.9 billion expenditure'.[72] It's misleading because it's *not* Aussie drama production. It is Aussie drama produced in Australia plus foreign drama filmed in Australia. And that year, for only the second time in 27 years,[73] more was spent making foreign drama than local: $874 million on 95 Australian projects, compared to $793 million on the production of 10 US shows and a further $246 million on post-production for 53 foreign projects.[74] It is easy to see why federal and state governments love the cash injection that comes from foreign productions coming to these shores.

Foreign and Australian drama production should be treated *completely separately* in such reports, as in, *never* combined. And total expenditure shouldn't be talked about breathlessly by Screen Australia for all the reasons this Paper has raised. It is arse about to give the impression that everything is fine because expenditure is up. Expenditure is just activity, not cultural value.

One last point about Screen Australia: Australianness and cultural value encompass many, many things, and keeping executives in their jobs for a long time prevents a range of views and knowledge about the country cycling through. Also, people learn a lot and gather extensive contacts in those gigs, and limiting the length of executive contracts would lead to more of this knowledge flowing out into the production sector.

Revel in exploring what's possible in drama

In 2021, ABC TV ran the six-part drama *Fires*, set amid the 2019–20 Black Summer bushfires. Said Sally Riley, then at the ABC:

> Tony Ayres came to us, just after the fires happened, and said 'We need to talk about this. The community needs a cathartic moment.' And we said 'yes' straight away.[75]

Ayres and Belinda Chayko created the show, which is available free on the streaming platform ABC iview. The cleverly conceived anthology series puts two young volunteer firefighters (played by Eliza Scanlen and Hunter Page-Lochard) at the core of the first episode and then uses them as linking characters across all the episodes, each of which focuses on different people. Only the most cold-hearted viewer would not feel the grief of Miranda Otto and Richard Roxburgh's dairy farmers Kath and Duncan. Mark Leonard Winter's portrayal of a methadone user reverses every prejudice about drug addiction.

I had to see *Fires* for work. I would not have otherwise because I had watched the Australian countryside burn, over and over, on the television news and didn't want that horror and shock again. But the mini-series left behind the sensation that I'd sat holding hands with the people who lived through the trauma, while they told their confronting stories. I didn't get that from the nightly news.

Screen Australia is given a lot of leeway under its enabling legislation, which suggests, among other things, that the agency is intended to ensure the development of a diverse range of Australian programs that 'deal with matters of national interest or importance to Australians, or that illustrate or interpret aspects of Australia or the life and activities of Australian people'.[76] *Fires* did exactly that—it illustrated the personal impact of climate change with devastating precision.

A serious tone and approach isn't mandatory for dealing with serious subjects. Filmmakers aged 14–35 could be invited via the media to pitch projects on subjects of national importance and told comedy will be treated most favourably. Screen Australia's new head of content, Grainne Brunsdon, says she wants to cater for this audience, and they might well respond better to material made by their peers.[77] Let's put aside the headlines of the day and have a public discussion about what's important. Revel in what's possible.

Why doesn't Screen Australia get enough good applications?

I worked at Screen Australia for three years part-time up to mid-2018. One day I suddenly clocked that there was rarely any enthusiastic talk in-house about brilliant projects that were coming in the door—the agency can only support what comes to it. The realisation was crushing. When I asked Screen Australia's chief executive, Graeme Mason, publicly at the 2022 SPA Conference if the agency received enough good applications, he said 'no'. That 'no' was not well received when it was delivered, nor when I repeated it in the first public version of this Paper. The agency was chastised for not making bold choices, and for being a closed shop that repeatedly funded the same production companies. Cultural value flows from shows that have great appeal. So, assuming Graeme's judgement is spot on, what he says is extremely important. What is stopping Screen Australia from getting more and better applications? Are people being prevented from even applying because of a lack of credits or contacts? Or are those who complain about not getting a look-in overestimating the quality of their work? Does the industry have a bedrock of experience and ample new talent? Who is responsible for replenishment? Screen Australia? Production companies? The states? Some think the states should be wholly responsible for new talent and project development—even though state governments unashamedly judge their screen agencies on economic goals. Is their sufficient creative and business training? Are filmmakers born or bred? So many questions.

Local content is distinctive globally

In the first version of this Paper, I wrote that 'just another cop show' shouldn't get Screen Australian funding. Producer Helen Bowden responded like this:

> First of all, crime drama is by far the biggest seller (attracting the biggest audiences) worldwide. 'Just another cop show' won't get you a sufficient international advance to finance it, that is the reality now. It wasn't the reality even five years ago. Because of the SVODs (and streaming by free to airs) the market is demanding better, more interesting, more diverse cop shows. But make no mistake they are still demanding cop shows. And isn't *Mystery Road* the ultimate, fabulous Australian cop show?[78]

The mention of *Mystery Road* brings me back to an ever-present gut feeling that once a drama hits the mark in terms of execution and its ability to stand up against the worldwide competition, the more Australianness it has, the more likely it is to sell internationally, because its distinctiveness makes it stand out from the crowd.

In a speech to the 2022 SPA conference, Minyoung Kim, a senior Korean-based executive at Netflix Asia Pacific, told the audience, the more authentic a story is, the higher its chance of it finding a Netflix audience outside its country of origin. She had a significant role in *Squid Game*, a very big worldwide success for Korea, and commented that there were many national social issues embedded within its storyline. It is an encouraging narrative, that the local has infinite global potential. People are watching closely to see if local breakouts come to represent the norm, and if the US will allow its cultural dominance to be threatened.

Let's end how we began. Less Australian drama is made, it's harder to find, its on-screen Australianness is being ironed out, and that's the elephant in the room. I invite you to come and look at the elephant with me. Come on.

Appendix
Interviews with two practitioners
Tony Ayres and Emile Sherman

Tony Ayres and Emile Sherman were asked to take part in an interview after pondering this question: 'How can more and better film and TV, with (on-screen) Australianness at its heart, be made and seen?' They had not read the Paper. A record of those interviews, conducted in May 2022, follows.

Tony Ayres says it's all about valuing writers

The eight-hour series *The Slap* traces the ripple effect of one dramatic incident at a lunch, the slapping of a child by an adult. Tony Ayres was one of the producers on that outstanding 2011 show, which had a big impact both in Australia and around the world. He also directed two episodes. He was then a partner in Matchbox Pictures and now works under the banner of its sister organisation, Tony Ayres Productions. He is at the top of his game in television.

The premise behind Matchbox, when it was set up in 2008,

was to create a company that writers wanted to work with, he says. The company would respect them, make them central to the process, and support them to be the best writers they could be. He still has that philosophy. He started in television and knows very well that, in Australia, power is in the hands of producers, but in the US market, writers are the stars:

> We need to really value writing. That's the middle, beginning and end of the argument. Producing the best work takes time. There is the potential you've not got it right and have to start again. You've got to keep the bar as high as you possibly can. Sometimes scripts are raced into production when they're not ready. Every industry does that and it is part of the condition of TV but it's something we have to rethink if we want to compete.

Tony co-created two 2021 Australian dramas, the six-part *Fires* and the eight-part *Clickbait*—he has a writer's credit on all *Clickbait* episodes. *Fires*, which was made for the ABC, got its finance from a range of sources and had a budget in line with other Australian dramas. *Clickbait* had way more:

> We had a 22-week writers' room [on *Clickbait*]—in Australia you'd have six weeks, maybe eight if you're lucky. And we paid writers to stay on the project for the whole process. They weren't dipping in and out, working on other things. It was eye opening. Here it's three drafts, three polishes and you're done. The recognition that maybe that doesn't give you the best possible version is a no brainer.
>
> I'm also an advocate of a showrunner/writer/producer overseeing creative development and production. It provides a backstop when the three-and-you're-out system doesn't work. Some producers

believe creative carriage is their job and a script producer's. A showrunner gives a more unified vision of the whole show. The way to make the best creative projects is to empower the creatives. It's not rocket science.

Moving to another point, Tony says that one of the joys of *Clickbait* was being allowed to make each episode the length it needed to be in order to tell the best possible story—in this case, a story that propelled itself forward. Making it fit into a conventional television hour of, say, 50-something minutes, is an obstacle when competing with international shows.

The work we [Australia] produce is phenomenal for the resources we have—the caveat is always 'for the resources we have'. In the UK, their shoots are so much longer than ours. They have the luxury of time. In America... they have the luxury of resources. We always start with a structural disadvantage: 20 metres back in a 100-metre race. The fact that we manage to produce the work we do, that it travels as well as it does, is a minor miracle.

We are in such a precarious position right now because, like so many industries around the world, we only exist at the scale we exist at, because of government subsidy and regulation. We all have to try and protect our industry in whatever ways we can. The strongest argument for why we want a screen industry is that we need to reflect our national identity as part of civil society, a coherent society. That is the function of culture.

Emile Sherman says create a garden that nurtures local content

Producer Emile Sherman has been nominated three times for the Oscar for Best Motion Picture, the most prestigious of all the Academy Awards. *The King's Speech* won in 2011, *Lion* was nominated in 2017 and *The Power of the Dog*, which won the BAFTA for best film, was nominated in 2022. Emile and UK-based Iain Canning established See-Saw Films in 2008 with offices in London and Sydney. The films *Shame* and *Tracks*, and the series *Top of the Lake*, are among many acclaimed productions.

Using the analogy of a garden, Emile says that creating an environment where more Australian film and television can be made, means more content with Australianness at its core can blossom. That's his first key point. The PO had recently been increased from 20% to 30% and he began with this:

> Thirty per cent for TV will super fertilise the soil for many, many years to come. It's hard to overstate how big this is. It is a simple measure that will fuel a lot of Australian production.
>
> We are at a great moment in the industry because the streamers are coming in and showing real interest in Australia, not just in Australian talent in US-set shows or in Australia as a location, but in Australian stories. It's up to us to deliver the quality that will cut through the crowded landscape.

He warns, however, that most of the SVODs are not just viewing platforms, they are also studios and production houses, and in the US it has become the norm for them to essentially commission themselves to make content. This must not be allowed to happen in Australia.

> You can't stop Netflix commissioning Netflix or Amazon commissioning Amazon, but we have to ensure a fair and competitive playing field, with multiple production houses. If something is Australian, 30% [of the budget] in taxpayer money is up for grabs, and it is absolutely appropriate that at least half of everything commissioned is done with arm's-length third-party production companies.
>
> And the production companies have to have meaningful ownership and upside in the project—not just be a hired-in producer. We need to use the 30% to supercharge an ecosystem with a lot of production companies—tiny little ones, big Aussie studios, some owned overseas, some not. You can't have a mature industry if most Australian content is made by a small group of foreign streamers. If we get this right, it will be incredibly good for the garden.

Emile recognises that on-screen Australianness is important, but believes that the broader the definition of what's Australian under the SAC test, the better our chances will be for creating culturally Australian content.

'When you back Australian creative voices—writers, directors, talent—a virtuous cycle comes into play', he says:

> We need to fuel those people. They might want to make shows or films in America or wherever else but as Australians they generally also want to make shows grounded in the world they live in. See-Saw makes international television [and film]. I naturally want to make a lot of things based in Australia because that's where I am and where my roots are. The current SAC test works well to balance

> the various components of Australianness, focusing heavily on the creative voices.

Emile also suggests that Australian voices can still be heard through productions that are set overseas or in stories that aren't Australian—although he describes this concept as cheeky. Baz Luhrmann, for example, brings something very Australian to his work.

His second key point is that a healthy industry needs safe places to experiment. Film and TV schools offer that, but so do Australian movies and television in general, because they are small scale, in the global context, and backed by a lot of government money. He acknowledges that Screen Australia has to back work that is popular and which reaches Australian audiences, but even if the films are less successful commercially, they also provide opportunities that have big flow-on effects. Cinematographer Greg Frasier, for example, worked on nearly a dozen features and as many shorts before he was nominated for an Oscar for *Lion*, and he subsequently won the Oscar for *Dune: Part One*. Having skilled Australian heads of departments gives Australia a competitive advantage.

Emile's third key point is that he would rather sprinkle a lot of low-budget movie seeds than focus on a small number of well-supported films within a controlled system. He'd use the PO for this, setting the rebate at 60% for expenditure of less than $5 million.

> It would be a good way of keeping things dynamic and iterating, because you never know what's going to be successful. It wouldn't cost much [in taxpayer funding] but it might be an incredible talent

generator. And that's what we need, to keep generating talent and experimenting. It's pre-venture capital, seed funding. It's what people do in businesses now: fail fast and learn.

We would be planting more and saying 'let's see what grows'. It would be a wilder, more dynamic ecosystem. Things might grow and die more quickly. You have to expect things to fail. Some things can go unseen and that's to be expected. We shouldn't be scared of failure if it's done at an appropriate budget level and is part of an ecosystem which can find and amplify the successes.

Smaller budget shows with more government subsidy may be of interest to the streamers, if they are driven by exciting creative voices. And streamers don't have to worry about using up limited slots like traditional broadcasters do.

Emile has often thought about implementing a sliding scale for the rebate too. An option for features would be to apply 50% to the first $10 million of expenditure, 40% to the next $20 million, then 30%. He questions why the PO is a flat 40% regardless of whether it's a $5 million independent movie or a very high budget studio-financed film.

I'm confident that, with the right incentives, knowing we have the right talent here, and with fair terms of trade, I reckon we'll be making a lot of Australian content. Some will be great, some less so, some very Aussie, some less so. We need to be open to seeing what emerges.

He describes the English series *Sex Education* as a US-leaning version of England, an interesting moment at which the streamers reached a different vision of a culture:

We have to be careful about holding on too tight to what it means to be an Australian. We're always reinventing ourselves. And if we have an ecosystem that's well fuelled, which supports a broad range of production houses that are empowered to unearth and support great Australian creative voices, we will have the best shot at continuing to grow an industry that we're all proud of.

Emile adds,

I do think, additionally, based on the conversation with Sandy, that there's an opportunity to more cleverly cross-fertilise Australian film and TV shows, so that audiences here and overseas appreciate what we're doing. At the moment it's very much project to project, and there's little sense of what we're doing as a whole industry.

Endnotes

1. '2019 Box Office results prove the enduring popularity of the cinema experience'. Media Release. Motion Picture Distributors Association of Australia, January 21, 2020. mpdaa.org.au.
2. 'Streaming Services Reporting and Investment Scheme Discussion Paper'. Commonwealth of Australia, February 2022, p. 11.
3. Ibid, pp. 12, 13.
4. 'Cinema Industry Trends: Films Screened'. Screen Australia. screenaustralia.gov.au.
5. 'CEO's 2021 Year in Review and 2022 Preview'. Media Release. Screen Australia, February 11, 2022. screenaustralia.gov.au.
6. '2019 Box Office results prove the enduring popularity of the cinema experience'. op. cit.
7. 'Cinema Industry Trends: Domestic Box Office and Share by year,

1977–2022'. Screen Australia. screenaustralia.gov.au.

8. *Screen Australia Drama Report, Production of Feature Films, TV and VOD Drama in Australia in 2021–22*. Screen Australia, p. 8. screenaustralia.gov.au.
9. Ibid, p. 4.
10. *Measuring the Cultural Value of Australia's Screen Sector*. Olsberg•SPI, November 11, 2016, p. 5. screenaustralia.gov.au.
11. Ibid, p. 15.
12. *Supporting Australian Stories on Our Screens—Options Paper*, Australian Communications and Media Authority, Screen Australia, March 2020, p. 6. infrastructure.gov.au.
13. Federal Register of Legislation, Income Tax Assessment Act 1997, Section 376–70 'Determination of content of film'. legislation.gov.au.
14. 'CEO's 2021 Year in Review and 2022 Preview'. op cit.
15. Karl Quinn, 'Australian show *Clickbait* tops Netflix charts around the world'. *Sydney Morning Herald*. October 5, 2021. smh.com.au.
16. 'Green Paper. Modernising Television Regulation in Australia'. Netflix. May 24, 2021, p. 18. infrastructure.gov.au.
17. Craig Mathieson, 'Sandstorms, a broken bone: the extreme lengths Zac Efron went to for a new film'. *Sydney Morning Herald*. January 24, 2022. smh.com.au.
18. Amanda D Lotz and Anna Potter, 'Effective Cultural Policy in the 21st Century: Challenges and Strategies from Australian Television'. *International Journal of Cultural Policy*, Vol. 28, no. 6, 2022, pp. 684-96. doi: 1080/10286632.2021.2022652.
19. *What Are Our Stories Worth? Measuring the Economic and Cultural Value of Australia's Screen Sector*. Deloitte Access Economics, 2016, p. 27. screenaustralia.gov.au.
20. *Supporting Australian Stories on Our Screens—Options Paper*. op. cit., p. 6.
21. *Screen Currency: Valuing Our Screen Industry*, Screen Australia, 2016, p. 8. screenaustralia.gov.au.

22. Chris Coughlan, 'Subscription Entertainment Lifts in Lockdown'. *ITWire*. September 23, 2021.
23. *Media Consumer Survey 2020*, Iso Edition, Deloitte, p. 20. deloitte.com.
24. Presentation by Nick Palmer from Screen Audience Research Australia to the Australian Feature Film Summit, May 12, 2022.
25. Clem Bastow, 'Ten Australian accents by foregin actors, from worst to best—sorted'. *Guardian*. April 4, 2022. theguardian.com.
26. 'Latest Release: Film, Television and Digital Games, Australia, 2021–22 Financial Year', Australian Bureau of Statistics. abs.gov.au.
27. *Screen Australia Drama Report*, op. cit., p. 19.
28. 'Latest Release: Film, Television and Digital Games, Australia', Australian Bureau of Statistics, June 15, 2017. abs.gov.au.
29. David Knox, 'Report: Commercial TV drama drops 68% over 2 decades'. *TV Tonight*. August 26, 2021. tvtonight.com.au.
30. *Supporting Australian Stories on Our Screens—Options Paper*. op. cit., p. 5.
31. 'Modernising Television Regulation in Australia, Media Reform Green Paper', Australian Writers' Guild submission, May 21, 2021, p. 18. infrastructure.gov.au.
32. Michael Schneider, '100 Most-Watched TV Shows of 2020–21: Winners and Losers'. *Variety*. May 25, 2021. variety.com.
33. 'Streaming Services Reporting and Investment Scheme Discussion Paper'. op. cit. p. 10.
34. Tess Connery, 'By the Numbers: The Most Watched Programs of 2021'. *Mediaweek*. December 22, 2021. mediaweek.com.au.
35. 'CEO's 2021 Year in Review and 2022 Preview'. op cit.
36. 'Television Industry: Top Drama Programs. Top 50 Drama Episodes on Free-to-Air Television, Metro & Regional, 2008–2019', Screen Australia. screenaustralia.gov.au.
37. *Screen Australia Drama Report*. op. cit., p. 17.
38. Ibid, p. 22.

39. Ibid, p. 15.
40. Scott Galloway, 'TikTok Boom'. *No Mercy/No Malice.* May 20, 2022. profgalloway.com.
41. Conversation between Cathy Payne and Sandy George, March 28, 2022 at the Screen Producers Australia conference, 'Screen Forever'.
42. This report previously at https://www.screenaustralia.gov.au/fact-finders/production-trends/feature-production/australian-feature-films has been taken down from the Screen Australia website since the time of writing. Screen Australia notes:

    'Trends in the production of Australian films since 1970. To provide more specific insights into production for different release platforms, Screen Australia re-categorised the titles that contributed to the 2021/22 *Drama Report*. These changes have been applied to the last five years of data in the report. It is Screen Australia's intention to apply these new categories to Fact Finders in 2023. In the interim, caution is urged when comparing data to the years prior to 2017/18.' 'Australian Theatrical Feature Production: Australian Theatrical Films since 1970'. screenaustralia.gov.au.
43. *Screen Australia Drama Report.* op. cit., p. 10.
44. Email exchange between Sangyun Lee, International Relations Team, Korean Film Council, and Sandy George, May 13, 2022 and August 28, 2023.
45. AFF Summit (2021–22), Australian Feature Film Forum. aff-forum.com.au.
46. Phone interview with Tim Bevan, March 21, 2022.
47. Chris Coughlan op. cit.
48. Tomas Eskilsson, *Public Film Funding at a Crossroads*. Film i Väst Analysis, p. 21. analysis.filmivast.se.
49. *Fact Pack, H2, 2022*. ThinkTV, p. 3. https://thinktv.com.au.
50. 'Spending by Subscription Video on Demand Providers: 2021–22 Financial Year', Australian Communications and Media Authority, Table 1. acma.gov.au.

51. Email exchange with Kim Dalton, May 19, 2022.
52. Sandy George, 'Head of drama at Australia's ABC talks competing with streamers'. *Screendaily.* March 29, 2022. screendaily.com.
53. 'CEO's 2021 Year in Review and 2022 Preview'. op cit.
54. Amanda D Lotz, Anna Potter, Marion McCutcheon, Kevin Sanson and Oliver Eklund, *Australian Television Drama Index*, 1999–2019. Working paper. Making Australian TV in the 21st Century Research Team, Digital Media Research Centre, Queensland University of Technology, and USC, August, 2021, p. 13. eprints.qut.edu.au.
55. Tim Dams, 'The Centrepiece interview: Sister's Jane Featherstone on the future of drama in an age of anxiety'. *Screendaily.* March 23, 2022. screendaily.com.
56. *Screen Australia Drama Report*. op. cit., p. 11.
57. Phone interview with Sally Riley, February 17, 2022.
58. Tomas Eskilsson, op. cit., p. 14.
59. Email exchanges and phone conversations with Rakel Tansley, Manager, Marketplace, Strategic Policy and Industry Insights, Screen Australia, between February 25 and May 20 2022.
60. Lotz et al, op. cit., p. 11.
61. Hon. Tony Burke MP, speech at the Make it Australian campaign launch, June 9, 2022. makeitaustralian.com.
62. Estimate provided to the author by a media adviser to the Minister for Communications, Urban Infrastructure, Cities and the Arts, Paul Fletcher, in an email on March 9, 2022.
63. *Screen Australia Drama Report*. op. cit., pp. 44-50, 61 and 62.
64. *Sculpting a National Cultural Plan. Igniting a Post-COVID Economy for the Arts,* House of Representatives Standing Committee on Communications and the Arts, Parliament of the Commonwealth of Australia, October 28, 2021, p. 31.
65. 'Australian Theatrical Feature Production Activity Summary: Number

of Feature Films Produced, Total Production Budgets and Spend (current dollars) in Australia, 1990/91–2020/21'. Screen Australia. screenaustralia.gov.au.

66. Estimates provided to the author by a media adviser to the Minister for Communications, Urban Infrastructure, Cities and the Arts, Paul Fletcher, in an email on March 11, 2022.
67. Karl Quinn, 'Inside story: How Bryan Brown and the Nationals saved Australian film'. *Sydney Morning Herald.* April 11, 2021. smh.com.au.
68. Bryan Brown AM, *Staying Focused*, National Press Club of Australia Address, July 12, 2023. youtube.com.
69. Hon. Anthony Albanese MP, 'Prime Minister's Foreword' in *Revive: A Place for Every Story, A Story for Every Place.* Commonwealth of Australia, January 2023, p. 4. arts.gov.au.
70. Hon. Tony Burke MP, speech at the national cultural policy launch, The Esplanade Hotel, Melbourne, January 30, 2023. minister.infrastructure.gov.au.
71. Tomas Eskilsson, op. cit., p. 6.
72. 'Aussie Drama Production Reaches Record-Breaking $1.9 Billion Expenditure'. Media Release. Screen Australia. December 8, 2021. screenaustralia.gov.au.
73. Email exchange with Patrick May, then manager of strategic policy and insights at Screen Australia, on June 30, 2022.
74. *Screen Australia Drama Report*. op. cit., p. 6.
75. Phone interview with Sally Riley, February 17, 2022.
76. Screen Australia Act 2008—Sect 6, Commonwealth Consolidated Acts, Australasian Legal Information Institute, classic.austlii.edu.au.
77. Phone interview with Grainne Brunsdon, April 13, 2022.
78. Email exchange with Helen Bowden, July 13, 2022.

About the Author

I've tracked the film and television industry for aeons as a journalist, in particular the business that sits behind it. Having access to that backroom is endlessly fascinating because what happens in there affects what stories find their way to the screen and what they look like.

I'm the Australian correspondent for the UK-based *Screen International* and *Screendaily.com*. I have been the editor of local trade magazines, a film writer for the *Australian* newspaper and the scribe behind hundreds of industry newsletters and reports, pitch documents and corporate communications. I've presented films on SBS TV, I regularly host panel discussions and Q&As at industry events and film festivals, and lecture on a range of film and television-related subjects.

So much Australian drama—and comedy and documentary too—has brought me wonder, enrichment and joy. It has made me feel about Australia like I imagine someone who believes in a god might feel. It has shown me aspects of society I would never have known about otherwise and has made me feel ashamed too. When I love a new drama, I can't shut up about it. When I don't, I keep my lips sealed because I know how tough it is to make great

Australian drama and get it to audiences—and I know that my taste isn't everyone's anyway.

My view of journalism is conservative in that I try and keep my personal opinions out of the picture. This Paper does the opposite. It is about something I feel strongly about and it feels both good to get that monkey off my back and kind of sad that I have to.

Staying Focused

Bryan Brown AM
Gadigal country

This is an edited version of an address given at the National Press Club of Australia on 12 July, 2023.

I would like to pay my respects to elders past and present on whose lands we stand today.

Good afternoon. My name is Bryan Brown and I'm a Westie. Born and raised by my mother in a housing commission house in the western suburbs of Sydney, I learnt all the skills required for life, playing in the Milperra Swamps, the streets of Panania, the Georges River at Picnic Point, the local Catholic church and the Panania picture theatre. For that I am grateful.

In 1968 I was working at the AMP Society at Circular Quay, studying to be an actuary. In those days actuarial studies wasn't included in any Australian university curriculum. It had to be done by correspondence from London or Edinburgh and it would take about seven years on average to complete. I was doing it because I was good at maths, having achieved honours in Maths 1 and 2 in the leaving certificate, and because I had no idea what to do after leaving school. University wasn't an option for me. I knew I would just use it as a social opportunity and fail any course I enrolled in.

It was coming up to the end of 1968 when a newsletter went round the Company informing the staff that the Drama Club—yes, there was a Drama Club and a Bike Club and a Sky Diving Club and quite a few other clubs—the Drama Club would be staging an end-of-year revue in the theatrette on the ground floor for three nights, and they would welcome any staff that wished to audition.

A day or two later I presented myself for the audition. This wasn't because I had any desire to act but, once again, it was an opportunity to take advantage of a social situation—maybe there would be some girls there I hadn't met yet.

That half-hour-or-so audition process led me on a journey that has taken me to some forty countries, seen me thrown into the Pearl River in Guangzhou, taken on a private tour of the White House, celebrate my fortieth birthday on top of a mountain in Rwanda, hurl bottles with Tom Cruise, sing with Paul McCartney and share a bath with Sigourney Weaver. Marry one of Hollywood's rising stars, Rachel Ward. Strange but wonderful happenings.

As a young bloke growing up in the western suburbs of Sydney in the 50s and 60s, I went to the movies most Saturday afternoons—saw a lot of John Wayne and Lassie and the odd Rank movie from England. That's RANK as in Rank

Organisation: a bloke with hardly any clothes on took a huge sledge-hammer and bashed a gong making an almighty boom. The Rank Organisation doesn't exist today.

There was *one* Australian film released during that time. It was a film of a great Australian play: *Summer of the Seventeenth Doll*. It was the story of two Queensland canecutters and their girlfriends in Melbourne. Every year, for seventeen years, they'd visit during the off season, and one of them would bring a doll as a gift.

The four actors telling this *great* Australian story were the Americans Ernest Borgnine, Shelley Winters and Anne Baxter, and the English actor, John Mills.

At school I don't remember reading any Australian book or play. Let's get it right: Australian history came second to English history—if it came at all. The sum of my knowledge of the Australian arts world was a poem that began 'I love a sunburnt country' and an Aboriginal artist called Albert Namatjira. Both definitely worth knowing, but a little limited as the sum of one's knowledge of one's own country's art and culture.

But back to the AMP.

Having read the audition script for the end-of-year revue, I became aware that I had no idea what I was doing. But then I was asked to read opposite another employee and something must have worked, because the powers that be told me to turn up after work the next day for rehearsals. Whatever rehearsals were.

Now I liked going to work. I enjoyed the people around me and I enjoyed the salary that gave me some independence. But that next morning was different to any other morning. I really couldn't wait to go to work because, at the end of the day, I was going to be doing this thing called 'rehearsals'. Thrilling beyond belief.

The revue went on before Christmas '68. I loved it. I couldn't rationalise why I loved it, but I wanted more. I gave up studying to be an actuary, became a salesman for AMP selling life insurance and joined an amateur theatre in Kent Street in Sydney: smart move because, as a salesman, no-one cared where you were as long as you got your figures in on a Friday. So, the amateur theatre began to take up a hell of a lot of my time. Reading plays, rehearsing plays and acting in plays.

By 1972 I knew I had a decision to make. Either give up this all-consuming side-line at the theatre and get on with a proper career or resign and become an actor professionally. I resigned, sold my car and bought a ticket to England, the home of theatre.

In fact, the reason I left Australia was because all I was seeing on Australian stages was Australian actors doing English and American plays in English and American accents. It seemed pretty silly doing that in Australia, so I went to England to do it first-hand. I would become a pom. I would become a professional actor in England.

My flight to England was via Athens where I took a boat out to the island of Mykonos, and it was there that my journey into English theatre began. I got talking to a young English boy who told me his father was in the theatre. Ears pricked up.

Yep, he was a fireman at one of the London theatres. All theatres had a steel fire curtain and a fireman in attendance at all performances. For some that might have been the end of the conversation, but I knew I had to get started and I was prepared to clean toilets, sell programs, anything.

The English boy said to look his father up and he would help me. And he did. Got me a job pushing scenery at the Victoria Palace, a major theatre where the hugely popular entertainer Max Bygraves was performing with dancing girls and a ventriloquist. I was in the theatre.

That led to me moving out to the provinces in the north of England, Billingham, where I was hired as a stagehand, and that led to the chance to be an actor with a theatre-in-education company playing in schools twice a day.

I continued with this company for a good six months, until the second half of 1973, and then went back to pushing scenery in London. I didn't have an agent but a theatrical paper, *The Stage*, advertised auditions that were going. One audition was for a prestigious company called The Actors Company that was headed by Ian McKellen. The company was going to the US to cover the universities there with a couple of Shakespearian plays. They needed a dogsbody actor who could also help out backstage. I auditioned. That night I was rung by one of the actresses to say they wouldn't be offering me a job—but they liked me and her sister, Gillian Diamond, was the casting director at the National Theatre of Great Britain, and now that Peter Hall had taken over from Sir Laurence Olivier, he was putting together a new company of actors—and would I like to audition? The answer was 'bloody oath'.

So a couple of days later I'm auditioning for Gillian with a Berowne speech from Shakespeare's *Love's Labour's Lost*. And, again, a call in the evening from Gillian asking if I would be available to audition for Peter Hall the next day...? Oh, and do I have a song, as the musical maestro for the National will also be at the audition.

So, it's on, and luckily I had been working with an opera mate who had been trying to get me to stay in tune on 'When the Red, Red Robin Comes Bob, Bob Bobbin' Along'. Yep, got a song.

The audition was at the Old Vic, the home of the National Theatre. There was one actor before me, so I was waiting backstage behind the curtain until he finished. I didn't really pay attention to his Shakespeare, but when he did his song I shat myself. It was an aria. *That* was what they meant by 'a song'.

I was brought on stage and introduced by Gillian who told them what my Shakespeare piece was, which seemed to go okay. Peter Hall asked me to do it a second time and slow down. I did as he asked. Then Gillian told Peter and the music maestro that I would be doing 'Red, Red Robin'. Peter smiled and I red, red robined.

The maestro gave a couple of notes and asked me to hold them and then it was over. Gillian shook my hand and said she'd be in touch. And she was. That night. I was offered a year's contract with the National Theatre of Great Britain. The whole of 1974. Eighteen months out of Panania. Pretty exciting. Got pissed that night.

When I visited Australia at the end of '74 to see my mother, theatre here had changed dramatically. Australian playwrights had taken over the stages and were presenting plays about Australians. David Williamson's *The Removalists, Don's Party, What If You Died Tomorrow?*, all spoke of us silly buggers. *How Does Your Garden Grow?* by the ex-con Jim McNeil was a powerful indictment of our prison system. Jack Hibberd and Alex Buzo had their plays performed in exciting venues all over the country. For me, there was no point in returning to England. We now had a voice and it was an exciting, fresh, new voice for all the world to hear, and I wanted to be a part of it.

It may be difficult for some of you to understand how exciting this change was. It was as though the shackles had come off and we were set free. Free to explore who we were, where we'd come from and where we were going, and to do it in our own way with our own people. Never again the *Summer of the Seventeenth Doll* experience. We hoped.

In January 1977 I did my first film. It was a fifty-minute feature funded by the Australian Film Commission called *The Love Letters from Teralba Road* that dealt with the disintegration of a marriage. I played a rather violent and sad young man. That was forty-five years ago and it was the early days of the resurgence of the Australian film industry.

They were heady days, the 70s. Making movies, we were like gunslingers from the wild, wild, west. Except this wild west was in Australia and we were making Australian films.

Australian films were reaching out to the world and the world was reaching out to us. Actors, writers, directors. Fred Schepisi tackled the brutally complex *Chant of Jimmie Blacksmith*, the story of an Indigenous man fighting to right the wrongs of racism. *Breaker Morant*, directed by Bruce Beresford, examined the politics of war. In Gillian Armstrong's beautiful period film *My Brilliant Career*, we witnessed a young woman's struggle to escape social expectations and become a writer. And *Picnic at Hanging Rock*, directed by Peter Weir, gave us a harrowing mystery with the disappearance of schoolgirls in outback Victoria. And not a car chase or crash to be seen. Not, of course, until George Miller's *Mad Max* reimagined the genre. And then Phil Noyce's *Newsfront* highlighted the social change that had rocked Australia after World War II, through the escapades of two newsreel cameramen.

Profound, complex, necessary questions about the human experience from creative and questioning Australian men and women.

You know, we had a thriving film industry way back. Way, way, back. The first Australian films were produced back in 1886, sort of home movies—us at the racetrack or arriving on the ferry at Manly wharf. Then in 1900 the Australian Salvation Army made the acknowledged forerunner of the feature film: *Soldiers of the Cross*, a multi-media religious production, with slides, ninety-second films and 150-odd performers. And it didn't stop there. Six years later the world's first full-length feature film was produced. And where was that? Yes, here in Australia. *The Story of the Kelly Gang* produced by Charles Tait. Significantly, Australia then went on to become the major source of film production in the world, and during the period 1906–1928 it produced a total of 150 films.

But then came the Depression, the introduction of costly sound technology and the lack of interest in Australian films from American-owned distribution companies.

So we had to wait until the late 60s for a resurgence. And what a resurgence it was.

The independent production of just one or two of those films I mentioned would make any industry extremely proud, but in the 70s and early 80s Australia sent out into the world some of the finest films *ever* made. And as an actor who was lucky enough to be a part of it, that was hugely exciting. We got paid—and a fair bit more than what we'd been getting doing theatre in all sorts of venues from pubs to the Sydney Opera House. And then it was exotic, flying to Adelaide or Melbourne or Brisbane. Very exotic to a bunch of young *broke* actors in the 70s. But the most exciting part of it was that we were telling our stories and telling them with our voice, our sensibility, sharing the Australian experience: the place, its people, its struggles, its history, its strengths and weaknesses.

So where did this creativity come from? Well, it was there in its people, wasn't it? All that was needed was a visionary government to recognise it and support it. And that's what John Gorton's government did. A modern Australian film culture was born and the film floodgates opened. And it has continued. Continued to be supported by both sides of politics. For that, we Australians can be very grateful.

I remember saying to Bill Hunter, one of our great film actors, 'You know, we make bloody good dramas and we're funny buggers, but we'll never make a comedy.' And then Paul Hogan made that statement, the crock that it was, *Crocodile Dundee*. And the world laughed and loved this Australian character.

And so comedies followed: *Muriel's Wedding* and *Strictly Ballroom* and *The Dressmaker* and *The Adventures of Priscilla, Queen of the Desert* and *The Castle*. And crime, which of course we had to be good at, given our convict past: *Chopper, Two Hands* and *Animal Kingdom*. And then Indigenous films with themes that challenge the past and present: *Rabbit-Proof Fence, The Sapphires, Samson and Delilah, Top End Wedding*. And *Sweet Country*.

I was lucky enough to play a role in *Sweet Country* and attended the screening at the Venice Film Festival with Sam Neill, the producer, David Jowsey, and the writer and director, Warwick Thornton. You could have heard a pin drop at the end of the screening, and then we faced a five-minute standing ovation from a highly sophisticated audience, lauding the extraordinary talent of Warwick Thornton, an Indigenous filmmaker who, that night, brought great acclaim to Australia with a tough, honest and beautiful film.

Many, many films have delivered through the years. Big hits with consistently good box office: *Australia, Ride Like a Girl, Lion, Ladies in Black, The Water Diviner, The Dry, The Odd Angry Shot, The Man Who Sued God, The Piano, Breathe, Rams, Penguin Blue, Palm Beach, Invisible Man, The Man from Snowy River, Looking for Alibrandi, Babe, The Year My Voice Broke, Moulin Rouge, Dirty Deeds, Lantana*.

I have touched on such a few.

And that's all we needed, was it? A resurgence and everything would be fine. Roll them out, and keep them rolling. No, of course it doesn't work like that. Films, and of course TV, need finance, and financing structures continue to change, especially now, as technology opens up so many new ways to deliver stories into people's homes.

Early on it was pretty straightforward. A combination of Australian Film Commission and State investment, a distributor's advance and some rules requiring commercial TV to show new drama, kids shows and documentaries on those few channels we had: a serve of our stories in our homes. But then we needed advances on overseas sales and that started to put pressure on casting. During the 80s there was 10BA, a 150% tax write off and tax payable on only 50% of the return. The money flowed but it was a flawed model. It was more about moving money around than making good films. We lost our way somewhat, but we kept producing.

Now we have the 'Offset': a tax offset for Australian film that gives a 40% rebate on the total budget. We nearly lost that in 2021. There was a move to reduce it to 30%. Then the government announced additional support for *offshore* production, American films and TV in the main, that *increased* their Offset to 30%, bringing it in line with Australian TV. And our film industry, the Australian film industry, the industry that told Australian stories, was going to pay the difference. Robbing *Crocodile Dundee* to pay for *Forest Gump*.

Yep, offshore production is encouraged to film here and the Offset is the incentive. Economically it makes sense. Overseas productions are always looking for ways to finance their budgets. A large part of that Offset will be spent in Australia and for Australian crews it creates work opportunities.

Offshore production is *fine* if it is balanced. I was filming in Toronto twenty years ago, on an American production. At the time there were 38 American productions being shot all over Canada, but mainly in Toronto. Good for the industry? Lots of employment? You work it out. If a Canadian filmmaker wanted to shoot a movie at that time they'd have had trouble putting together a twentieth-rate crew. The cinematographer would most probably have been in first year at film school. Offshore production is exactly that: offshore, with its allegiance offshore.

Decreasing the Offset from 40% to 30% for Australian film would have been the death of our industry. The government listened and the 40% was retained.

They say, if the film is good enough the market will finance it. Well, this *is* the market place: the Offset. And offshore production is here for that. Let's not kid ourselves. If Bulgaria or Hungary or Brazil or wherever comes up with a better deal or a better offset, then our offshore production will become their offshore production. And then they will become a suburb of LA.

There will be changes, and sometimes those changes will threaten our Australian film industry, and the industry will come again to Canberra, to remind the government of the day how important our film culture is. And that is why we must remain vigilant, committed, disciplined and persistent.

If our ability to present ourselves on film is taken away, we will become unsure of ourselves, in awe of others and less as a people. A thriving film and television industry presents who we are to the world.

In 1981, a miniseries I did for Channel 7, here in Australia, was shown on TV. It was hugely successful and set a benchmark for quality television that still stands today. The show was a six-hour television adaptation of Nevil Shute's *A Town Like Alice*. It was sold all over the world, and in the US it went out on the prestigious *Masterpiece Theatre* on PBS Television. Until then Masterpiece had really only shown the best of English television: *I Claudius* and *Brideshead Revisited*. Once again *A Town Like Alice* proved itself to be hugely popular and received glowing praise and reviews all over the US, and it won an International Emmy.

A number of months later I received a call from a gentleman who was the editor of a major Washington newspaper and a guest in Australia speaking on the role of the media in society. He introduced himself and explained that he'd been asked to track me down by a Nancy Reynolds, who was a great friend of his, and it seems, a great friend of the White House. Nancy Reagan was her best friend. Both Nancys had loved the show and they offered to take me on a personal tour of Washington and the White House if I was visiting the States at all in the near future. As it happened, I was on my way to the US in a couple of weeks' time, to promote *Breaker Morant*, so I jumped at the invite.

Nancy Reynolds was an extremely lovely and generous lady and for two days I was wined and dined with US senators and Washington journalists and taken through the White House by Nancy Reagan. It was a great experience. I met many of the staff and was taken to restricted areas.

At lunch I was taken to meet the Vice President, George Bush senior, who was cordial and charming and inquisitive about Australia. As we left that afternoon Nancy, informed me that they had arranged for me to meet the President, Ronald Reagan, but there had been a last-minute change of plans due to the Saudis arriving for a meeting to buy one billion dollars' worth of planes. Fair enough excuse for getting shunted, I thought.

But what I couldn't help thinking about was the power of television. All because of a miniseries that had caught the American public's imagination, doors had been opened to me that business people would have given their eye teeth for. And the hunger for knowledge about Australia was obvious. Their imagination had been pricked. It was both the country itself and the spirit of the people portrayed in *A Town Like Alice* that had grabbed them.

My early years at the National Theatre had shown me what a huge part the arts play in the sophisticated cultural life of Great Britain. In many ways the arts define Great Britain. It is for its cultural life that so many tourists visit. Take the great arts institutions out of the UK—the British Museum, the Royal Shakespeare Company, the National Gallery, the Royal Opera, close down the theatres in London and the provinces—and it becomes a bleak old place.

Why is it we know so much about other countries? Why is London so familiar to those of us who have never been there, or

New York or Paris or Rome? Why is it that our kids say 'butt' now instead of 'bum' and wear baseball caps turned to the side? The answer is obvious. Television and film. Its power is so great. We know how the Mafia speak, dress and where they live. The American Wild West is better known to us than our own outback. Powerful stuff film.

And that power was of enormous benefit to Australian tourism when the shoe was on the other foot and 'Croc Dundee' hit the States. *Crocodile Dundee* was a phenomenon that happens not often. But both before and after it came, television and film kept people all over the world aware of Australia, interested in it and inquisitive about its people, what we do and who we are.

I believe that what film, television and literature do is introduce us to the spirit of a people. *Crocodile Dundee, Muriel's Wedding, Breaker Morant* and Tim Winton's *Dirt Music*, the wonderful novels of Tom Keneally and Kate Grenville, and our musos, Midnight Oil and Yothu Yindi, present to the world the spirit of a people that is exotic and different from other people's.

Our spirit is different, and it is a spirit that continues to be carried onto the world stage by our present Australian actors: Sarah Snook, Liam and Chris Hemsworth and Margot Robbie, all got their start through the local industry. It's different because our journey is different—from convict ships to pioneers in a vast continent, with millions of inhospitable square kilometres; fighting in strange wars in far-away places in support of our allies; whipping the arses of larger nations at sport; and colonising a culture that had been 65,000 years in the making, the struggles that brings. So different and so much to explore. We have still only touched the surface.

Back in 1987 my agent rang to say that Michael Apted wanted to meet with me in London. He was about to direct a film on the life of Dian Fossey called *Gorillas in the Mist* starring Sigourney Weaver and they were interested in me playing the *Nat Geographic* photographer Bob Campbell who was Fossey's lover. I flew to London a couple of days later to meet with Sigourney and Michael.

Now, I had seen *Greystoke*, the film of the fictionalised life of Viscount Greystoke who became Tarzan. It was a great film with blokes dressed up in monkey suits all running around Pinewood Studios in London. I imagined that's where *Gorillas in the Mist* would be shot. After my meeting with Sigourney and Michael I was offered the part. I asked when I'd be needed in London and was told 'no', the film would be shot in Rwanda, in Africa. Cool. Never been there. Good idea, more authentic.

On flying to Rwanda, I asked, who were the actors who would be wearing the monkey suits? 'Oh, no', I was informed, we would be shooting with the real gorillas. Cool. More authentic, I agreed. My first day out, there were about two hundred porters carrying gear up the side of the mountain where the gorillas were. After some two hours, an army-type fella with a rifle came out to say that the gorillas were about two hundred metres into the jungle. We stopped, got into costume and make up. Camera was offloaded and the film loaded into it. I was very happy to see the bloke with the gun. Next, we were told to accompany the guard into the jungle. Just four of us. Sigourney, myself, focus puller and camera operator. That's all that was allowed. Not even the director. And a researcher with a pad and pencil.

We followed the guard into the jungle and then he called us forward and pointed to the gorillas: a huge silverback, a smaller huge silverback, about ten females and maybe five youngsters.

And then, as the gorillas moved off, he waved us to follow them. I looked to the researcher and asked if the bloke with the gun would be with us and was told it wasn't allowed. Just the five of us, with a pencil as our only weapon. I wasn't all that keen on authenticity at that point.

We followed them for four hours as they ate their way through the jungle, before they finally stopped to rest. This was my moment to move among them, photographing them, and waiting for my head to be lifted from my shoulders and my body thrown over the cliff.

It didn't happen. I filmed amongst these extraordinary animals for some time. In front of them, with my back to them, amongst them. When they asked 'what was it like?' when I got back to camp, I didn't have a word to describe the experience: relief to be alive, excitement to be among these creatures, the delight as they played together. It was overwhelming. An impossible experience, made possible by making a film. I turned forty up there. Could I have ever imagined that? Not in my wildest dreams.

As I mentioned earlier, with the resurgence of the Australian film industry, the world—or Hollywood, same thing—came calling and our producers were now lent an ear. They were now able to build a business, get in bed with the major studios, and retain some IP (intellectual property) ownership at the same time. And that meant a library and further royalties down the track. A business.

But now there's a new game on the block for our industry: streaming. Australian audiences are loving streamers and we hand over a few billion dollars in revenue each year to the streaming companies. We need some of that revenue put back into Australian stories. And I mean *Australian* stories, not stories filmed in Australia with American accents. We've been there. That spells cultural death.

Canada and France have legislated that a percentage of the revenue from their countries must go back into local production. In France it's over 25%. In Australia, a 20% reinvestment obligation, complemented by strong and sound IP arrangements, would help secure the future of our industry and keep it vibrant. The streaming companies will fight hard against legislation—they are a business—and we must fight just as hard for our culture.

I'm sure that, once again, we will all find an answer and so move forward. We owe it to Australians, Indigenous peoples, old migrants and new, to keep telling our stories. Our Australian stories. And what a story the Australian story is. The oldest living culture colonised by one of the most powerful empires the world has seen and handed to a bunch of misfits to make it work.

Good luck. Good stories.

The more I've travelled the more I've noticed that, as different as our origins may be, and as far apart as we may live, the world is inhabited by people with very similar needs. Our hopes for our families are the same. Our conflicts no different, whether they are personal or political. Our desire to be challenged just as strong, and our need to express ourselves is overwhelmingly important to us.

That is why, when we see a film or TV show that works, it's because, in that story we recognise our own humanity. No matter what its country of origin, whether we laugh or cry, whether we are thrilled or astounded, film brings us together. So, let's do everything we can to support each other in our endeavours, to produce good Australian stories.

Thank you.

About the Author

BRYAN BROWN AM has appeared in over 80 films in a career that spans more than forty years. He has been nominated for both an Emmy and a Golden Globe, and received numerous Australian acting awards, including the Lyall Longford Award in 2018, for his contribution to Australian Film and Television.

He achieved international success in the early 1980s, receiving critical acclaim for his performances in *Breaker Morant* and the TV series *A Town Like Alice*. A stream of Australian hits and Hollywood productions followed: *The Thorn Birds, Gorillas in the Mist, FX, Newsfront, The Shiralee, Cocktail* and, in 1999, *Two Hands*, for which he won the Australian Film Institute's award for Best Supporting Actor for the second time.

He also played major supporting roles in the box-office smash, *Along Came Polly*, for Universal in 2004, and alongside Nicole Kidman and Hugh Jackman in Baz Luhrmann's *Australia*, in 2007.

His latest film credits include *The Light Between Oceans, Red Dog: True Blue* and *Sweet Country*, directed by Warwick Thornton, which was awarded the Venice Critic's award for Best Film; and he produced and starred in *Palm Beach* directed by

Rachel Ward. His television credits include *Bloom* and *Caught* for Stan, *Darby and Joan* for Acorn and *Boy Swallows Universe*, based on the much-loved Australian novel, for Netflix. In 2023 he completed filming *Anyone But You* for Sony.

In 2021 *Sweet Jimmy*, a collection of short crime stories, was published by Allen & Unwin and a full-length novel, *The Drowning*, will be released in November 2023.

Diversity and Inclusion: Building the Good Life in Australia

Jeremy Neideck

Morwenna Collett

no. 5

March 2023

Terminology

ADEI	Access, Diversity, Equity and Inclusion. ADEI and diversity are used interchangeably throughout Morwenna Collett's Paper. The collective term ADEI is explained in detail within the essay.
BIPOC	Black, Indigenous, people of colour.
CALD	Culturally and linguistically diverse.
Cisgender or Cis	A person whose gender identity aligns with their identified sex at birth.
Deaf and d/Deaf	Deaf is capitalised when referring to members of the Deaf community (typically Auslan users), and d/Deaf is used as a wider term that also encompasses people who may be deaf but do not consider themselves to be members of the Deaf community

Introduction

Harriet Parsons
Wurundjeri country

What does the 'good life' mean to Australians today? We have come a long way from the life of masculine leisure George Caiger described a in *The Australian Way of Life* in 1953. That life, he wrote, was built on the foundation of female domestic labour and 'a kind of good-humoured casualness towards other peoples' (except when it came to our economic interests). But behind this idyll, Australians were wracked with deep anxieties. The baby boomers were reaping the benefits of a strong post-war economy, but the 'fair go' asked them to share their good fortune with others.

In the first essay in this issue, 'Queer(y)ing the Australian Way of Life', performance maker Jeremy Neideck argues that a contemporary cis-straight fantasy of those 'relaxed and comfortable' days is polarising Australian society. Nostalgia for this non-existent past is heightening the fear of losing its supposed rewards.

Liberation from this fantasy, he proposes, is to be found in the work of queer artists, who are reconceiving the good life in Australia by engaging in a process of 'nationhood as creative practice'. Artists Justin Shoulder, Sarah Stafford and Joel Bray are his interlocutors in this thought experiment. As creative practitioners, parents, friends and lovers, he argues, they are using queer ways of being, knowing and understanding to explode the false ideal of cultural homogeneity and redefine the good life, both on stage and off.

'More Risk, More Play: Creating an Inclusive Culture', by arts consultant Morwenna Collett, asks what Australia would look like if we actually embraced diversity 'in all its glory'. Creating an inclusive culture, she argues, is about more than prioritising the needs of particular groups, it is about ensuring that everyone who wants to participate in the arts, whether as a member of the audience, in the administration or on stage as a practitioner, is made to feel welcome.

Writing as a proud disabled woman, Collett points out that everyone will have 'accessibility issues' at some point in their lives, whether it is due to illness, accident or old age, or the social and psychological barriers that make people feel like they just don't belong.

But accessibility is always a trade off. Every decision an organisation makes puts culture within the reach of some, and out of reach for others. The barriers can be economic or geographical, linguistic or technological. Ultimately, ending discrimination and creating equal access, so that we can all enjoy 'the good life', comes down to examining how we treat each other in all of our relationships.

Acknowledgements

In my first essay for Currency House, 'The Cost of Cultural Ambition', I wrote about the love I have for the extended family of artists who are negotiating a good life between South Korea and Australia.[1] To the family I have chosen to share this working life with: REM Theatre, LATT Children's Theatre, Motherboard Productions, Offset Art, Imaginary Theatre, Staff Seoul, Ten Spoons, Kiosk and Company Bad, thank you for collaborating on what at times has felt like an impossible dream.

To the family I have chosen to share my personal life with: Nathan, Fi, Thom, Bec, Maisie, Flora, Younghee, M'ck, Dave, although we are, once again, spread out across the globe, I can't wait to be with you again. Thank you for everything.

To the family I didn't choose: thank you for your love and your pride.

To Julian Meyrick, Harriet Parsons and the team at Currency House, thank you for investing in my development as a thinker and a writer.

To Joel Bray, Justin Shoulder and Sarah Stafford: thank you for showing me many of the ways that queers can live a good life in so-called Australia.

Queer(y)ing the Australian Way of Life

Jeremy Neideck
Whadjuk Noongar Boodjar country

This is a work-in-progress.

I wonder if, by the time you read this Paper, any clarity will have emerged from the messy and incoherent desire-lines that urged me to pitch it to the editorial team at Currency House.[2]

My starting point is a hunch: there is something queer about the past, present and future of life in Australia.

Messiness is queer.[3] I'm queer. I find value and pleasure in exploring ways of forming knowledge outside of the hierarchies of institutions. Avoiding mess, for me, is a futile business. But I am beginning to wonder if some clarity can be found in the messy and incoherent desire-lines that have shaped my life in so-called Australia.

Lauren Berlant has written about something she calls cruel

optimism—an affective state where we confuse the struggle to attain the good life with the good life itself.[4] It is the point at which we lose sight of the good life, and the daily grind and the crushing weight of living under late-stage capitalism perversely becomes our goal in and of itself. One way to think about the good life is that it is a combination of the moral, the intimate and the economic, underpinned by the principles of enduring reciprocity that hold people together in relationships as couples, families, political systems, institutions, markets and businesses. When conditions are such that these relationships begin to fracture and fail, cruel optimism seduces us into attaching ourselves to myths and fantasies that are harmful or even impossible to achieve.

In a 2022 opinion piece celebrating the launch of the Centre for the Australian Way of Life at the Institute of Public Affairs, former Prime Minister Tony Abbott wrote that there had 'never been less racism and never been better treatment for minorities' in this country.[5] Ghassan Hage skewered Abbott's vision when he was writing about his predecessor, John Howard, nearly two decades earlier, in 2003:

> The Prime Minister has publicly declared himself 'offended' on many occasions; he even went as far as being 'outraged' once when faced with the term 'racism'.
>
> More offended by it than by the sight of the dehumanising concentration camps he has used to cage third-world-looking asylum seekers. In fact, in Australia today those offended by the term 'racist' almost outnumber those offended by racists.[6]

The landscape of Abbott's fantasy was first mapped out in *The*

Australian Way of Life by the editor George Caiger in 1953. He described Australia as a nation of people who were 'engaged in remoulding an inherited tradition in a fresh environment', a people yearning for a greatness but frustrated by an 'insistence on equality and uniformity', whose society was dependent on the 'heavy domestic demands upon the womenfolk' and who demonstrated 'a kind of good-humoured casualness towards other peoples except where economic interests are affected'.[7]

The cruel optimism of the pursuit of the Australian way of life has become a serious impediment to the wellbeing of our nation. For straights there is liberation to be found in queerer ways of being, knowing, understanding and animating the world. Tracing these desire-lines has become one of my obsessions. Company Bad is a collective of performance makers who are my lovers, friends and collaborators. A driving force behind Company Bad's approach is the negotiation of points of transition and transformation between audiences and performers as they create new worlds together.

The 2010s was a period of sustained resourcing of new and emerging performance makers in Queensland. Queer world-building became a cherished part of this independent theatre boom, which has been described by Hannah Brown as the 'new new wave'.[8] To understand why, Nathan Stoneham, Younghee Park, M'ck McKeague and I have been re-evaluating 지하 *Underground*, the formative work we made during that period.[9] This Paper builds on that critical reflection, and looks further afield to the ways in which our friends elsewhere have been contributing to queer ideas of Australia.

Julianne Schultz writes in *The Idea of Australia: A Search for the Soul of the Nation*:

> In seeking to articulate an idea of Australia that is now fit for purpose, there is a need to... isolate and cauterise the unexamined and unlovely DNA that will otherwise pass epigenetically from one generation to the next. Transformation is at the heart of the Australian story, though rarely celebrated as a guide for the future.[10]

For those who find themselves queer in Australia and at odds with the 'unexamined and unlovely' aspects of nationhood, no amount of speculative isolation and cauterisation will make their lives commensurable with an environment soaked in cis-straight fantasies.

That initial hunch of mine is becoming stronger now. It's a proposal: Patterns of potential for the future of the Australian Way of Life are encoded in the work of queer performing artists and, through them, the diverse hopes and dreams of their communities.

Hoping and dreaming in Australia

I was a twink for about nine months in my twenties, bald by thirty and skipped both the twunk and hunk stages to settle on the flabby side of daddy at nearly forty. I'm sitting in my 70s red brick flat surrounded by vintage earthenware; printouts of this week's lecture slides and lesson plans strewn across a pile of coffee table books full of artistic nudes. Paintings and prints and ceramic tiles are neatly arranged on the walls around me, displaying messages like 'REST YOU BEAUTIFUL, BUSY IDIOT'[11] and 'HOW TO MEET HORNY MARRIED DADS IN YOUR AREA IN A GOD-HONOURING WAY'.[12] I take a moment to scroll past unread messages from ex-lovers and ex-students on my phone as I once again cancel plans for dinner with one of three friends I have in Perth, the city I moved to twelve months ago to take up my dream job, leaving behind my young family of almost a decade.

In 'The Decay of Lying', Oscar Wilde unsettles Aristotle's concept of mimesis by asserting that it is life that imitates art: art creates an ideal version of the world that life attempts to copy.

Art shapes the way we perceive reality.

But who would buy a ticket to watch the cruel optimism of an anxious, nervous, husk of a man writing and then deleting the same six sentences over and over all weekend?

Is it that art is my life, or that life is my art?

Fuck it. Clarity is for straight people, and I am sick of straight people.

Is this a sudden heterophobic outburst or the product of some deeper angst?

Living queer *and* in Australia seems incommensurable, and I am sick of worried straight people. Sick of the blatantly queerphobic delusion spouted by right-wing ideologues, that gays are grooming children by reading them stories in drag. Sick of the subtle handwringing of left-leaning Gen Xers who fret about how they could possibly talk to and about trans and gender non-conforming Zoomers. Sick of watching a screenplay about the bent nature of queer love and relationships die the death of a thousand straight cuts at the hands of executives who lack the imagination to invest in anything that contradicts the cis straight fantasy of the hero's journey.

I am appropriating Hage's thesis from *White Nation* in this harangue. One passage has reached out and shaken me from my malaise:

> If there is a single important, subjective feeling behind this book, it is that I, and many people like me, am sick of 'worried' White Australians—White Australians who think that they have a monopoly over 'worrying' about the shape and the future of Australia.[13]

Substitute 'cis-straight' for 'white' and that 'single important, subjective feeling' is what I am experiencing right now. It is a topic that occupies my conversations with friends, ex-lovers, ex-students...

There are many people for whom worrying is the last available strategy for staying in control of social processes over which they have no longer much control.[14]

My argument may prove tenuous or even problematic, but at least my hunch is finding its form: the fantasies of Australia as a cis-straight, white nation are being actively dismantled by certain artists who are engaging in a project of nationhood as creative practice.

Nationhood as creative practice

I want to give a wide berth to what David L Eng has described as the colonial dynamic of 'white folks (straight and gay) saving brown homosexuals from brown heterosexuals',[15] and the instruments of assimilation and destruction which, as Sandy O'Sullivan (Wiradjuri) reminds us:

> gaslight every historic iteration of gender diversity and sexuality outside of the heteronormative, and every Indigenous iteration of kinship that challenged the western patriarchal system.[16]

White folk have done enough damage here, and in this country non-Indigenous queers have much to learn from Indigenous critiques of the colonial project. I am white. I benefit from privileges inherited from successful intergenerational navigation of the penal-coloniser-settler industrial complex. I am not the one to lead us down the desire-line trod by O'Sullivan and others, but I do want to beat a path alongside it, that weaves around it, that intersects with it.

Whitney Monaghan has written that the queer notions of the good life that young people aspire to do not follow the same milestones as their hetero and homonormal peers and they are not often celebrated.[17] Over one in five participants in the *2021 Australian Youth Barometer* survey aged 18 to 24 identified as a member of the queer community;[18] and, compared with the general population, they were more than twice as likely to declare that sharing a similar ethnic or cultural background with others was 'not at all important for them to feel like they belong'.[19]

In 2022 Tony Abbott was writing that 'our school students deserve better than politically correct brain-washing, with every subject taught from an [I]ndigenous, sustainability and Asian perspective'.[20] What would happen if we abandoned the cruel optimism of cultural homogeneity and searched for the good life in queer models of reciprocity?

There is important work being done right now in representing and illuminating queer lives, histories and practices for a wider audience. In *Queer Performance*, a special edition of *Australasian Drama Studies*, the editors, Jonathan Bollen, Alyson Campbell and Liza-Mare Syron (Birrbay) offer to:

> trace the LGBTQI+ desire-lines linking artists and audiences—crossing social, cultural, political and regional boundaries and reaching out queerly across time and place.[21]

Zoë Coombs Marr and Nayuka Gorrie (Kurnai/Gunai, Gunditjmara, Wiradjuri, Yorta Yorta) recently led a parade of Australian LGBTIQ+ personalities across our screens in *Queerstralia*, facilitating conversations that unsettled the dominant narratives of Australian culture and identity while celebrating its contemporary queer life. The parade continued in our streets and on our stages as some of those same personalities appeared at 2023 World Pride in Sydney. Rising above the crowd was Tiwi sistergirl Crystal Love, an icon of Indigenous queer people in Australia who uses her platform to highlight the challenges they face and their opportunities.

This Paper is a work-in-progress that is messy, personal and in transition. It uses queer modes of 'associative argumentation and evidencing' to braid together analyses of Australian life provided by authors such as Ghassan Hage, Aileen Moreton-Robinson, Chelsea Watego (Mununjahli and South Sea Islander), Sandy O'Sullivan and Julianne Schultz, and landmark works on American life by José Esteban Muñoz, Lauren Berlant and Jack Halberstam.[22]

It will paint a series of scenes that describe the affect of three contemporary queer performance makers: Joel Bray (Wiradjuri), Justin Shoulder and Sarah Stafford.

Berlant writes that:

> affective atmospheres are shared, not solitary… bodies are continually busy judging their environments and responding to the atmospheres in which they find themselves.[23]

There isn't space here for a close reading and analysis of the work of these three artists, but by exploring the worlds they inhabit bodily on stage, and the atmospheres they conjure up, these aesthetic interlocutors may act as guides for readers through the dense and sometimes obscure affect theories that underpin a lot of queer studies.

Through the use of thick description, I propose to show that these artists are engaging in a project of nationhood as creative practice, or, to borrow from Álvaro Luís Lima, that they are imagining 'queer nationalism by attempting to complicate the representations of power'.[24] In doing so, I want to make space for future projects that archive and critique the work of artists who are contributing to the contemporary canon of queer performance in Australia. Above all, I want to witness, love, and celebrate the work of Joel, Justin and Sarah.

***

It's late September. The best time of the year to be in Brisbane. Festival time.

JOEL: 19 SEPT 2019 4:06 PM

Hey babes! Can't wait to see you next week! Two things though...

1 - I need a fresh guy as an audience plant in each show. I would love if you would be the one.

2 - If you know any other guys who would be good, could you suggest some?

Anyway, hope you are super well and can't wait to see you!!

Drink after the show?

Babes. Fresh guy. The one. Other guys. Can't wait. I'm nervous. Joel Bray is coming to Brisbane Festival.

I haven't seen Joel since last year. I was in Melbourne for a conference and I smoke-bombed on an afternoon panel session to meet him at a pub for dinner. On our agenda was talking business, art and love. Swapping the kinds of stories that would shock our mothers but are part of daily life for certain artistic queers. Rich fodder for Joel's new work *Daddy*. The pretext for our meeting however is that our friend Justin Shoulder is in town with his latest show, *Carrion*. We're excited. The reviews are delicious:

> A costume of bones is prepared in reverent solitude, knuckles clattering on the floor in the quiet. That endearing yet unsettling masked figure becomes riotous, and tears down a cloudscape so that it lies in a heap in the rising smoke. A pink, flouncy enormity rises up, the size of a house, burping, gluttonous, like a spirit gorging itself, and then sinks back down into the earth.[25]

I'm full of expectation. I haven't seen Justin since 2010. We were in Seoul creating dancing creatures for the inaugural Roger Rynd

International Cultural Exchange. The 'pink, flouncy enormity' sounds suspiciously like a beast that manifested as a pile of pink tissue paper under a Christmas tree in the foyer of Seoul Art Space_Mullae. I can't wait.

> He carefully dresses himself, transforming before our eyes into a masked creature with bones on the outside of his skin, at once insectile and birdlike. Around him is a jungle of mechanical parrots that imitate speech—I see you!—in between their recorded whistles. He makes bird noises: is he trying to speak to them? Is he simply curious?[26]

I'm suddenly regretful. I now remember that I spent the last night of the Cultural Exchange drinking an entire bottle of vodka in a taxi and making out with a straight friend in an alley on Homo Hill before making a menace of myself at the Wolfhound, a notorious Irish pub. I woke up in a strange bed with no memory of how I got there. I was so late to check out of our accommodation that we had to sprint through Incheon Airport, desperate to make our flights home. It's been years though. I'll be fine.

> And then he's a giant pulsating polyp, or perhaps a partially sentient intestine, that grows a human face. Then he's the masked bird-insect-human again, bereft of words, at once sinister and innocent. Hungry. Predatory.[27]

Even though I am desperate to prolong my engagement with Joel, I can't hang out after *Carrion* because another mate is also in town, and he mentioned that he might want to catch up for a drink.

No, it's not like that.
No, he's straight.
No, I haven't heard from him.
No, I don't know where we are going to meet.
Well, you know how it is...
How these straight boys always have us in a chokehold...
No? Ok, I guess I'll see you next time.

This is a good life.

1
Justin Shoulder

For the last decade and a half Justin Talplacido Shoulder has been occupied with a project of transformation that has seen him mutate into fantastic creatures—fabulous beasts—that explore his ancestral Filipinx mythologies and speculate on future possibilities for humanity. His esoteric, archetypical and exquisitely sculptural performance personas gestated in Sydney's subaltern queer nightlife to be birthed onto stages across the country and around the world.

Carrion was his first foray into the post-human. It showcases a creature that sometimes writhes, sometimes stalks, sometimes inflates, in its quest to reveal the role humanity is playing in the Earth's destruction. *Carrion* has evolved from a work of theatrical performance into a transmedial saga, its shapeshifting form challenging the binary opposition of human and animal, natural and artificial, life and death, in a rich exploration of alternative modes of being and belonging. It destabilises the myth of progress that, as Alison Croggan pointed out in her review, is built on crippling trauma and the human capacity for forgetting:

> We're also very good at making myths. This, like most human capacities, is both marvellous and catastrophic: myth-making is one of the ways we make narrative sense of the worlds we inhabit, and often how we learn to see more clearly. But some of our most pernicious myths, the myths that are undoing our very existence, are invisible.[28]

The queerness of *Carrion* isn't just in the way that it fucks with binaries and unsettles deeply held myths about humanity, it's also in the creative process that fucks with the boundaries between Justin's professional and personal lives.

Growing up closeted and deeply Pentecostal on Queensland's Sunshine Coast, I had no role models or mentors to point me towards queer patterns for a good life that strayed outside the heteronormative. The closest I got to coming out to my parents was telling my mother at sixteen that I would never give her grandchildren.

In *Gender Trouble* Judith Butler discusses the idea of 'the refusal', a personal rejection of participation in the binary performances of gender that are expected by our societies.[29] In *No Future*, Lee Edelman takes this even further by arguing that because queers have historically been excluded from participation in reproductive models of the future—a society built around the fulfilments of the child—that we should embrace what he calls the 'death drive', and refuse to invest in the future and instead focus on the present.[30] As a young person, I saw no positive examples of refusal, and had no language to express the death drive that was taking root in me.

Queer young people can have markedly different experiences of belonging and exclusion from each other.[31] Benjamin Law's book *Growing Up Queer in Australia* starts with a list of things he yearned for as an adolescent: nice clothes, clear skin and 'wavy hair like the local hot white surfer boys'; three things, however, proved hard to find: queer people, queer stories and depictions of queer sex, 'and I craved them with a desperation that bordered on hunger'.[32] The importance of representation for marginalised groups in the media, arts and cultural production is well understood, but what comes after representation?[33]

Representation wasn't especially helpful to me as a guide to living in the early 2000s. One of my overwhelming memories of being with my first love, Nathan, is that it felt like we had discovered something special and unique. In a time just before we had the entire corpus of human knowledge at our fingertips: we were inventing everything for the first time. Flirting. Sex. Breaking up. Reconnecting. Seeing other people. Seeing the same people. We binged *Queer as Folk* and I internalised the mortal dread of turning thirty—an age which would render me worthless. Season one featured a soap-operatic parenting narrative about a one-night stand between a gay man and a lesbian that resulted in an unexpected pregnancy and was further complicated by a convoluted and dramatic IVF storyline in season two. And so, I promised my best friend that if we were both still childless by thirty we would get out the turkey baster and she could keep the kid. In season four, when a gay comic store owner and his academic partner foster a teenaged HIV-positive sex worker I thought that maybe that would be an option for me. But thirty came and went, as did any prospects of a family life—being, as I was, an independent artist with crippling creditcard debt, share-housing with strangers in a run-down inner-city workers' cottage.

The first concrete model of queer family life I had was in my late twenties, getting to know Justin and hearing him talk about life with his partner and collaborator, Matt Stegh, a prolific designer and costumier. Hearing about ways they thrived as co-parents in a non-nuclear living arrangement, and inside a community in Sydney that is constantly organising and reorganising itself to accommodate families in flux, radically expanded my horizons.

Justin's creative family extends from the Glitter Militia—the politicised and avant-garde artist incubator he inaugurated with Matt in 2008—to Club Até—the collective he formed in 2014 with Bhenji Ra, contemporary dancer and Mother of the Western Sydney vogue house, Slé. Club Até's most recent work is *In Muva We Trust*, a community-led intergenerational event that poses the question: 'In the face of an uncertain future, how do we, as queer communities of colour, cultivate hope and create possibility?'[34] For Justin, extending his work into forms accessible for children and families is an exciting and important part of his creative practice.[35]

Justin's work embraces the forces of negativity, irony and disruption to rehearse strategies, born out of the rich, transgressive alterity of his personal and social lives, that imagine the world on the other side of the looming apocalypse—whether it manifests as a climate emergency, a nuclear tragedy or a disaster generated by artificial intelligence. His refusal to accommodate or assimilate to the social and symbolic orders of the cis-straight nation fantasy of Australia cultivates a vision of hope and possibility that is inspiring and should be celebrated.

By 2015, my first love and I were romantically independent. In Brisbane we got to know networks of queer and BIPOC families whose adults were arts and cultural workers and whose children benefited from collective caregiving. Two of our best friends, Fi and Thom, found a large home that none of us could ever afford alone and pitched the idea of moving in together. Nathan and I would live on separate floors and there was enough space for us all to work from home and raise children when the time came. It was a milestone I could never have imagined as a teen and would certainly never have thought of it as a good life, but when the opportunity arose, it was an easy proposition to say yes to.

***

It's late September. The best time of the year to be in Brisbane. Festival time.

> JEREMY: 20 SEPT 2019 AT 09:41 AM
>
> Hey. I would love to be your plant... I'm coming along on the Friday night. ☺
>
> Can't wait to see you. I'll put my feelers out for other willing boys.

It takes two minutes to walk directly out of my office, across the street and catch a band, some stand-up, indie theatre, cabaret, performance art, my housemate DJing for an outdoor dance party.

This year the festival is bigger than ever. 'Revels, Revelations and Romances', the marketing screams. 'Music! Theatre! Fire!' the headlines read. The Artistic Director is going out with a bang.

JOEL: 21 SEPT 2019 AT 08:49 AM

Thanks so much!

This month I've rarely been at home. I am busy teaching. Rehearsing a show. Wrapping a show. Planning a show. Today I'm meant to check in on Sarah Stafford at the bowls club. She was one of my first students when I took on teaching work during my post-grad. By some twist of fate, it turns out that her high school drama teacher was my best friend. Now Sarah is one of my best friends. The queer circle of life. She is at the bowls club three afternoons a week, wrestling hours of family video into something truly iconic. I'm her outside eye. She didn't really listen to me when she was my student, and she isn't really listening now, but I am just happy to be coming along for the ride.

My big housemates only see me if we catch a show together, bump into each other at the artist bar, make the trek out to the suburbs to watch the expensive festival centrepiece. We rename our group chat in homage to the experience. My little housemate only sees me during our morning ritual: she sits on the bottom step with me as I put on my shoes, checks that I have everything in my backpack, confirms that I am walking and not taking my car, reminds me that today mum is going to work and dad is staying home with her. 'Bye uncle!', grandma sings out as I head into the street.

This is a good life.

2
Sarah Stafford

Sarah Stafford is the doyenne of Brisbane's queer club performance scene. She performs her signature mashup of absurd mundanity, grotesque clown and vain arrogance as Amaro Mayfair in the band 'The Architects of Sound' with her long-term collaborators David Stewart (Valencia Low-Fi) and Sampson Smith (Sutro). They describe their sound as being forged 'in a Bray Park garage during a fierce electrical storm in 2012',[36] but, as one reviewer has noted, they aren't musicians: 'they're far more important, far more conceptually insightful and artistically refined, percipient guardians of the zeitgeist'.[37] The Architects are a mainstay of the 'new new wave' of independent theatre in Brisbane, but Sarah has for the last couple of years also been striking out on her own.

At a solo performance in a packed nightclub one night in 2019, I watch her paint her nails while eating discounted lobster tails from a plastic deli bag, attempt to assemble a $59 IKEA Grimsbu bed, then give up and take a nap on the mess she has made.[38] Sarah's most popular creation, the heavily pregnant Donna Jane Lesbian Lee (she insists you MUST call her UK DJ LESLEY), rides a hoverboard while snorting a bag of flour before giving birth to a packet of Arnott's biscuits.[39]

Sarah's work took a gothic turn in *Again, You Have Trusted Me*, a camp, gritty, and violent portrait of her working-class family in Queensland's deep north that powerfully reanimates the intergenerational trauma that has left lasting scars on the women in her family:

Look at them, aren't they gorgeous? That's my family. My mother's side. That's Nanny. Jacqueline is my mother. Ugh beautiful feisty little cow. Gayle, we love her. Toni, beautiful Toni. Karen, hello Karen. And Poppy, bless his soul.

[A FAMILY PHOTO APPEARS]

Mum told me this photo was taken because Nanny (Ivy) was going into emergency surgery and everyone was freaking the fuck out so they decided to sit for this portrait in case something happened while she was under. I think that's the story but also I wasn't really listening so I could be wrong. And actually, I haven't asked again/decided not to fact check that so...[40]

These are the battlers whose mythologies animate our image of the Australian way of life. They are riven with internal contradictions that, as Julianne Schultz writes, lull us into complacency by defying analysis 'so that we don't have to take responsibility'.[41] *Again, You Have Trusted Me* is a prime example of the anti-social[42] nature of queer storytelling and the 'temporal drag'[43]—adopting a persona that switches times rather than genders—that exposes Peter Dutton's 'forgotten Australians' to the antiseptic of the theatrical spotlight.[44] Nadia Jade wrote in her review of the show when it was remounted by Backbone Youth Arts in 2022:

What is Australian gothic when you drill down into it? When you discard the sports jokes and the cliches of white suburban life? Is it a reckoning with the incongruity of us, broken people from a hundred countries, all chasing a better life, trying to find ourselves

> in this red desert land where the true way of life is completely foreign to our limited understandings? Alongside the lucky country jibes the colony offers us up the very darkest of gallows humour. Is it the callous truth that ours are scarred people? Maybe we're white trash just trying to hold on with both hands to whatever joy we can scrape out of the colony. What is shocking to a people immured in generations of violence?[45]

Through her work Sarah is rebuilding Australian nationhood in an act of creative practice. Whether she is providing live commentary on a home video of the women in her family moments before they come to blows, or using a home-made green screen to recreate Australian Olympic gold medal wins in a pub,[46] or hoverboarding onto a nightclub stage to sit on a discounted Woolworths mud cake,[47] or stringing together all of her greatest hits in a red clown wig as a truly unhinged durational Pauline Hanson parody,[48] Sarah embodies the absurdity of Australia's suburban, working-class pantheon of battlers in ways that even Chris Lilley could never pull off.

In 2021 she was interviewed on a Brisbane talk show that was livestreamed from an inner-city ex-government building. The host seemed to think that his laddish charm would be enough to elicit a meaningful conversation, but Sarah was deeply uninterested in discussing 'what else is going on in your life' or 'where does your mind go when you get into character'. So thoroughly and uncomfortably confounding were her answers that he was repeatedly forced to apologise, finally admitting, 'I'm just jamming my foot in my mouth tonight'.[49]

This wasn't a difficult interviewee letting the vain arrogance of an on-stage persona bleed into her personality off-stage. Her queerness—her ability to play on the podium of a nightclub on a Saturday night and on the field of a suburban soccer club on a Sunday morning—allows her to confidently occupy the complicated social and political landscape that seems to worry so many of her straighter contemporaries. So, Sarah wasn't being difficult, she just wasn't letting him get away with falling back on cis-straight fantasies as the default mode of social interaction.

Most recently, Sarah has recently been working with All The Queens Men to facilitate the Brisbane chapter of their LGBTIQ+ Elders Dance Club, bringing multiple generations of our community together to share social space. For its participants, this this is a life-changing project that is happening on a local scale.

***

It's late September. The best time of the year to be in Brisbane. Festival time.

JOEL: 27 SEPT 2019 AT 5:03 PM

Hey babe,

Agh! Forgot to ask you. Could you arrive at 8:40 today for a quick onstage briefing? Just make yourself known to FOH and they'll bring you through.

x J

It's Friday and my workmates are off to the pub, but I need to be back in tomorrow. A day full of work before Sarah's birthday party extravaganza at Ben's Vietnamese in Woolloongabba. I should be sensible.

I have a show to go to.

JEREMY: 27 SEPT 2019 AT 5:03 PM

Yeah no worries.

The pub. A much needed debrief and a glass of prosecco. A bottle of prosecco. Two bottles. I'll order tapas, that'll slow things down.

JOEL: 27 SEPT 2019 AT 8:16 PM

Legend!

I have a show to go to.

Let's all go for a walk. Prosecco is on special at the bottle-o. I can definitely act sober enough to be served at the bottle-o. Just one more drink.

I'm not fooling anyone.

JEREMY: 27 SEPT 2019 AT 8:30 PM

Hey babe. I am so sorry... I am not going to be able to make it back tonight... I know this is going to totally put you out RE the audience plant. All the best. Xxxx

No reply.

I'm on the veranda of a Queenslander, and everyone agrees that I should stay. Wait. That was unprofessional. I made a promise. Shit.

I have a show to go to.

> <u>JEREMY: 27 SEPT 2019 AT 8:31 PM</u>
>
> Lies. I'll make it! I'll just be late.

No reply.

I have nine minutes. Will it be quicker to sprint down the hill or get an Uber?

No reply.

Eight minutes now.

> <u>JEREMY: 27 SEPT 2019 AT 8:32 PM</u>
>
> Ok. I'll make it!!! But like 4 minutes late.

I am at front of house. I give my name. Act sober.

I'm not fooling anyone.

The room is hazy. The lights are dim. Joel is beautiful in a bath robe. Now he's telling me what I'll have to do. It's hard to focus, but I've got this. It's a couple of simple cues. At some point he'll give me a signal, the crowd will part and we will dance. Was I meant to part the crowd or would that just happen? I can wing it. Act sober.

I'm not fooling anyone.

He tells me it will be sexy, intimate. He'll put his hand on my head and I'll pretend to go down on him. It is an important moment of audience interaction. It is meant to look spontaneous, but he has thought it all through and wants it to be safe. Safe, and sexy. Okay. Act sober. I can do safe. I can do sexy.

I'm not fooling anyone.

> JEREMY: 27 SEPT 2019 AT 10:48 PM
>
> That was so beautiful.
> I have to be at work at 7:30
> tomorrow morning so I had to run.
> You're a fucking star. Xxxxx

I order an Uber. Confess to the producer that I think I ruined the show. I was not contributing to making a safe space... And I was definitely not sexy.

I'm home. My keys are at work. I climb the back fence. Quietly. The little one is sleeping. Break in through the veranda door. No noise upstairs. Sneak to the fridge room. Uncle Jeremy's fridge, aunty Bec's fridge, side-by-side under the stairs. Find an egg. Fill a pot. Open the *ramyeon*. Turn on the stove. Set off the fire alarm. Wake the whole house. Shuffle to my room. Pass out.

> JOEL: 28 SEPT 2019 AT 12:11 AM
>
> Thanks babes. Love ya!

This is a good life.

3
Joel Bray

Joel Bray is a Wiradjuri dancer who performed in Israel with some of its most dynamic contemporary dance companies for a decade, before returning to Australia to forge a new practice as a choreographer and performance maker. We first met at the National Indigenous Dance Forum in 2017 and bonded over our shared experiences growing up regional, Pentecostal and queer.

As Bray sees it, pre-coming out, queer kids learn to live two very distinct lives. The straight-passing one that helps navigate parental and peer expectations, 'the good son, the boyfriend to the girls at school' and the queer internal life: 'On the inside you're indulging your fantasies. When you watch a Disney film, it's Prince Charming you're looking at.' It's this dual life, he believes, that set him, and many queer kids like him, in good stead for a future in performance.[50]

In *Considerable Sexual License*, Joel recontextualises his familial history in an immersive dance-theatre experience which weaves together storytelling and audience participation to 'ponder a past (and perhaps an imagined future) of the sexual ecology of Australia before the Coloniser and the Bible'.[51] The work unsettles the mythology of what Aileen Moreton-Robinson calls the 'Good Indigenous Citizen'—an identity in which Aboriginal and Torres Strait Islanders willingly conform to colonial norms—and undermines its false doctrine that Indigenous cultures were homogeneously heteronormative at the time of first contact. Troy-Anthony Baylis (Jawoyn) has also challenged this notion:

> It is as if history has constructed Aboriginality as being so pure and so savage, so purely savage, that if tainted by the complexity of sexuality, mixed ethnographies, mixed geographies and mixed appearances, the whole look would be ruined. Aboriginal people would be regarded as not pure, not savage.[52]

Julianne Shultz asks 'what does it take to acknowledge the past, make amends and forge a new future?'53 According to her, the main challenge is how to 'synthesise ancient and modern ways of being, both temporal and physical' to resolve the fundamental contradiction on which this nation is founded, but Joel's answer is different.[54] *Considerable Sexual License* foregrounds the queerness of incommensurability to show that living in the tense space between black and white, in and out, godly and blasphemous, is not a place to 'settle', but a place where we may thrive.

***

The stark reality is that those who live at the intersection of Indigeneity and queerness here in so-called Australia have never been afforded the things that the cis-straight white fantasy of Australia lives in terror of losing: loss of status, loss of wealth, loss of opportunity, loss of respectability. Does that make us any less Australian? Do we even want to be Australian? Should nationhood even be an endeavour queers engage with? Writing of South Africa in the wake of apartheid, at the intersection of art, queerness and national identity, Álvaro Luís Lima argues that 'a queer consideration of nationhood already implies the... subversion of what nationalism can mean.'[55] My long-time collaborator M'ck McKeague said to me on reading this Paper,

'I don't know any queer people looking to the future, who are tied to Australia as part of their identity.'

Australia is a work-in-progress. Aboriginal and Torres Strait Islander arts and cultural workers, their communities and leaders have started to make sure that any work made in and on this country respects their histories and is responsive to their futures. And Australia is also a country steeped in mythologies. Some of these mythologies nourish the people living here and help them to sustain their communities, and some of them are frustrating, if not downright destructive: *terra nullius*, the Aussie battler, the migrant threat, the idea of progress itself... All of these myths ignore and deny the complexity, diversity and contingency of human experience. But I think that we might have a chance of breaking the shackles of cruel optimism that bind us to the cis-straight fantasy if we pay keen attention to those artists who are devoting their lives to the project of nationhood as creative practice. If art shapes the way we perceive reality, then it is artists who are shaping the world that we live in.

Schultz says that a spirit of transformation lies at the heart of the Australian story, but it is rarely celebrated as a guide to the future. My response, I guess, is it depends whose celebrations you are going to.

Endnotes

---

1. Jeremy Neideck, 'The Cost of Cultural Ambition'. QUT ePrints, 2016. eprints.qut.edu.au.
2. The term 'desire lines' is borrowed from Jonathan Bollen, Alyson Campbell and Liza-Mare Syron, 'Editorial: Queer Performance'. *Australasian Drama*

Studies, no. 81, *Queer Performance*. October 2022.

3. Alyson Campbell and Stephen Farrier, 'Queer Practice as Research: A Fabulously Messy Business'. *Theatre Research International*, Vol. 40, no. 1, March 2015, p. 83. doi:10.1017/S0307883314000601.
4. Lauren Berlant, *Cruel Optimism*. Duke University Press, 2011.
5. Tony Abbott, 'Tony Abbott: Don't be brainwashed by revisionist history, we're still the lucky county'. *Daily Telegraph*. March 31, 2022. dailytelegraph.com.au
6. Ghassan Hage, *Against Paranoid Nationalism: Searching for Hope in a Shrinking Society*. Pluto Press, 2003, p. x.
7. George Caiger (ed.), *The Australian Way of Life*. Columbia University Press, 1953, p. xiv.
8. Hannah Brown, 'Brisbane's New Theatre Boom and the Turquoise Elephant in the Room'. *Guardian*. July 9, 2015. theguardian.com
9. Jeremy Neideck, Nathan Stoneham, Younghee Park and M'ck McKeague, '"We'll meet you underground": Transcultural performance practices in queer space and time'. *Australasian Drama Studies*, no. 81, October 2022, pp. 203-36.
10. Julianne Schultz, *The Idea of Australia: A Search for the Soul of the Nation*. Allen & Unwin, 2022, p. 24.
11. Samuel Leighton-Dore, 'Rest Smile Tile'. 2021. sadmanstudio.com.
12. Zain Curtis, 'Horny Married Dads'. 2021. happydevilboy.com.
13. Ghassan Hage, *White Nation*. Routledge, 1998, p. 10.
14. Ibid.
15. David L Eng and Jasbir K Puar, 'Introduction: Left of Queer'. *Social Text*, Vol. 38, no. 4, *Left of Queer*, December 2020, pp. 1-24. doi: 10.1215/01642472-8680414.
16. Sandy O'Sullivan, 'The Colonial Project of Gender (and Everything Else)'. *Genealogy*, Vol. 5, no. 67, 2021, p. 4. doi:10.3390/genealogy5030067
17. Whitney Monaghan, *Queer Girls, Temporality and Screen Media Not 'Just a*

Phase'. Palgrave Macmillan, 2016, p. 14. doi:10.1057/978-1-137-55598-4.

18. Blake Cutler, Beatriz Gallo Cordoba, Lucas Walsh, Masha Mikola and Catherine Waite, *Queer Young People in Australia: Insights from the 2021 Australian Youth Barometer.* Monash University, Centre for Youth Policy and Education Practice, 2022, p. 3. doi:10.26180/19719532.
19. Ibid, p. 8.
20. Tony Abbott, op. cit.
21. Jonathan Bollen et al, op. cit., p. 2.
22. José Esteban Muñoz, *Cruising Utopia: The Then and There of Queer Futurity.* New York University Press, 2009, p. 3.
23. Lauren Berlant, op cit., p. 15.
24. Álvaro Luís Lima, 'Screw the Nation! Queer Nationalism and Representations of Power in Contemporary South African Art'. *African Arts,* Vol. 45, no. 4, *Gender and South African Art,* Winter 2012, p. 46. jstor.org/stable/41721404.
25. Cleo Mees, 'Liveworks: CARRION: Magnificent mutancy'. *Realtime.* November 8, 2017. realtime.org.au.
26. Alison Croggon, 'Carrion: The intimacy of strangeness'. *Witness.* June 29, 2018. witnessperformance.com.
27. Ibid.
28. Ibid.
29. Judith Butler, *Gender Trouble.* Routledge, 1990.
30. Lee Edelman, *No Future: Queer Theory and the Death Drive.* Duke University Press, 2004.
31. Blake Cutler et al op. cit., p. 1.
32. Benjamin Law (ed.), *Growing Up Queer in Australia.* Black Inc., 2019, p. 1.
33. Whitney Monaghan, 'Lesbian, Gay and Bisexual Representation on Australian Entertainment Television: 1970–2000'. *Media International Australia,* Vol. 174, no. 1, February 2020, pp. 49-58. doi: 10.1177/1329878X198763.

34. 'MCA Australia Announces Major Exhibition Ultra Unreal—New Myths for New Worlds'. Media Release. Museum of Contemporary Art Australia. May 16, 2022. mca.com.au.
35. Steve Dow, 'Justin Shoulder Discusses His New Performance for Liveworks 2017'. *Art Guide Australia*. October 16, 2017. artguide.com.au.
36. '*Titties in Paradise,* The Architects of Sound, Review'. *Triple J Unearthed*. January 27, 2014. abc.net.au.
37. Kristy Stanfield, 'Rough, Red and Raw | Architects of Sound'. *Nothing Ever Happens in Brisbane*. April 9, 2023. nothingeverhappensinbrisbane.com.
38. Sarah Stafford, 'LOBSTER'. Instagram. June 2019. instagram.com.
39. Sarah Stafford, *Poly Lez Slut*. 2022. sarahstafford.com.au
40. Sarah Stafford, *Again You Have Trusted Me,* creative development script. 2019.
41. Julianne Schultz, op, cit., p. 27.
42. Edelman, op. cit., p. 43.
43. Elizabeth Freeman, *Time Binds: Queer Temporalities, Queer Histories*. Duke University Press, 2010.
44. Jessica Bahr, 'Peter Dutton promises to target "forgotten Australians" after elevation to Liberal leadership'. *SBS News*. May 30, 2022. sbs.com.au.
45. Nadia Jade, 'Again, You Have Trusted Me | Sarah Stafford'. *Nothing Ever Happens in Brisbane*. November 9, 2022. nothingeverhappensinbrisbane.com.
46. Sarah Stafford, 'GRN SCRN'. Instagram. May 2021. instagram.com.
47. Sarah Stafford, 'DJ LESLEY'. Instagram. December 2020. instagram.com.
48. Sarah Stafford, 'PAULINE'. Instagram. April 2019. instagram.com.
49. Superordinary, 'Superlate S02E05'. Sunday 15 August 2021. twitch.tv. This video has been taken down. Editor.
50. Stephen A Russell, 'Growing Up Queer and Indigenous: "I Make My Art Out of That Tangle"'. *SBS Pride*. January 10, 2019. sbs.com.au.
51. Ibid.

52. Troy-Anthony Baylis, 'The Art of Seeing Aboriginal Australia's Queer Potential'. *The Conversation*. April 16, 2014. theconversation.com.
53. Julianne Schultz, op. cit., p. 7.
54. Julianne Schultz, op. cit., p. 16.
55. Álvaro Luís Lima, op. cit., p. 46.

Acknowledgements

I'd like to acknowledge the leaders, artists, audience members, board members, staff and volunteers and other stakeholders from under-represented groups engaging with the arts and cultural sector. Your continued advocacy, activism and action is shaping us into a more inclusive industry which is producing better art. Thank you for everything you do and for allowing me to walk alongside you, learn from you and play my part in supporting you.

I would particularly like to acknowledge my trusted advisors and friends, Tandi Palmer-Williams, Sherryl Reddy and Trish Adjei, for providing invaluable guidance and support in the development of this Paper; and my editors Julian Meyrick and Harriet Parsons—thank you for showing me the ways of a Platform Paper and for helping to bring out my voice in an authentic and, I hope, engaging way.

***

The variety of language and terminology used in this field is rapidly evolving, shifting and changing. Language preference is a personal and a political choice. I have chosen to use language that resonates with me, and specific language used by those I am quoting or referencing. However, there are widening views on language preference in Australia and internationally.

More Risk, More Play
Creating an Inclusive Culture

Morwenna Collett
Gadigal country

Content warning: This section describes an example of racism towards First Nations people. Please take care when reading. This Paper was written on unceded Gadigal country, which always was and always will be Aboriginal land. I pay my respects to the traditional custodians, to their Elders past and present and to all Aboriginal and Torres Strait Islander Peoples. First Nations Peoples are the oldest living culture on the planet, with over 65,000 years of history and continued connection to the land, sea and sky. Australia's arts and cultural sector is built on this foundation and is the richer for it.

It's the opening night of my first show of the year, at one of Australia's best known and loved festivals. The house lights have gone down, we're all settling in and a First Nations Elder is invited to the stage to offer the Welcome to Country. There is some mumbling from the seat behind me, but I'm concentrating on the words and taking a moment for quiet reflection. At the close, someone behind me starts booing. It's horrific. Others in the audience think so too and we all start booing the heckler. My heart goes out to the Elder leaving the stage and the trauma this will cause her and the performers waiting behind the curtain to begin their show. The heckler doesn't leave and the show goes on. It's incredibly uncomfortable and we're in shock that this has actually happened. It's 2023 and sitting in that theatre, I realise, wow, there is still so much work to do.

Fast forward to the last show I see at that festival. It is in a recently re-opened performing arts centre. It has been significantly upgraded and includes new accessibility features. The venue management has chosen to re-open with a First Nations show, and not only that, it's one for kids. My three-year-old loves it, as does everyone else. It's delightful and spine-tingling: a sign of great things to come in the program.

For many, the Welcome to Country at the beginning of a cultural event helps to ground us in our surroundings and provides an important moment for reflection and learning. It might be a child's first experience of art or their introduction to First Nations history and culture. The arts have the power to shape and change hearts and minds. They allow us to see the world from different points of view. They give us time and space to reflect and focus on important issues and think beyond ourselves. This is a small illustration of how the arts has the power to create spiritual and political shifts in our society—to point us towards a more accessible, diverse, equitable and inclusive future. Our theatres, galleries and other arts spaces should be inclusive environments and spaces, where everyone feels welcome.

We're on the brink of a global shift towards equity and social inclusion. Movements like #MeToo and Black Lives Matter (and Indigenous Lives Matter here in Australia) are showing that we can no longer ignore the injustices happening around us. Slowly, this is translating into stronger diversity requirements in government funding programs, the appointment of Diversity and Inclusion (D&I) Managers in organisations in Australia's arts and cultural sector, and more discussion about diversity and inclusion issues in our national forums and our culture as a whole.

But is our sector truly ready for this coming change around access, diversity, equity and inclusion (ADEI)? Many of our large arts institutions still appear to be run by white, able-bodied people, often men, from metropolitan, middle-class backgrounds. In 2021, the Australia Council's *Towards Equity* report showed that only 3% of the current cultural leaders of major arts organisations receiving multi-year investment were d/Deaf or disabled; and only 16% were culturally and linguistically diverse, compared with 18% and 49% respectively of the general population.[1] Why should we bother with these issues anyway? Is it out of genuine commitment or just because we feel like we should? And are arts organisations only complying because funding bodies are starting to demand it?

In this essay I argue that celebrating diverse perspectives and embracing other kinds of lived experience is essential if the Australian arts and culture sector is to remain relevant, continue to produce exceptional art and sell more tickets. What will it take to do ADEI successfully, whose responsibility is it, and how could it inform the hearts and minds of arts practitioners and audiences across the country? I explore what the arts sector has found hard about embracing diversity in the past, and where it has failed to answer important questions. I look at the increasing appetite for meaningful diversity across the mainstream arts sector and how we've got to where we are today, just how inclusive our current practices really are, and where we need to get to in the future. In short, I ask how ADEI can have an impact on all stakeholders in the cultural sector, empower artists, arts workers, audiences and the wider public—and get more bums on seats.

I write as a proud disabled woman and an experienced practitioner. I have worked in the arts and for arts funding bodies all my adult life. That's taken some doing and I acknowledge my good fortune in being able to do it when the barriers for many others are too high. My views have been shaped by my own experiences and those of the people and organisations I've worked with, and I'm sharing now the things I think we need to think about, and what the future could look like if we act.

As the Australian arts sector recovers from the impact of COVID-19 and responds to the government's latest national cultural policy, *Revive*, I want to paint a picture of what could happen if we did, truly, prioritise diversity. What would it look like if we supported and nurtured it in all its glory? What sort of art might we make? How do we 'walk the talk' and make space to do things differently? What steps can individuals and institutions take to make meaningful change?

It is important to note that contemporary ADEI is very much a 'live' issue and the discussion is rapidly evolving. There's a chance that some of the issues I raise here may quickly become obsolete. That's okay. Some authors write for all time. I write this essay with the hope that, in the not-too-distant future, it will be redundant.

1
The case for ADEI

Across Australian society we've got a lot of 'isms' relating to marginalisation, and sometimes it can feel like these are growing rather than shrinking. Forms of discrimination which are currently alive and well include racism, ableism, ageism, sexism, homophobia, transphobia, intersex discrimination, social stigma and many others. Put simply, difference is not something everyone is comfortable with, and some may view diversity as 'background noise' rather than an issue that is genuinely important.

Access, Diversity, Equity and Inclusion are essential to Australian culture, not just in the arts but in everything we do and everything we are. It's about fairness, it's about basic human rights, it's about representation and most of all it's about belonging and community. Ultimately, ADEI is about ending discrimination by finding its root causes in the way we treat each other. It's about recognising that people have different needs and building workplaces that work for everybody by removing barriers to participation—it's common sense and responsible business practice.

Most of us would consider these values as the basic components of a just society, so why is ADEI still an issue in 2023? What's holding us up?

Towards Equity provides some basic principles for supporting diversity in and through arts and culture:

- Participation in arts and culture is a human right.
- An arts and cultural sector that reflects all Australians will drive positive outcomes, including a more inclusive,

cohesive and just nation and great art.

- Inclusive leadership is critical.
- Data and reporting support action and accountability.[2]

These principles are a useful starting point for explaining why action is needed and to help us to think about what sorts of incentives and regulations might best support these actions.

'Diversity' and 'inclusion' are being used frequently now, along with 'equity', 'belonging', 'access' and 'representation', but what do these terms actually mean? One of the obstacles to transparent discussion is the terminology which is loose, changeable and poorly understood. If we're not careful, we can spend more time trying to articulate what we're doing, rather than getting on and doing it. I use the definitions proposed by ADEI scholar Dr Antonio Cuyler:

> Access—removing barriers to participation (this is about who is included or not).
>
> Diversity—qualitative and/or quantitative assessment of human difference and representation (this is about how people are represented).
>
> Equity—fairness in addressing the historic injustice of under-representing certain groups (this is about policies and practices to ensure success).
>
> Inclusion—belonging, one of many measures of quality of life (this is about people feeling welcome).[3]

When we talk about diversity, who exactly is under-represented? Because of the lack of overarching equality legislation in Australia, and the fact that much specifically ADEI legislation is outdated, this is not something that can be definitively expressed. *Towards Equity* focuses on the following demographic cohorts:

- First Nations
- Cultural and linguistic diversity
- Disability
- Gender
- LGBTQIA+
- Regional, rural and remote
- Children and young people
- Older people.

Class (social and economic) as well as religious affiliations and beliefs could also be included in this list. All these groups have experienced marginalisation in various ways, both historically and in the present day. But people's lives are also multi-dimensional—we all have many facets to our identities—and it is important to recognise that these groups overlap as well. We know for example that 45% of First Nations people[4] and 39% of LGBTQIA+ people aged 14–21[5] experience disability or long-term health conditions. This can have a compounding effect on the disadvantages and discrimination one individual experiences. In 1989 Kimberlé Crenshaw coined the term 'intersectionality' to describe how the various aspects of a person's identity may expose them to multiple forms of marginalisation.[6]

It is impossible for anyone to speak for all under-represented groups. Our lived experiences of the world are different. This is partly why working in the ADEI area is so challenging. In fact, when invited to write this essay, my first response was to go out and interview a range of diversity leaders in the cultural sector to give voice to their views and opinions. It makes me slightly uncomfortable to rely only on my own experience and the ADEI conversations and programs in which I have participated. Having made that caveat, I do my best to take a helicopter view—to be inclusive about the issue of inclusion.

Some initiatives for engaging with equity issues for under-represented groups in the arts are common and foundational, such as targeted outreach and engagement activities to welcome specific communities. Others are more bespoke: working well with the Deaf community requires a tailored and ideally Deaf-led communication approach.

As arts organisations, we should question whether to approach inclusion for these groups all at once, especially when each demands tailoring and thought. Do we want to be a jack-of-all-trades and potentially master of none? Or do we want to start our ADEI journey by focusing on a few areas first? Can we create a 'one-stop-shop' overarching Diversity Plan, or do we also need to have specific plans such as a Reconciliation Action Plan, Disability Inclusion Action Plan and Gender Equity Action Plan?

There are no simple answers and no one way of doing things. But the *ABC's Diversity & Inclusion Plan 2019–22* is a good model:

> To enable us to make some real, sustainable and accelerated change with the resources we have available, this Plan will focus on five key diversity areas:
>
> - Cultural and linguistic diversity (CALD),
> - Aboriginal and Torres Strait Islander people,

- Disability,
- Gender,
- LGBTQI+.

> However, the initiatives and actions set out in this Plan focus on fostering an inclusive work culture and practices for everyone. Other diversity markers, such as age, geographic location and socioeconomic status, are also very important to the ABC. This work will benefit all under-represented groups—and the workforce as a whole. An inclusive and diverse workplace is better for all of us.[7]

A long shopping list of under-represented groups can be overwhelming for an under-resourced arts organisation. Just knowing where to start can seem like an impossible task, but it is better to dive in and get on with something, than sit back and try and figure it all out in advance while doing nothing at all.

2

Case study: spotlight on disability

Having provided a brief overview of ADEI and under-represented groups, I want to focus on a specific area to clarify some of the issues involved and to illustrate these through the lens of my own experience of disability. This is a key part of my identity, which has shaped my relationship with the arts over twenty years. I live with invisible disability which I hid for many years to avoid social stigma, only 'coming out' as disabled in the arts sector once my career was well established. Disability became part of my life when I was studying music at university. Due to the lack of accessibility provisions in the classical music industry twenty years ago, this changed the course of my career from performer to administrator. Meeting other incredible disabled artists and administrators gave me the courage to do so, and now I couldn't imagine my life without it.

Disability is a very broad category. According to the 'United Nations Convention on the Rights of Persons with Disabilities', it includes those with 'long-term physical, mental, intellectual or sensory impairments which in interaction with various barriers may hinder their full and effective participation in society on an equal basis with others.'[8] The international symbol for disability, the blue wheelchair, doesn't help holistic thinking. Only 4% of people with disability are wheelchair users.[9] Eighty per cent of us live with hidden disability,[10] including myself, raising complicated issues about identity and disclosure. Disability can include groups such as people living with mental health conditions (which have risen exponentially since COVID-19),[11] people with neurodiversity and people from the Deaf community, who, if they are sign language users, may identify as culturally and linguistically diverse.

It is not always helpful to think of people with disability as one group. There are many different barriers to access that people with disability can experience, and many different types of solutions—and in some cases, these may even compete with each other. For example, a captioned video or performance that works well for someone with hearing loss may be distracting for someone with cognitive disability. Our needs are so different and, in an arts context, targeted engagement strategies are required to reach different pockets of people with different access needs.

Disability can sometimes get left out of diversity and

inclusion conversations and thinking. That's one reason I like the acronym ADEI—it gets access in there, nice and early. When we hear the words diversity and inclusion, our minds may initially gravitate to People of Colour or First Nations or women, which are vitally important under-represented groups. However, diversity is broader than race and gender, and disability is often an afterthought or forgotten altogether. It's challenging, because disability requires practical and sometimes expensive changes to ensure access, such as capital works or booking access service providers like Auslan interpreters. For these reasons, disability can find itself left in the 'too hard' basket, particularly in Australia where much of our arts activity takes place in inaccessible heritage-listed buildings. Disability needs to be prioritised and supported with appropriate financial technical and human resources—it's the only diversity area which we can all become a member of at any time!

People with disability have a keen interest in the arts and are in fact more likely to create art, volunteer in the arts or even give money to the arts.[12] Sadly, this high prevalence of engagement doesn't translate through to the professional artist community, with only 9% of professional Australian artists identifying as disabled in 2017.[13] Accessibility hasn't become an embedded priority in the sector as much as other diversity concerns.

People with disability are an important, culturally-engaged group and we're all missing out if we don't plan for accessibility for our diverse communities. If there's one thing we can all do straight away, it's to start talking about access and get comfortable with it. The simple question 'Do you have any access requirements?' gives people permission to say what they need and takes away the emotional labour of wondering whether I'm being a pain if I tell you I need a seat at your standing gig, or a wheelchair accessible toilet. Ask everyone—artists, audience members, staff, any of our stakeholders: it is a question that can open up a new conversation. Ultimately, it's that conversation that will push us to meet the demand for an accessible and inclusive arts sector.

3

Why bother: reasons to be inclusive

As an arts consultant specialising in ADEI, people come to me for help and advice for a range of reasons. Sometimes it's because they know government legislation is changing or their current action plan will soon expire, and they are looking ahead. Or it might be because a complaint has been made against them, perhaps through a body like the Australian Human Rights Commission. Sometimes there's a genuine desire to do better, and sometimes it's about how to make it all go away.

No matter the reason, I love working with everyone on ADEI solutions. I often find myself playing the role of 'critical friend' or guide, as we work through the barriers together to resolve them, with the help of various communities. Whether I'm helping to set priorities, develop a strategy or action plan, provide practical advice on programming and audience development, deliver training or run a diversity program, it's all working towards building more ADEI competent and confident organisations.

From my vantage point, I have observed five main reasons arts organisations want to address ADEI:

1. Moral principles
   Because fundamentally, most of us see including everyone in our work as the 'right thing to do'. It's about values and being good human beings.

2. Funding and legislative requirements
   Arts organisations are realising that funding agencies are starting to make this a priority and addressing these issues may make them more competitive. As a result, more organisations in the National Performing Arts Partnership Framework grant program now have ADEI related plans. New legislation is also on the radar. Victoria will be introducing a new Disability Inclusion Act in the next twelve months and some organisations are already on the front foot to respond to it.

3. Artistic potential
   A reason not frequently cited, but to my mind the one that is the most important, is to ensure that we are telling diverse stories that are told by diverse artists. Not only is it ethically important that our stages and screens reflect the world we live in, but the art is bloody good. Diverse artists are making some of the most exciting, interesting, relevant, risk-taking, experimental work on the planet. Some organisations are starting to realise that they are missing a trick if they aren't showcasing diverse artists in their programming.

4. Business case
   The notion that being inclusive is good for business is slowly gaining traction. Economic arguments for inclusion are cited

more often overseas, with places like the UK measuring the spending power of disabled households: in 2020, the 'Purple Pound' was estimated to be worth £274 billion.[14] If even a small percentage of that amount is spent on arts and cultural activities, that's a significant investment in arts institutions. In Australia, the most recent Audience Outlook Monitor research shows that in Australia, 26% of audiences were affected by access issues in some way in 2022. This included people who were disabled or immunocompromised, or close to someone who was.[15] That is a big part of the market.

5. Diversifying our workforce
   Arts organisations are currently experiencing high levels of staff turnover, burnout and 'quiet quitting' across the country.[16] Attracting and retaining staff and volunteers is essential and their long-term viability depends on their ability to recruit people from all backgrounds.

At the end of the day, there are many reasons to take ADEI seriously, including innovation, wider talent pools and happier staff and customers. To do the work of diversity, we need to use our heads, our hearts and our hands.

4

Who cares: who does ADEI affect?

ADEI issues can impact multiple people in multiple ways. They affect the entire cultural sector, including audiences, artists, boards, volunteers, staff and other stakeholders. Sometimes when

ADEI is in the responsibility of a 'People and Culture' team, it can get focused mainly on actions relating to staffing rather than audiences, artists, and other stakeholders. In areas of ADEI that seem harder to tackle such as disability, there can be a tendency to start with audiences.

Audiences

Audience diversity is tangible. For Deaf people, it is easy enough to book an Auslan interpreter for a show and 'tick it off the list', but it is much harder to build a relationship with the Deaf community and encourage them to attend. The company needs to choose the right show and the right session to interpret and the audience development work needs to be ongoing and meaningful.

Artists

While starting with audience diversity is good, artists are the heart of arts organisations. Some of the most transformative experiences come about when diversity and inclusion are considered from an artist's perspective. Working directly with artists is personal, so it can humanise ADEI work. Seeing more diverse artists on our stages is important, particularly in high-quality works of scale. This is a powerful act of inclusion that can shift perceptions, both at a societal level and by providing role models for under-represented communities: 'you can't be what you can't see.' I remember a story shared by a disabled colleague who said that for years she just assumed she wouldn't survive until adulthood because she'd never seen a character with her impairment who was an adult. Cultural representation conditions expectations.

When Wendy Martin was working on the inaugural Unlimited Festival (which was part of the Cultural Olympiad for the Southbank Centre in London, as part of the 2012 Olympic and Paralympic Games) she developed relationships with some of the world's most talented disabled artists. This experience and the artworks they made stayed with her, and her pitch for her next position as the Artistic Director of the Perth Festival featured artists with disability. This priority has remained permanently embedded in the program beyond her tenure. The ripple effects of transformative experiences like this can be felt by individuals and organisations for years to come.

I attended Wendy's second Unlimited Festival in 2014, having negotiated to work as the program's first International Intern. It was the most impactful and transcendental arts experience of my life. I saw more work by disabled artists in one week than I was able to see on average in a year in Australia, including work by internationally renowned disabled artists. I saw work so powerful that it still moves me today. I met artists who have become lifelong friends. I saw a major mainstream cultural organisation showcasing work by artists who are so often forgotten by the mainstream theatres, and audiences flocking to see the work. I saw what was possible when barriers are removed. It was this arts experience that led me to start identifying more openly as disabled when I got back home to Australia.

In respect of programming and diversity, there is debate about the benefits of the spotlighting or targeted strategy (e.g. The All About Women festival, centred on female-identifying speakers and topics) versus an inclusive mainstream approach (a general festival which includes artists/speakers from under-represented groups, without making this the sole focus). In my view, both have a role to play. Spotlight events like the Unlimited Festival at London's Paralympic Games can elevate the profile of d/Deaf and disabled artists in an unprecedented way. High quality mainstream events can promote diverse artists to a wider audience and avoid the 'preaching to the converted' syndrome that can be present in the ADEI field. Artists need both sorts of opportunities—as do their audiences.

Administration

We are beginning to have discussions about the importance of diversifying boards and governance structures, though too often the focus is on gender alone. In fact, the Governance Institute of Australia and Watermark Search International only include gender, cultural background, age, skills/experience and tenure/independence in their annual Board Diversity Index.[17] That doesn't sound particularly diverse to me.

Diversifying our boards means going beyond lawyers and accountants, and appointing members who have a variety of types of lived experience, including working with diverse communities. In the last twelve months, the Australian Institute of Company Directors has created scholarships for people with disability, to ensure that more of us are represented on boards in the future.

We're talking about Skills Matrices on our boards, but we need to be talking about Diversity Matrices as well. While there is some acknowledgement within the business sector that boards need to represent the breadth of the communities they serve, in the arts, many boards are still not as diverse as they should be. Many good, diverse board members from minority groups are being stretched too thin across too many commitments. If we want to see real change, this is where it starts—every ADEI related plan should contain actions around board diversity.

Kate Larsen Keys has been conducting some excellent research into how we can re-think arts governance and start to do things differently and better by moving away from current hierarchies based on industrial, patriarchal and military structures imported from overseas as part of ongoing colonisation. Diversity is a core component of this and a 'decolonised board could embed access, equity and anti-oppression into its structure, composition and fabric.'[18]

Staff, volunteers and other stakeholders

When it comes to staff and volunteer diversity, capturing data regularly is critical—and not just at the recruitment stage, when someone may be uncertain about disclosing. Explaining the purpose of such data, how it will be used and alleviating concerns about privacy is also important. One mechanism for monitoring which recruitment measures are actually working, is to track diversity data through regularly administered staff engagement surveys. The next level is transparency: publishing the data, targets and progress.

Finally, diversity needs to be a consideration across all other stakeholder groups. People from diverse backgrounds are our contractors, donors, sponsors and suppliers. Having proactive and diverse protocols, to procure services from Supply Nation for example, helps shift us towards a more equitable sector.

5
The global context: how does Australia stack up?

How does Australia compare with the rest of the world, when it comes to the arts and ADEI? Confession time—sometimes I just really want to go and move to the UK. Brexit and other issues aside, they are at least very aware of diversity issues and talk about them out loud. As someone with hidden disability, when I visit the UK, I feel seen as a disabled person: arts organisations ask me what I need in order to participate. This is thanks in part to the Equality Act which legislated in 2010 to protect people against discrimination and promotes a fair and more equal society. It replaced more than 116 pieces of anti-discrimination legislation with a single Act, making the law easier to understand and closing loopholes. It lists nine protected characteristics specifically: age, disability, gender reassignment, marriage and civil partnership, pregnancy and maternity, race, religion or belief, sex, and sexual orientation. It is a handy list that provides clarity around the meaning of the words 'diversity' and 'inclusion'. Naming things helps us to understand what they are, and where our focus needs to be.

The UK also puts its money where its mouth is. Arts Council England has had a 'Creative Case for Diversity' since 2011, and regularly reports on what the sector is doing across a range of legally protected characteristics including Age, Disability, Race, Sex and Sexual Orientation. As part of the organisation's new Inclusivity and Relevance investment principle there is a stronger focus on workforce, leadership, governance and how organisations become more relevant to the communities they serve to complement the ongoing commitment to the Creative Case. The shift has also seen a stronger focus on socio-economic background and class in addition to responding to the Equality Act.

Historically National Portfolio Organisations (multiple-year funded organisations, or NPOs) were required to provide Equality Action Plans and… drum roll… have responding to the Creative Case for Diversity mandated into their funding agreements. The new National Portfolio announced in the autumn includes more organisations across the country that are either Disability or Black, Asian and Ethnically Diverse-led, including significant awards to We Are Unlimited, Autograph ABP, New Art Exchange and Bradford Literature Festival of £1m or more annually. The significant increase in funding to diverse-led organisations responds directly to the organisation's equality objective ambitions to address historic inequity in the distribution of public funding. The 2023–26 funding round also addressed the need to diversify investment geographically to increase the level of funds available to organisations based outside of London. These decisions show that Arts Council England realises that if nothing changes, then nothing changes when it comes to ADEI. The Creative Case for Diversity has been around for so long now, that it's well known by the sector—and for the most part, they are just getting on with responding to it. At a forum in London in 2022, Tarik Elmoutawakil, Artistic Director of Browntown Abbey made the comment that the Creative Case for Diversity is now 'closed'. This is a great example of a funding agency guideline, which has led to sector-wide change.

Another interesting example of leadership in ADEI policy is in the USA. Americans are notoriously litigious and, there, the fear of being sued is a key driver for taking action. The conversation around race is live and constant, and for gender as well. They're big on 'compliance'—I've even walked past a fishing platform that boasted compliance with the Americans with Disabilities Act. I can't imagine seeing anything like that in Australia.

The UK and USA offer two different approaches to ADEI that Australia could follow. There's lots to like in our new national cultural policy, *Revive*. It provides significant new funding overall and offers hope for improving ADEI, with a new First Nations-led board, and $5m for a new and well overdue National Arts and Disability Plan. While ADEI is not one of the five Policy 'pillars', there are several principles and programs that target diversity, many with funding attached. This is a promising start to our next chapter of cultural awakening.

6

Carrots and sticks: encouraging ADEI success

Power and privilege lie at the heart of any discussion on equality. In the arts, we need to take control of decision making, programming and the purse strings, and be consciously responsible for who has advantage and influence over others. Those in positions of power and privilege can utilise their advantages for good. Although I am a disabled person, I am still white, middle class, cis, heterosexual and based in a metropolitan city—so I try to use my advantage to amplify the voices of others, to be an ally and champion to lift them up. According to the *2022 Credit Suisse Global Wealth Report*, Australia has the highest median wealth in the world,[19] but we currently rank

23rd on a list of 34 countries in respect of supporting culture.[20] Those in charge of money, commissions and employment can lead the agenda.

When we think of power in the arts in Australia, we often think of government and funding bodies, even in what has been a shrinking arts funding landscape over recent years and decades. Ultimately, for ADEI in the arts to succeed, governments have to play a significant role. Change will only be possible if it is built into our government systems and structures and supported with funding.

Funding bodies define the selection criteria, the composition of selection panels and mandate the conditions of the grants that shape what sort of art is made, how it is made and who sees it. The City of Sydney, for example, recently mandated that funding they provided to an arts festival had to contribute towards a certain number of accessible performances and exhibitions. The festival in receipt of this funding then did not have a choice as to whether they would prioritise certain kinds of access—which, luckily, they were already planning to do—the funder took the tyranny of choice away. They had to do it, if they wanted the money.

The funding framework for Major Performing Arts Organisations changed in 2019 for the first time in twenty years. The new National Performing Arts Partnership Framework that replaced it refers to diversity for the first time:

> Priorities may include but will not necessarily be limited to...
>
> iii. Developing First Nations arts and increasing Aboriginal and Torres Strait Islander representation within programming, new works, organisational workforce and leadership;

iv. Addressing barriers and improving performance across key diversity areas (including disability, gender, LGBTIQ+, age and cultural diversity) in arts practice, programming, employment, education, training, engagement and participation.[21]

While I would like to see this language strengthened, arts organisations now have to stop and think about ADEI—some perhaps for the first time. It sets a government expectation that barriers to participation will be addressed. The proof will be in the pudding. We will see whether the performance of these organisations on ADEI has an impact on their funding in the future, as it did for the applicants to Arts Council England. Only time will tell.

Every arts funding body has a different approach to ADEI. Creative Victoria not only has a First Peoples stream for assessment, but also one for d/Deaf and disabled people. Through Creative Victoria, d/Deaf and disabled creative practitioners can also apply for additional funding, on top of the grant category amount, to cover any specific access costs to help remove the barriers involved in their project. All grant applicants are actively encouraged to think about and include costs associated with making activities accessible to d/Deaf and disabled audiences. This is an example of a funding body using their power to create cultural change and equity across their sector, and a government giving them the money to do so.

Other key influencers with power (and money) in our arts community are programmers and commissioners. They choose what appears on our stages and on our walls. They have immense influence and the ability to curate trends and encourage others to try work that they might not otherwise have seen. Festivals and commissions can provide diverse artists with opportunities to make works of scale that would not possible without their support. Making works of scale, and having bigger budgets increases the chances of high-quality work being produced which will resonate more strongly with audiences. They are an opportunity for artists to learn and grow.

Under Wesley Enoch's tenure, the Sydney Festival ran a three-year arts and disability programming initiative. By committing to this area of practice over a significant period of time, the Festival gave a platform and voice to some of the most marginalised artists in the country.

The Melbourne Fringe has been championing diversity and inclusion for a long time. It had already been employing an Access Coordinator for three years before it announced a new Radical Access Program in partnership with Arts Access Victoria in 2022.[22] A ten-year program for social change, it moves the conversation beyond the provision of access services to one of cultural equity and imagines a radical version of best practice accessibility for the independent arts sector. It includes commissioning big, bold new works for d/Deaf and disabled artists, providing research and development opportunities, running workshops, masterclasses, mentorships and employment opportunities, with the aim of significantly increasing access and inclusion for d/Deaf and disabled artists across the independent arts sector. Chunky Move has come on board as a co-commissioning partner for a $40,000 new work for a d/Deaf and disabled artist by Fayen d'Evie.[23] What an excellent carrot to dangle!

In 2013, the Australia Council estimated that less than 2% of program applicants identified as having a disability.

Acknowledging the under-representation of disabled artists in programs, the Council developed targeted arts and disability initiatives in 2014. However, due to substantial changes in investment, decision-making and data collection limitations outlined in *Towards Equity*, direct comparisons between 2013 and current data are not possible. Nevertheless, there is evidence indicating that disabled artists' participation and engagement in Australia Council programs have significantly increased over the past decade.

The 2018 report *Creating Pathways: Insights on Support for Artists with Disability* showed that the number of artists with disability interacting with the Australia Council and those actually receiving support had increased. Of the applicants to the dedicated funding program, 66% were applying for the first time, and 12% of those were successful. Those who had previously applied to the Australia Council had a 25% success rate.[24]

Outside of the dedicated arts and disability funding programs, *Towards Equity* showed that the number of individual applicants with disability had risen from less than 2% to approximately 7%—perhaps not yet on par with the population but a significant improvement on a decade ago.[25] And amazingly, while it has morphed and changed over the years, the Australia Council's commitment to dedicated funding in this area has remained strong, showing there is still a great need in a group traditionally locked out of funding opportunities.

These days, we are used to seeing positions advertised for First Nations people. Identified positions carve out a space for under-represented groups which are usually accompanied by support and education. New positions are also cropping up in disability and others areas. By making space, we invite change.

It takes thought and planning to prepare someone for success. When there are so many barriers to accessible and inclusive employment pathways, internships and traineeship programs such as the Create NSW Createability program are very useful.[26] This program matchmakes talented interns with disability across the arts and screen sectors to work with major organisations who provide support, advice and training. Some interns have gone on to secure ongoing roles with their host organisation and many others have secured work in related organisations. The benefits of programs like these are not just for the interns—they demonstrate to mainstream organisations that employing staff members with different access needs is not as hard as it may seem. As a learning opportunity, it can lead to more diverse staff being employed across our sector in the future.

However, for these positions to be effective, they have to be real jobs that are interesting and designed in consultation with the community. Otherwise, they simply 'tick a box' that gives the appearance of doing the 'right thing' with little care for cultural safety. So often, diversity-specific employment is for entry level positions. There has to be room for growth and employment beyond the position. We need to see more support for promoting people from under-represented groups into leadership positions. In both closed diversity-led organisations and 'mainstream' programs a gap remains around capacity-building and development. In recent years, the Australia Council has expanded its Leadership Programs and taken practical steps, such as providing targeted information sessions and workshops, to significantly increase the diversity of participants. Following these interventions, the number of First Nations applicants to the Future Leaders program increased from one in 2018 to seven in 2020, and the number of CALD applicants increased from eleven in 2018 to 53 in 2020 (an increase of 382%).[27] The Australia Council also delivered the Sync Leadership Program that specifically catered to the needs of d/Deaf and disabled artists and arts workers. These strategies for diversifying our leadership were long-term investments in the leadership of our industry.

7
Quotas and targets

Quotas often confuse and divide people. You might love them or hate them but there's no two ways about it, they force change and ultimately lead to a different outcome.

Time for my second confession: sometimes I wish I worked in the screen industry. While it's not perfect either, it is a place where diversity and inclusion are regularly discussed and action is taken. The release of Screen Australia's 'Seeing Ourselves: Reflections on Diversity in Australian TV Drama' in 2015 acknowledged that our screens were looking a little 'same same' and the authors wrote it with the goal of providing useful benchmarks for the industry on questions of diversity:

> It also explores some of the potential barriers that have limited change. We know this is an issue that will require an industry-wide approach. The support for this study across the industry has suggested a great willingness to engage with the issues—we seek to carry this enthusiasm and momentum forward.[28]

The recent second iteration of this report, covering the period 2016–21, shows that things are changing but the pace remains slow. Levels of diversity had increased since 2016, including higher representation for First Nations people (7.2%, up from 4.8%), disabled people (6.6%, up from 3.6%), LGBTIQ+ people (7.4%, up from 4.5%), and non-European people (16%, up from 6.9%). However, several Australian communities remained under-represented on-screen compared with the general population and disability representation in particular remained critically low.[29]

Data is a powerful tool and measuring demographics allows progress to be tracked. The Everyone Project initiated by the Screen Diversity and Inclusion Network (SDIN), a group of major Australian broadcasters, screen funding agencies and trade organisations, provides a methodology for measuring and reporting on diversity in the Australian film and television industry. In its latest *Everyone Counts* report for 2021–22, it counted 2,811 cast and crew working on over 70 film and TV productions across 2021–22.[30] Some broadcasters have taken this a step further: in 2021, both the ABC and SBS released equity and diversity-related commissioning guidelines. The SBS guidelines included some hard targets for people who identify as culturally and linguistically diverse, First Nations people, people with disability, LGBTQ+ people and women in order to increase the representation in front of and behind the camera across its commissioned programs.[31]

Table 1: SBS Inclusion Targets: Unscripted

Inclusion Targets: Unscripted	On Screen	Off Screen
Culturally and linguistically diverse	35–40%	25–40%
First Nations	3–5%	3.5%
People with disability	5–10%	5–10%
LGBTIQ+	8–12%	8–12%
Women	45–55%	45–55%

Table 2: SBS Inclusion Targets: Scripted

On Screen Meet all three categories	Off Screen Meet all three categories	
1. Main characters to include at least two CALD and/or First Nations people. 2. Broader cast to include (a) 33.3% from the four groups & (b) 50% women 3. Inclusive casting. Producers to demonstrate best efforts to (a) Practice open casting for all characters who are not specifically written to be Anglo-Celtic & (b) Cast extras that are from the four groups.	If the series focuses on a particular under-represented community: 1. Writing team to include at least (a) two key roles for people from this community & (b) 50% women 2. Other Key Creatives: Directors/ Producers to include at least (a) one other creative from this community e.g. At least one producer or at least one director & (b) 50% women.	If the series does not focus on a particular under-represented community: 1. Writing team to include at least (a) two key roles from the four groups (including one CALD and/or First Nations writer, to align with our SBS Charter goals as Australia's multicultural and Indigenous broadcaster) & (b) 50% women.

Table 2: SBS Inclusion Targets: Scripted cont.

On Screen Meet all three categories	Off Screen Meet all three categories	
	3. Production team to include at least (a) one Head of Department (HOD) 8 from the four groups & (b) 50% women	2. Other Key Creatives: Directors/ Producers to include at least (a) one other creative from the four groups e.g. At least one of the producers is CALD, First Nations, a person with a disability and/or LGBTIQ+ & (b) 50% women 3. Production team to include at least (a) one Head of Department (HOD) from the four groups & (b) 50% women.

Are those numbers reflective of the general population? Not at all, particularly when it comes to disability, but at least it's a start. When we take action, some things begin to shift, and while targets do make some people uncomfortable, these will change who is making the work shown on SBS for years to come. Imagine the impact such a change could have on the performing arts sector if festivals used diversity guidelines for commissioning new work or by funding bodies used them for multi-year funding decisions? I guarantee the sector wouldn't look the same in a decade if we were brave enough to use this sort of incentive.

Is dangling a carrot in front of an arts organisation enough to lead to actual change right now? Is it juicy enough when there are so many other things to worry about? What's more, as our carrots have been getting smaller, the sticks have been getting bigger. Perhaps the carrot and stick are complimentary strategies that work best in tandem. Both help set higher standards. We need tastier carrots *and* heftier sticks. And we need these incentives and deterrents to be there right at the beginning, when things are funded, commissioned and programmed. Adding requirements as an afterthought is acting too late.

8

Why it's hard: challenges and failures

If there are so many great benefits to ADEI, why doesn't the Australian arts sector have it sorted? What makes it so hard? Where do we fail? And what can we learn from this?

When the pressure is on, it can become harder for arts organisations to do things like ADEI voluntarily. Intentionally or not, agendas and priorities are cast aside or slip through the cracks, unless they are mandated. If our systems won't support it, to what extent is change even possible? As a consultant, I've seen a lot of willingness to do better when it comes to ADEI on the part of organisations, but without funding avenues and support, how can they make practical changes?

Here are some of the common ADEI obstacles I have observed from experience.

Fear

I believe the number one challenge around ADEI is fear—fear of getting it wrong, fear of missing the mark or being inappropriate, fear of using the wrong language (is it CALD or People of Colour or multicultural? Is it people with disability or disabled people? Is it Aboriginal and Torres Strait Islander or First Nations?). And fear freezes us—it stops us in our tracks because many of us would rather do nothing than feel the embarrassment of getting it wrong. We don't do failure well, and this can lead to inertia and reluctance to experiment and take risks as we figure things out.

Lack of knowledge

ADEI issues can be overwhelming. How do we know where to start? There's so much to tackle. Lack of knowledge can be a real block. Should we be trying to do everything all at once or is it okay to go softly, softly? How do we know what's right and appropriate for our organisation? If we add something into our program about diversity, could this highlight all the other ways in which we're failing? If I'm not an expert in ADEI and don't have lived experience myself, how do I know I won't get it completely wrong?

Time and resources

Arts organisations were stretched before COVID. Now we're trying to do even more with less. Making up for lost years and trying to support communities of artists and audiences who've been in fires, drought or floods, it can seem as if no-one has any time for anything, certainly not anything 'additional' that might cost more or, worse, require a significant outlay. Sometimes people say they're interested in ADEI but they just don't want to do the work. It's not high enough up the list of priorities. I had a recent experience working with a range of different organisations to improve their accessibility as part of a wider project. At the outset, all of them were very excited and waxed lyrical about how much it was needed, but when it required action from them—actually tweaking their websites or completing a survey—nothing happened. It didn't make it to the top of the priority pile.

Yet ADEI presents us with is a rich tapestry for learning and growth. Some years ago, the Sydney Festival received a complaint via the Australian Human Rights Commission from a wheelchair user who had been unable to access an event in its program. Sadly, it is not that uncommon for Australian festivals to program events in venues that are inaccessible to wheelchairs, but instead of trying to make it all go away, this festival did something remarkable: they listened, they reflected and they learnt. The experience led them to becoming one of the first festivals in Australia to have their own Disability Advisory Committee, made up of people with lived experience, to provide them with feedback on their program and production considerations. They now produce a more inclusive festival which more of us can enjoy and continue to set new and higher ADEI standards.

Ultimately, we need a little more risk-taking, a little more experimentation and a bit more play when it comes to ADEI. We need to learn from people with lived experience and pay people to share their expertise with us. We need to prioritise this work, carve out space for it and provide the resources to actually do it.

Arts organisations aren't going to wake up tomorrow and become magically more diverse. It requires purposeful action. Otherwise, cultural homogeneity will remain our status quo.

9

What does it actually look like? Doing the work

Each of us has a role to play in building a more inclusive arts and culture sector, whether we have lived experience of diversity or not. Individual actions can lead to organisational step-changes that create cultural shifts from which there is no turning back. There are a million tips and tricks and cheat sheets out there, from how you can make your website accessible for screen-reader users, to what words to use in your Acknowledgement of Country. That's not the purpose of my essay. I want to point to the high-level changes that individuals and organisations can take to truly prioritise and celebrate ADEI.

Be a good ally

Read, listen, watch, converse. Educate yourself and learn. Lead by example. Call things in and call things out. Create space for others—if you're not someone with lived experience of diversity yourself, ask whether someone with lived experience has been booked for the panel you've been invited to speak on and if not, recommend someone—offer to give up your seat. Think about how things can be done differently, more fairly and more inclusively. A beautiful ally/friend recently told me how she'd applied for a job she really wanted, but, conscious of the value of that leadership role, she proposed a job share with a diverse artist in the interview. That's an example of a good ally to me.

Plan for it

Benjamin Franklin was onto something with his aphorism, 'by failing to plan, you are preparing to fail.'[32] ADEI progress doesn't happen overnight, only if you chip away at it over time. Develop a strategy, policy or plan—whatever floats your boat. And take inspiration from others. We don't have to re-invent every wheel. There's much to love about the Sydney Opera House's Diversity, Inclusion and Belonging Strategy.[33] I'm sure they won't mind if you borrow a bit.

Resource it

If you want to do things, they might cost some money. Has your organisation got a line for accessibility and DEI projects in its budget? Get people behind it and the budget line so that action happens. There can be debate about whether you need a Diversity and Inclusion Director or Manager (please don't make them an Officer or Coordinator—this stuff is hard). *Or...* do you just make ADEI part of everyone's role? Both options can work, and there's no right answer. What I like about the defined job is that someone is paid to focus on the issue. That means something gets done. Appointing everyone to a task can be a dangerous game with no-one ultimately responsible, but you also have to keep an eye out for the dangers of 'siloing': 'I don't have to do that ADEI thing in my area that is actually my job, because our D&I Manager should do it!' None of that, please.

Find the carrots and sticks

Consider where you can actively encourage diversity and discourage homogeneity in your workplace. Identify both incentives and disincentives. Set quotas, targets or KPIs for diversity in your work. Can you offer an opportunity to someone or a group of people from an under-represented background? Can you expose a lazy department or division that has got its head in the sand when it comes to diversity? Be creative: we're arts organisations after all.

In the end, just start somewhere. It doesn't have to be perfect on day one. We're all learning, but take responsibility and ownership for the things you can control and look for opportunities to influence others. That's where sector-wide change really takes hold.

10
What's next

It's 2033, a decade from now. Australia looks different. We have our First Aboriginal Prime Minister, and she's a woman. Creative Australia is run by a person of colour. 30% of our National Performing Arts Partnership Organisations have a CEO, AD and/or Chair who is from an under-represented group, and a few are on Fair Notice for failing to meet their diversity and inclusion KPIs. The fourth iteration of the *Towards Equity* report shows that we've at least doubled all statistics since 2020. Our small to medium sector is continuing to push boundaries and program ground-breaking diverse work—and it's accessible. Most festivals have stopped presenting work in physically inaccessible sites and are regularly providing major commissions to diverse artists. Diverse artists, arts workers and leaders are supported across all parts of the arts ecology. Pathways to training and employment have opened up. It's exciting, and the art is good. No, it's better than that: it's great.

That's what it could look like if we all got to work on building an inclusive future for our Australian arts and culture sector right now. Take a moment to imagine what might happen if we truly prioritised diversity in all its glory across our sector. What might it look like? Who might we become? What sort of art might we make? How might arts organisations, and artists, have shifted their imaginations?

Those in positions of power need to help us do this work. Because change won't be possible unless our systems and processes support it. In an industry with competing priorities, we need to be encouraging and celebrating good diversity work. We need to put our money where our mouths are—offer those commissions, provide those jobs, open up those targeted funding programs and set those high expectations to exceed our KPIs and quotas. How about a tiered accreditation system to help organisations improve their accessibility? The sky is the limit for what we might invent and the avenues we might create to provide support and encouragement.

To those who have the power to take things away: even though it's hard, you need to be bolder.

To funding bodies: imagine the change you could create if you mandated that all grant applicant budgets need to show at least a 20% spend on ADEI-related costs. Heck, you could even design things so that 50% of your organisational project funding one year (or one decade?!) goes to diverse arts organisations. Both carrots and sticks are useful, and we shouldn't be shy to use them—they can help nudge us along and show us the way. Why should a $40,000 commission for a d/Deaf and disabled artist be called radical? It really shouldn't be. Let's hope it's not by 2033.

The time for ADEI has come and the arts now need to respond through incentives and disincentives, because that is what it will take. We need to encourage genuine commitments from individuals and institutions to ADEI that are embedded in their practices. We need transformation from the top down and the bottom up—from those working on the ground, to our leaders at the helm. According to Diversity and Inclusion expert Sherryl Reddy, 'the change we need rests in leadership composition, intention, lived experience and exposure.'[34] The arts and culture have the power to change hearts and minds and drive societal change. To ensure that Australia's future is an inclusive one, let's lead with diverse (and great!) art.

Endnotes

1. *Towards Equity: A Research Overview of Diversity in Australia's Arts and Cultural Sector,* The Australia Council for the Arts, June 8, 2021, pp. 19, 16, 15. creative.gov.au.
2. Ibid, p. 37.
3. Antonio C. Cuyler, 'Access, Diversity, Equity, and Inclusion (ADEI) in Cultural Organizations' in Anthony Rhine and Jay Pension (eds.) *Access, Diversity, Equity, and Inclusion (ADEI) in Cultural Organizations: Challenge and Opportunities*. Routledge, 2022, pp. 83-104; p. 87.
4. '4714.0—National Aboriginal and Torres Strait Islander Social Survey, 2014–15'. Australian Bureau of Statistics. abs.gov.au.

5. 'Snapshot of Mental Health and Suicide Prevention Statistics for LGBTIQ+ People'. LGBTIQ+ Health Australia, May 13, 2021. lgbtiqhealth.org.au
6. Kimberlé Crenshawe, 'Demarginalizing the Intersection of Race and Sex: A Black Feminist Critique of Antidiscrimination Doctrine, Feminist Theory and Antiracist Politics' in *University of Chicago Legal Forum*, no. 1, 1989, pp. 139-67. The Victorian government provides a summary of the concept at vic.gov.au, 'Understanding Intersectionality', reviewed February 8, 2021.
7. *Diversity & Inclusion Plan 2019–22*. Australian Broadcasting Corporation, p. 13. about.abc.net.au.
8. 'United Nations Convention on the Rights of Persons with Disabilities'. United Nations. social.desa.un.org.
9. 'Disability Statistics'. Australian Network on Disability. Retrieved April 26, 2023. and.org.au.
10. 'What is a Hidden Disability?' Hidden Disabilities Sunflower Scheme. hiddendisabilitiesstore.com.
11. 'Mental Health Impact of COVID-19'. Australian Institute of Health and Welfare. aihw.gov.au.
12. *Connecting Australians: Results of the National Arts Participation Survey*. The Australia Council for the Arts, June 2017, pp.18, 20, 45. creative.gov.au.
13. *Making Art Work: A summary and response by the Australia Council for the Arts.* The Australia Council for the Arts, November 2017, p.10. creative.gov.au.
14. 'The Purple Pound Infographic'. We Are Purple. wearepurple.org.uk.
15. Bianca Mulet, 'How the pandemic has changed audience accessibility'. October 2022, p3. thepatternmakers.com.au.
16. 'Australia is experiencing the "great burnout"'. Arts Hub *News*, March 24, 2023. artshub.com.au.
17. *2023 Board Diversity Index. Governance Institute of Australia and Watermark Search International.* governanceinstitute.com.au.

18. Kate Larsen-Keys, 'We Can Do Better Than Boards', February 7, 2023. larsenkeys.com.au

19. *Global Wealth Report 2022: Leading Perspectives to Navigate the Future*, Credit Suisse, p. 5. credit-suisse.com.

20. 'Australia lags behind OECD in cultural funding'. Arts Hub, *News*, February 16, 2022. artshub.com.au.

21. Meeting of Cultural Ministers, National Performing Arts Partnership Framework, n.d., p. 9. creative.gov.au.

22. 'Radical Access'. Melbourne Fringe. melbournefringe.com.au.

23. 'Radical Access Commission'. Chunky Move. chunkymove.com.

24. The Australia Council for the Arts, *Creating Pathways: Insights on Support for Artists with Disability*. September 19, 2018, p. 10. creative.gov.au.

25. *Towards Equity*, op. cit., p. 76.

26. 'Createability Internships EIO'. NSW Government. nsw.gov.au.

27. *Towards Equity*, op. cit., pp. 54, 65.

28. *Seeing Ourselves: Reflections on Diversity in Australian TV Drama*. Screen Australia, 2016 p. 1. screenaustralia.gov.au.

29. *Seeing Ourselves 2: Diversity, Equity and Inclusion in Australian TV Drama*. Screen Australia, April 2023, p. 1. screenaustralia.gov.au.

30. *Everyone Counts: Preliminary Data on Diversity in the Australian Screen Industry from The Everyone Project*, Screen Diversity and Inclusion Network. 2022, p. 5. sdin.com.au.

31. *SBS Commissioning Equity & Inclusion Guidelines*. Special Broadcasting Service, February 2022, pp. 6-7. sbs.com.au.

32. 'Thoughts on the Business of Life', attributed to Benjamin Franklin. Forbes Quotes. forbes.com.

33. *Diversity, Inclusion & Belonging Strategy, 2021–23*. Sydney Opera House. sydneyoperahouse.com.

34. Interview with Sherryl Reddy, Diversity and Inclusion practitioner, January 27, 2023.

About the Authors

JEREMY NEIDECK is a performance maker and academic who has worked in Australia and South Korea for the last two decades. His work models inclusive social realities on stage by interweaving cultures at the intersection of queer identities. His productions include 지하 *Underground*, co-written with Nathan Stoneham for Motherboard Productions; *Deluge*, an experimental dance theatre work; and *Shimchong: Daughter Overboard*, a re-imagining of the traditional Korean tale of Shimchong which combined *pansori*, poetry, and political satire. He currently works with Company Bad, an international collective of artists that experiments with transcultural collaboration and friendship as a methodology for facilitating arts and cultural projects.

He has been awarded scholarships by Aphids, the Australia-Korea Foundation, Asialink and Brisbane City Council and residencies at the National Art Studio of Korea, the National Changgeuk Company of Korea, and the Necessary Stage, Singapore. As an academic he lectures and tutors in the areas of contemporary performance theory, post-dramatic theatre, queer identities in performance, intercultural studies, independent theatre production, event and festival production, directing and performance in digital spaces. He taught at the Queensland University of Technology (QUT) for a decade before taking up his current position as the Course Coordinator of the Bachelor of Performing Arts at the Western Australian Academy of Performing Arts (WAAPA), Edith Cowan University (ECU), in Boorloo (Perth).

He is the co-convenor of the Queer Futures Working Group of the International Federation for Theatre Research (IFTR). 'Queer(y)ing the Australian Way of Life' is the part of the research project 'Fabulous Heroes' which has been awarded pilot funding by the ECU Early Mid-Career Researcher Grant Scheme

Morwenna Collett is an accomplished leader, consultant and facilitator with fifteen years' experience in government, the arts, not-for-profit and university sectors. She has worn the hats of CEO, Board Director, senior leadership team member, project manager, lecturer, researcher, trainer and advisor.

As a senior arts consultant specialising in access, diversity, equity and inclusion, she is deeply committed to working towards a future where everyone has equal access to participate in arts and culture and in society more broadly. A champion of inclusion, Morwenna is an agent for change who is sought after nationally and internationally for her expertise. She has worked closely to support a range of large and small organisations to help them improve their practices, acting as a critical friend, challenger and cheer leader. She has positively impacted many organisations, changing hearts and minds via her work on strategy, planning, policies, evaluation and through thought leadership, discussion and training.

Morwenna has a background as a musician and works across

all artform areas. Recent consulting clients include the National Gallery of Australia, MONA, the Sydney Opera House, the Australian Chamber Orchestra, the National Library of Australia, Opera Queensland, the Australia Council, Sydney World Pride, Diversity Arts Australia, People with Disability Australia and Taronga Zoo.

She is the Chair of the Sydney Festival's Access Committee and helped establish committees for Perth Festival, Sydney Fringe and Sydney World Pride. She is also a Director of Arts Capital, an arts centre management company in Canberra, and a member of the Contemporary Music Board at Create NSW. She is an Affiliate of the Association of Consultants in Access Australia (ACAA) and a member of The Inclusion Circle network.

She has previously been the CEO of Accessible Arts, the Chair of the Sydney Arts Managers Advisory Group and has held various management roles at the Australia Council. In 2020, she completed a Churchill Fellowship, exploring inclusive music programs, venues and festivals which actively engage disabled people across the USA, UK and Ireland. Her work is influenced by her own lived experience as a musician with disability. Read more at morwennacollett.com.

FIGURES 1–2

Top: Photographing *Les sauvages de la mer du Pacifique*, Joseph Dufour and Jean-Gabriel Charvet, 1804–05, at the National Gallery of Australia, Canberra, circa 2007.

Photograph by Lisa Reihana.

Bottom: Lisa Reihana, video still from *in Pursuit of Venus [infected]*, 2015–17. Captain Cook and Tupaia exchanging gifts.

FIGURES 3–4

Right: Pantochronometer, an instrument which combines a compass, sundial and universal time, showing the locations of then newly charted islands such as 'Owhyhee' (Hawai'i) and 'Otaheite' (Tahiti). Accession no. 1922.373.

Museum of Archaeology and Anthropology, University of Cambridge.

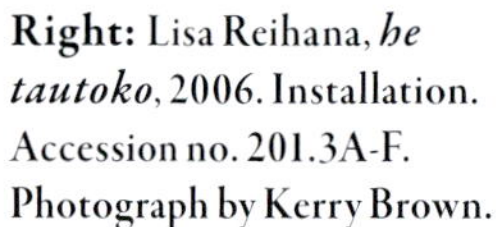

Right: Lisa Reihana, ***he tautoko***, 2006. Installation. Accession no. 201.3A-F. Photograph by Kerry Brown.

Museum of Archaeology and Anthropology, University of Cambridge.

FIGURES 5–7

Left: Tupaia, a chief mourner of Tahiti, BL add ms 15508 no. 9.

Photograph entered into the public domain from the British Library's collections in 2013.

British Library, London.

Left: Lisa Reihana and Professor Nicholas Thomas looking at the *parae* of a chief mourner's costume at the Museum of Archaeology and Anthropology, Cambridge University.

Photograph by Lisa Reihana.

Below: Lisa Reihana, video still from *Tai Whetuki—House of Death*, 2015.

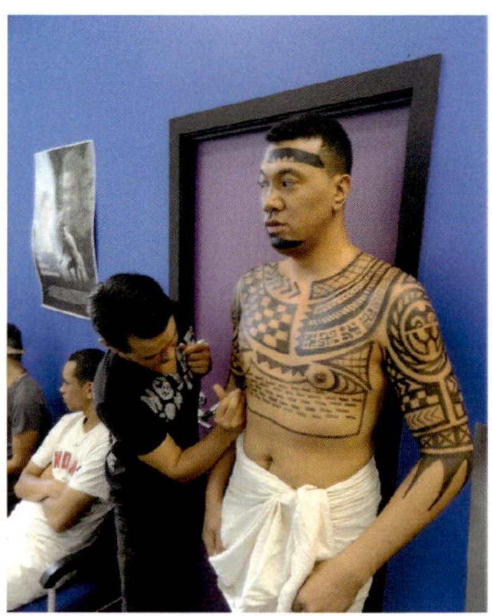

Figures 8–11

Above left: Tupaia, Māori bartering a crayfish, BL add ms 15508 f. 11, no. 12.
Photograph entered into the public domain from the British Library's collections in 2013.

British Library, London.

Above right: Tattoo artist and anthropologist Tricia Allen applying a design to actor Ali Foa'i for a scene in ***in Pursuit of Venus [infected].***

Photograph by Lisa Reihana.

Far Left:
Lisa Reihana,
A Māori Chief,
2016

Left:
Lisa Reihana,
Sydney Parkinson,
2016.

FIGURES 12–13

Above: Lisa Reihana, ***Groundloop***, 2022. Two installation views.

Commissioned for the Sydney Modern Project.

Photographs © Art Gallery of New South Wales.

FIGURES 14–16

Left: Goethe-Institut, Singapore

Photograph entered into the public domain in 2015.

© *Zairon.*

Left: Australia House by Andrew Burns, Architect at Echigo-Tsumari Art Triennale.

Photograph by Nakamura Osamu.

Below: China Culture Centre, Bangkok, Thailand.

Photograph by kind permission of the China Cultural Centre Sydney.

© *www.aey.me.*

The Arts and Australian Soft Diplomacy in Asia, India and Indigenous Foreign Policy

Keynote speeches and discussions from the
Currency House Authors Convention
July 7, 2023 (online)

NO. 6
December 2023

Introduction

Harriet Parsons
Wurundjeri country

The Currency House Authors Convention was created to renew debate in the arts by putting practitioners in conversation with other thinkers. In the first year we talked about the meaning of value with an economist and philosopher; in the second, we invited a constitutional lawyer to discuss the place of Aboriginal sovereignty in Australian culture and the arts. The theme of the 2023 Convention was suggested by a promise of the last election for an Indigenous Foreign Policy. Senator Penny Wong, now Minister for Foreign Affairs, said this would be a policy 'that weaves the voices and practices of the world's oldest continuing culture into the way we talk to the world, and the work of the Department of Foreign Affairs and Trade'.[1] This vision turned the discussion outwards, to reflect on the art of soft-diplomacy in Australian foreign affairs.

China's recent expansion of its Belt and Road initiative into the Pacific has brought nations such as the Solomon Islands to prominence in the strategic negotiations of the US and its allies; and India too has begun exerting its influence in our region. This year's keynote speakers have each acted as cultural interlocutors in the regions of the Pacific, India and Asia.

Our first speaker shot to fame in 2017 when her video installation, *in Pursuit of Venus [infected]* was chosen to represent New Zealand at the Venice Biennale. As a Māori artist practicing her craft on the international stage, Lisa Reihana sees her work as continuing in the tradition of First Nations diplomacy. Tupaia, a leading character in Reihana's video, was a First Nations envoy of the modern era. He met Captain James Cook in Tahiti and travelled to Aotearoa and Australia on the *Endeavour* with the intention of going to England. *Tupaia's Sketchbook* has given us the iconic images of first European contact in the South Pacific and in Reihana's address, she explains how the use of creative practice in her own work has nurtured rich cross-cultural relationships between her homeland and the First and Second Nations of Australia and the world.

Our second speaker, Peter Cooke, has similarly nurtured countless international relationships in his role as a teacher and the former administrative head of two major drama schools in Australia and the US: NIDA and Carnegie Mellon. As a visiting professor at the National School of Drama in India since 2004, Cooke has observed the close bonds that develop between artists across cultures through practical learning.

He writes:

> Myriad conversations took place in the construction workshops, rehearsal rooms and ultimately the theatre. I believe the students' direct creative involvement in the production was an invaluable part of their learning process. I have kept in touch with that and subsequent classes, helping them with advice about further educational opportunities abroad, fellowships and scholarships and a sea of references.

Creative exchange produces an atmosphere of collegiality that returns long-term dividends at both the individual and institutional level. Our final speaker, Alison Carroll, was the founding director of Asialink's arts program in 1989, which has funded regular exchanges between Australia, Asia and India for more than thirty years. It was established as a joint initiative of the Commission for the Future and the Myer Foundation under the guidance of the director of the Foundation's board, Carrillo Gantner. In 2012 Carroll and Gantner co-authored *Finding a Place on the Asian Stage* for Currency House in which they argued that the support that was needed to reap the dividends of international exchange at the national level was lacking. They put forward a plan for an Australian international cultural agency on par with the Alliance Française, the Goethe-Institut and the Japan Foundation. Carroll revisited this plan in her address to the Convention. While she notes that the need for an international agency is now greater than ever, in her observation, things have gone backwards since 2012.

Carrillo Gantner believes the turning point came when trade was added to the Department of Foreign Affairs. In closing comments he remarked that DFAT had become transactional. This was certainly the indication of the *Indigenous Diplomacy*

Agenda that was released by the Morrison government in May, 2021. The Agenda's four policy areas were:

- foreign policy
- trade and economic policy
- development policy and
- corporate policy.

A plan for Indigenous diplomacy with no room for culture is hard to imagine. The authors' vision was of a world where 'open markets facilitate the free flow of trade, capital and ideas for indigenous businesses, and where indigenous peoples are participants and beneficiaries of the international system.'[2]

The new Labor government has appointed Gooreng Gooreng man Justin Mohamed to develop its Indigenous Foreign Policy as Ambassador for Indigenous Foreign Affairs, and Wong's brief outline gives reason to hope that the arts may yet play a part. However, within DFAT itself, there appears to be what can only be described as a siege mentality. It was a great disappointment to us that we were unable to deliver an invitation via email to Ambassador Mohamed to attend the Convention—or anyone from the Department who might have an interest in this new policy. Gantner and Carroll, having breached the walls, reported a similarly disappointing reception inside the Department. They were sent back to the Australia Council, now Creative Australia, and we will see how international relations fare under the latest restructure of this once much-loved arts institution. What seems clear from all the speakers' experience is that close ties in our region are not achieved through self-promotion but in the way we conduct ourselves in our international affairs.

Endnotes

1. Hon. Penny Wong MP, 2022 Foreign Affairs Debate with Marise Payne & Penny Wong, at the National Press Club of Australia, May 10, 2022. youtube.com.
2. *Indigenous Diplomacy Agenda*, Australian Government, Department of Foreign Affairs and Trade, May 2021, p. 1. dfat.gov.au.

Picturing History:
Rewind, Fast Forward, Revise...

Lisa Reihana CNZM
Aotearoa

Ko Ngātokimatawhaorua tāku waka
Ko Te-Hokianga-nui-o-Kupe tāku moana
Ko Puhanga Tohoroā me Ninihi āku maunga
Ko Ngā Puhi tāku iwi

Greetings, my name is Lisa Reihana, and I'm speaking to you from Tamaki Makaurau in Auckland, Aotearoa New Zealand.

I'm going to talk about the research for my video *in Pursuit of Venus [infected]*. It is based on a French wallpaper called *Les sauvages de la mer du Pacifique* that was created by Joseph Dufour and Jean-Gabriel Charvet in France in 1804–05. I encountered it at the Australian National Gallery in Canberra in about 2007 and I took a photograph of myself photographing it with a little iPhone (figure 1). This photograph shows two artists, two-hundred years apart, really pushing technology: Dufour and Charvet in France in the early nineteenth century, and me, the 'discovered', in the place they were imagining, Australia and the Pacific, in the early twenty-first century. I took the picture because I could see an opportunity to use digital technologies to investigate this wallpaper and understand why it became so popular in Europe, what it meant to people then and what it means now. The artists intended it to represent European encounters with Indigenous peoples around the Pacific, but they were completely unrecognisable. To me, it was an extraordinary cultural misreading.

in Pursuit of Venus [infected]

I have a fascination with wallpaper. As a young child I used to stare at the patterns, trying not to blink until the images appeared to levitate off the wall. I saw this design and wanted to recreate that child-like feeling of bringing a wallpaper to life, so I began my research by trying to understand who these characters were and why they were in this utopian Tahitian landscape—and then use that to unpack some of the many issues that followed Captain Cook's arrival in the Pacific.

Cook arrived in Tahiti on the *Endeavour* in 1769 to observe the transit of Venus for the Royal Society. He named their campsite Point Venus, but his crew and other European explorers also introduced sexually transmitted diseases into the Pacific. The Māori word for love is *aroha* (in Hawaiian, *aloha*): it refers to breath and the giving of life. Venus is the goddess of love, but the title of the work was also meant to stop people in their tracks and make them wonder about the infection.

One of the characters in my video is Tupaia. Tupaia was an *ari'oi*, a navigator, priest and artist, from a very high chiefly family. His *marae*, Taputapuatea, is on Ra'iatea, an island near Tahiti. Māori have another name for Ra'iatea: Hawaiki, the homeland. It's part of our origin story and it is both a physical and spiritual place. Hawaiki is the place our spirits return to after we depart this earthly realm.

In figure 2, Tupaia is the orator at a ceremonial gathering. In front of him are Captain Cook and Joseph Banks. They are exchanging gifts with Tupaia and the *Endeavour* can be seen in the harbour behind them. Tupaia decided to join Cook on the *Endeavour*'s expedition to travel to England. Polynesian navigators had been exploring the Pacific for hundreds of years, charting the routes to islands and transmitting the information through oral traditions, memory and the amazing stick maps that you may have seen. But when they landed here, on Aotearoa, he was the first person to come down to this part of the world from Ra'iatea in five hundred years. This was an incredible opportunity for Māori because he was reconnecting them back to Ra'iatea, to the homeland and their ancient histories. He spent a lot of time speaking with elders and chiefs who recognised him as a person of *mana*, a person of power and prestige, and because they revered him, they assumed that the *Endeavour* was captained by him.

Figure 3 is a pantochronometer, a wayfinding device from around 1826 that combines a compass and sundial to calculate the time in locations around the world, including the then newly charted islands of 'Owhyhee' (Hawai'i) and 'Otaheite' (Tahiti).

It also has Lisbon, London and Nootka Sound, so it shows how Pacific and European networks were beginning to intersect and their importance for global trade. These connections between the Pacific and Europe were first established through the exchange of gifts. Many *korowai* (woven cloaks) and countless *taonga* (works of art) were gifted in the spirit of reciprocity, as a gesture of diplomacy towards these visitors. The cloak Joseph Banks wears in the Benjamin West's 1788 portrait and many of the 'curiosities' surrounding him include gifts to Tupaia that were claimed by Banks after he died on the voyage. Cook and Banks gave trinkets in exchange, so their understanding of the real value of these prized possessions, and the level of engagement that was expected of them, was not there, and often it still isn't. Many *taonga* have ended up in European collections around the world, and some continue to be traded today.

he tautoko

I enjoy the challenge of working with museums. It makes a contrast to working in the white cube of the art gallery, and it brings up different concerns and conversations. If I know customary works from home, Aotearoa, are on display, I'll visit them at the beginning and end of each day to talk to them. Māori see *taonga* as living entities. During our research for the *Pasifica Styles* exhibition at the Cambridge Museum of Archaeology and Anthropology in 2006, Māori and Pacific artists were allowed to touch the taonga from their country or tribal area with ungloved hands.

There was just one carving in their collection that had come from a place near my father's tribal homelands in the Far North and I worked with it for my installation, *he tautoko* (figure 4). I would uncover the crate to converse with this ancestor, an ancestor who had lost their name. It was lovely to imagine the artist giving their time and energy and breathing life—*aroha*—into the native wood and transforming it into an ancestor. Whose ancestor was this, and who brought it to life—who was the maker?

Māori often speak of taking up tools, any tools—like these works of art—and using them for our own purposes, which is what we should do. But when a *taonga* enters a museum, it is removed from its living traditions. The installation *he tautoko* was a bit like a catch up. I used audio and visual material, recorded songs in New Zealand, and added sound devices to the cabinet so that the audience could mix their own unique soundtrack. From the time we first met, the carving seemed to change colour and become more chocolatey when he was on show. This ancestral figure commanded the focus of the audience and they spent quite some time with him. I tried to evoke empathy, new feelings without telling the audience what to think. I just wanted people to pause and take a moment to see another way of viewing the world.

POV

We called in Pursuit of Venus 'POV' for short. To filmmakers this stands for 'point of view'. POV was very much a deep dive into thinking about how you read situations, and how visual material can be read from different points of view. Tupaia's watercolour of a chief mourner (figure 5) inspired several scenes in the video. Cook acquired—or traded for—the ceremonial garments, *heva tūpāpā'u*, that are now in the British Museum in Tahiti, on his second Pacific voyage. Years later I was able look at the parae, the incredible mask, with Professor Nicholas Thomas (figure 6). It is such a high-status item, made of pearl and coconut shell and the feathers of tropical birds.

I wanted to understand more about what this revered figure represented and its deeper meaning by recreating the costume. I wrote a script called *Tai Whetuki—House of Death*, so that I could see it in the real world and I was thrilled when we managed to produce a reasonable simulacrum (figure 7).

This ceremonial garment is very heavy and the mask has just one small slit to see through and it makes the wearer move in a very particular way. We filmed at Karekare Beach, a wild and beautiful landscape on the West Coast of Aotearoa. Not the utopian backdrop of *in Pursuit of Venus [infected]*, but a sad and haunted place where Nga Puhi caused a massacre. It felt apt to reenact the chief mourner there, but it was also scary because we were invoking not just the memory, but its associated energy and bringing it back into the world. These very powerful vestments call the gods down to earth, and in the past villagers would have been terrified at the sight of them and might just have died of fright.

The history of Captain Cook can be told in different ways: Cook can be portrayed as a hero or a villain, and learning how to read a situation means trusting your gut and being open to understanding what's happening in front of you. When the *Endeavour* arrived in present day Gisborne, the first encounters with the Māori were fatal. The local *iwi* (people) may have been performing a ceremonial challenge which the crew mistook for an attack and Ngāti Oneone chief Te Maro was shot and killed. The next day, when Cook returned with Tupaia to smooth over relations, another chief was killed and three youths were also abducted. So—hero or villain?

On that same trip, Tupaia painted an image of Joseph Banks trading with a Māori for a crayfish (figure 8). The exchange of information here is taking place on multiple levels. Here is a Pacific man who has co-opted a European illustrative form, he demonstrates keen observational skills which are entirely different to the Tahitian drawings of his time. His penmanship leads me to think he must have been absorbing these drawing skills by watching the hard-working illustrator, Sydney Parkinson.

I tried to put myself in the shoes of the European artists as well—Sydney Parkinson on the *Endeavour* or John Webber and William Hodges on Cook's second and third voyages—to understand their experience. Surely they couldn't—or wouldn't—have been drawing portraits of local *iwi* accompanied by marines. Thinking about how images have been made, not just what they show, provides insights into how relationships were being built. These artists were intrepid and brave. That's the skill of an artist: you may not know the language, but if you read the cues, there's a lot of information to draw upon.

There's a well-known Māori principal of engagement: *kanohi ki te kanohi*, 'face to face'. There are many different ways of reading situations and dialogue creates a space for understanding. Indigenous people know that the best thing you can do is talk: talk to the elders first, do it in person, share food and build relationships. *In Pursuit of Venus [infected]* provided an opportunity to create a space for dialogue, where I could invite Pacific actors and performers into the space of the studio and the utopian backdrop of Dufour and Charvet's Tahiti. It's an honour as an artist, filmmaker and researcher, to be able to write words on a page and then translate them into living, breathing performances.

Dufour and Charvet's Tahiti does not exist, it is a non place. I prepared scripts and talked about my vision for the work, but I also offered the performers the opportunity to make their own responses to the legacies of Captain Cook—he is condemned by Indigenous peoples and the wallpaper is a post-colonial confection. The people in this video are a living link to ancestors, some of whom may even have been at these historic events.

Dufour and Charvet relegated the darker-skinned races to the background and they are derided by some members of the *Endeavour* in the journals. *In Pursuit of Venus [infected]* enabled me to bring these people into the foreground and include their stories to make this work feel complete. I worked with the Campbelltown Art Centre in Western Sydney where I was able to talk with local elders and hear the stories that they were happy for us to tell. We recorded Koomurri mob, a male dance troupe performing a Welcome to Country, Aboriginal women weaving and Amala Groom singing her grandmother's medicine song. We also timed video shoots to coincide with the annual Pacifika Festival which is hosted by Auckland. It's a massive undertaking and people come from all around the region. It's very expensive for Island nations to travel down here, but it is a highlight of the year, where artistic goods, knowledge and performances are shared.

We share information and exchange what we think in many ways, and how it plays out in practice is complicated. Working with Tricia Allen, a Hawaiian tattoo artist and anthropoligist, was an eye opener. I had a very clear idea of the design I wanted for our actor, Ali Foa'i. Black work was very popular in the 1980s, but Tricia told me that this style was introduced by the missionaries to black out traditional designs. I didn't want to perform yet another act of erasure and was guided by Tricia's research. We recreated the body designs from a drawing of a man from Bora-Bora. Even using a felt tip pen, it still took eight hours to complete—but Ali looked fabulous (figure 9). Pacific tattoos carry a mass of information and artists must have been gaining knowledge from European bodies the same way as they adorned them with western drawings and symbols.

In an offshoot project, I made photographs of some of the characters in the video and placed them against a background of my own contemporary weaving patterns. When shown together the backgrounds form diamonds and suggest a dialogue between the characters. The contemporary background skews time, connecting past and present. The characters look outwards from their own time, with *mana* and power (figures 10–11).

Groundloop

I recently completed *Groundloop*, a video work twenty metres long and five metres high, for the atrium of the Sydney Modern Project at the Art Gallery of New South Wales (figures 12–13). It tells the story of a First Nations crew on a *waka hourua*, an ocean-going canoe. *Waka* traditions are really important and part of my continuing interest in travel. They reveal the histories of trade, movement and encounters. Not only are these vessels designed to move people around, they have metaphysical meanings and the navigators who sail them are a community unto themselves. I chose to have a woman as the navigator of this futuristic *waka*. I wanted to show her navigating traditionally, by the stars and ocean currents, in harmony with nature. There has been a growing movement for quite some time now to revive traditional sailing techniques right across the Pacific, and in Australia I see there is a growing interest in reviving knowledge around *nawi* and *wuuyi* or river canoes.

We probably have the highest number of residents from other Pacific Island nations here in New Zealand, so these relationships are very important and we've always kept them current. *Groundloop* reflects on the history of my relationships with Aboriginal and First Nations artists in Australia, and envisages our togetherness by recognising the cultural exchange between our countries. My long association with Australia began with a residency at the Australian Centre for Photography in Sydney in 1988, the year after I finished art school. It was supported by Brenda Croft, the director of Boomalli, which was in its second year as an urban Aboriginal art gallery. A lot of the political ideas I encountered then continue to inform my work and thinking today.

It's not easy to go into someone else's country and tell their stories: it can be very fraught. Indigenous people know that when you come to a new place, the the first people you go and talk to are the elders: you do it face to face, share food and chat to build relationships. But that all-important dialogue was delayed for *Groundloop* when COVID hit us all. Creating a narrative around Indigenous people coming together was going to be tricky, so it was a huge relief—and felt amazing—when I was finally able to come to Australia last year to start work on it with local artists and groups. I worked with artists and filmmakers on both sides of the Tasman. Riffing off the term 'past, present and emerging', I decided to set the work in an indeterminate future where the people of our region travel and connect with one another freely, honouring Indigenous customs and cultural knowledge in an atmosphere grounded in the Sydney Modern Project's inner-city locale. *Groundloop* embraces Indigenous spirituality and highlights that living consciously alongside the land and sea is the way forward for a sustainable, culturally positive and hopeful future, and it recognises the respect that traditional custodians of Country—*mana whenua*—hold for the land.

It is called *Groundloop* because I wanted to suggest that the ocean floor of the Tasman Sea was a connector. Māori and Pacific people use the ocean as a superhighway between far-flung places and the ground connects Hokianga, my tribal area, with Australia. Animals transcend boundaries and I wanted to include other living beings as well, so there is a mullet run and migrating eels with designs created by the animation company Studio Gilay. At the end of the loop, the First Nations crew arrive on Gadigal land. A group of culture men from Kempsey perform a *nawi* dance and the crew are welcomed with a smoking ceremony, which finishes with a celebratory gathering. I worked with members of the women's dance troupe Jannawi, who performed a fire stick dance.

He Wai Ngunguru—Nomads of the Sea was a different story of encounter. It's about Charlotte Badger, a convict turned pirate, who incited a mutiny in 1804 and stole the brig *Venus* to sail to Aotearoa. Her advesary Puhi is a *taiaha*-wielding warrior who defends her people's rights without hesitation. It takes artistic license from the half-truths about the first white woman to reside in Aotearoa.

Tupaia's tradition

Words can only communicate so much. This is why it is so important to include artists in foreign diplomacy. In our region it's important to think about who is best placed to lay down the *kaupapa*, the philosophical foundation, who holds the power and who has the right to speak. Working this way offers deeper levels of engagement, an this is about more than funding the arts. Working through artistic practice with objects and traditions, as a cultural interlocutor, is a very different proposition to walking into the white cube of an art gallery where the space is wiped clean of the previous exhibition. You have a personal reckoning with the history and culture of pieces and traditions that you're encountering.

When I was making *in Pursuit of Venus [infected]* it was important to make it as big as it deserved to be. I started just as the global financial crisis hit and largely funded it myself. The result is a work that is now travelling worldwide, and it occurs to me, as I'm writing this today, that I am working in a tradition that was laid down by Tupaia. I am an envoy, using the knowledge and skills I've gained as an artist, to stitch together the Indigenous stories of Australia and Aotearoa and their histories.

Thank you, everybody.

Drawing the Line: Two Decades of Theatre Design Teaching in India

Dr Peter Cooke AM
Jagera and Turrbal country

Good morning. It is my great pleasure to be with you. This morning I would like to speak about the creative connections that I have made within the Indian arts community, both serendipitously and intentionally, as a teacher, theatre designer and administrator in Australia, the USA and India. I was the Head of Design at NIDA in Sydney, as well as Assistant and then Deputy Director, for 22 years, before I moved to the USA in 2009 where I was the Head of the School of Drama at Carnegie Mellon University in Pittsburgh, Pennsylvania. I am currently a teacher and consultant and about to travel to Kerala and Telangana in

August for two months at the invitation of the new Director of the School of Drama and Fine Arts at Calicut University, Dr Abhilash Pillai.

First contact

My introduction to the Indian performing arts began in my teenage years in Malaysia. These early experiences instilled in me a deep attachment to the arts of South East Asia, the Pacific and India. Looking back over my twenty years teaching theatre design in India, I can readily identify person-to-person contact through creative practice, as a change-making activity that has led to mutually beneficial relationships between schools, students and professionals. Working alongside international peers, whether in education or professional practice, has a value beyond what can be achieved by simply meeting at conferences and seminars.

My interest in the Indo-Asian-Pacific region was inspired by my colleagues and mentors at NIDA, John Clark (Director from 1969–2003) and Aubrey Mellor (Director 2004–08). Mellor, started the ball rolling in 1973 when he travelled to Delhi on a Churchill Fellowship to 'study Asian theatre from Japan to India'.[1]

On that visit he made contact with Ebrahim Alkazi, a noted fine arts connoisseur who became the Director of the National School of Drama (NSD) in 1975. It had been established in 1959 as a Unit of the Sangeet Natak Akademi and in 1975 it became an autonomous institution financed by the Ministry of Culture. NSD also runs short-term workshops in urban, rural and remote areas of India, manages a professional Repertory Company which tours nationally, and oversees a Theatre in Education Company as well as a publishing arm.

Mellor connected Alkazi with John Clark who subsequently visited NSD to direct a production of Thornton Wilder's *The Skin of our Teeth*. Then in 1980 Clark invited Alkazi's successor, BV Karanth, to direct the folk-theatre epic, *Hayavadana* at NIDA as part of an Indian-Australian Government Cultural Agreement.[2] Aubrey Mellor was the assistant director on that production, and so began a long and fruitful collaboration between the two schools.

I first visited New Delhi to teach a theatre design workshop in 2004. I was working with the final third-year design/directing students. At the time there was no specialised theatre design course offered in India. Most often the director designed the production with artisans who created the set, costumes and props. My approach to pedagogy when working with Indian director/design students is to offer them a way of working that adds to their accumulated set of skills and knowledge. No one teacher has the gift of unlocking every student's imagination, so adding to their creative tool box is always my aim.

Some basic ground has to be covered early in our studio work, in terms of communication, so that we are all on the same page before we embark on the more complex area of working with each student's directorial hat on. A text is chosen to explore during the workshops with the students and their teachers and we analyse it together in depth before researching visual prompts from the internet and other sources to support each student's production ideas. I tend to work by sitting at a large table with the students around me as they generate rough sketches on paper of possible visual landscapes for their productions, before moving on to model boxes of a theatre space of the students' choosing. From then on, the process is to look at and refine ideas with a focus on characters, the visual landscape for the production, scale, space, lighting, iconography, clothes and budget. The students' understanding of imagery and iconography varies according to each individual's background, education and life experience.

Devendra Raj Ankur, who invited me to lead these workshops in 2004, works in the area of theatrical adaptation. Taking short stories, novels and articles of journalism, he develops compelling and undecorated performances through rigorous and imaginative improvisational techniques. While design in his own work is minimal, he recognises the value of specialised training in order to support directors and performers and open up employment opportunities for designers nationally and internationally in the theatre, television and film industries.

In 2005 Ankur invited me to return to design a large-scale production of *The Trojan War* with the students I had taught the year before and John Clark directing. Practical learning was clearly taking place and close bonds were formed. Not only did the group understand my process from our classes, but they now could see how the results were being achieved by working side by side with me. Myriad conversations took place in the construction workshops, rehearsal rooms and ultimately the theatre. I believe the students' direct creative involvement in the production was an invaluable part of their learning process. I have kept in touch with that and subsequent classes, helping them with advice about further educational opportunities abroad, fellowships and scholarships and a sea of references. These are some of the unplanned results that eventuate through artist-to-artist contacts.

The directorship at NSD is restricted to five years and I have now worked with four on my visits to Delhi. Following the retirement of Ankur in 2007, I continued my yearly workshops under the enlightened leadership of Anuradha Kapur, a distinguished and imaginative theatre director who often incorporates visually startling metaphors into the designs of her productions. She was succeeded at NSD by a further two directors over a ten-year period, who were supported on the Australian side at NIDA by John Clark and his successor Aubrey Mellor.

Interestingly, throughout the many years of our collaborations, there was never an official agreement between NIDA and NSD, it just happened because the Directors and Faculty at each school were committed to such interaction.

The NIDA years

The Indian performing arts training community and profession is a large and complex matrix of central government, state government and locally supported educational institutions, performing ensembles and community-based organisations. There is also a vibrant commercial theatre scene, active touring circuit and a healthy theatre festival culture throughout the country, as well as of course—Bollywood. From visiting drama schools high in the Himalayas, to the tropical South, I have seen what is available to a local theatregoer, aspiring drama student, educator or inquisitive arts practitioner who is prepared to reach out, explore and form bonds within the Indian performing arts community. I have also experienced the wish of many Indian students, faculty and performing artists to study or perform aboard and participate in the global creative arts industry.

While I was at NIDA one of the many pluses of my teaching trips to India was witnessing the interactions between faculty, staff and students, from both institutions, grow over time. Indeed during my NIDA years we hosted the Director of NSD, Devendra Raj Ankur; Registrar, AN Roy; Professor of Theatre Architecture, Suresh Bhardwaj; Professor of Voice, Hemma Singh; Visiting Faculty, Rita Ganguly, and students who have gone on to have substantial careers in the Indian theatre and film industries, including Dolly Ahluwalia and Bapi Bose. Both of the latter attended NIDA as part of a Government of India Cultural Exchange Agreement. With each visit, guests held workshops, directed productions or attended classes within the teaching programs.

The return arrangement from NIDA to NSD was more challenging. While John Clark, myself, acting teacher Jennifer Hagan and properties master, Krishna Thomas, visited, held workshops and seminars and directed or taught at NSD over many years, no Australian student exchange took place. Encouraging NIDA students to take a semester out of their program was always a challenge. It meant missing out on a play production, and that they would not be seen by agents and managements in a fully-mounted production in Sydney. Furthermore, NIDA's undergraduate degrees are three-year programs compared with the USA's four years, where study abroad is much more popular. The difference provides USA students with an extra year to be seen in productions by the professional community if they undertake study abroad.

Nevertheless, when students and faculty from NIDA and India, Japan, Papua New Guinea, Singapore, the USA, Tonga, Vietnam, Slovakia, the Philippines, Indonesia and South Korea collaborated, the texts studied in History of Theatre, scene study and studio projects and the works that were staged in the play production program noticeably broadened, as well as producing changes in my own pedagogy. While there is much work to be done in this area, when I left NIDA in 2009 the teaching programs, studios projects and productions were more diverse than when I joined in 1986, thanks to the initiatives led by Clark, Mellor and senior faculty, myself included.

One of Clark's interests when he became Director of NIDA in 1969 was to broaden the History of Theatre course to connect to the Asia-Pacific region and include works outside the established European canon. This led to a more inclusive play production program through the engagement of an increasingly diverse range of writers and directors. NIDA faculty always saw the rehearsing and mounting of productions as a core part of the curriculum, in which the involvement of in-house, local or international guest directors, area specialists, cultural advisors and teaching activities were intertwined with learning outcomes.

As a result of the faculty's interest in expanding the pool of applicants across all courses, students from Papua New Guinea, Singapore, the USA, India and increasingly from second and third-generation immigrant communities began to be enrolled. In 1997 Korean director Kim Sujin was invited to direct *A Cry from the City of Virgins* by Kara Juro, which in turn led to the NIDA students Jodie Fried and Fiona Crombie designing the Tokyo production, which then played in New York City.[3]

Throughout the 1990s NIDA faculty were also firmly focused on attracting and supporting Indigenous students and producing works of First Nations relevance when appropriate casting could be achieved. A production of *Dead Heart* by Nicholas Parsons for the NIDA Company in 1993, directed by Clark and with my designs, saw an equally-weighted Indigenous and non-Indigenous cast assembled on the Parade Theatre stage, including Glen Shea, Kevin Smith, Tom E Lewis and David Ngoombujarra.

As a current member of the NIDA Company and its Foundation Trust, I see the current administration and faculty working with considerable focus to decolonise the canon and place diversity and inclusion at the centre of all activities. The appointment of three Indigenous staff members shows a commitment to this endeavour.

USA–India connection

Moving to the USA to Head the Carnegie Melon School of Drama in 2009, I continued my visits and teaching role in Delhi, and facilitated reciprocal visits between staff, students and graduates from India and Australia to CMU. Indeed, I made it a condition of my contract that CMU supported my teaching visits to Delhi and return visits to Australia on an annual basis.

CMU has had a formal Study Abroad program with NIDA for many years that has seen Pittsburgh based students attend NIDA for a semester of training, most often in their fall, our spring. NIDA grew to become popular with our Pittsburgh-based students because of the success of NIDA alumni on stage and screen in the USA. Another factor was NIDA's tuition fees, which are well below CMU's, so students traveling to NIDA for a semester of training would receive substantial fee relief according to their individual tuition packages.

The Indian reciprocal arrangements with CMU were, unfortunately, not so successful. Although Anuradha Kapur and I signed a Study Abroad agreement between our two schools in 2012, no student exchange took place. We almost had one CMU actor visit Delhi for a semester, however her visa application was turned down as her father, a director specialising in puppetry on television, was Pakistani. Cost is most certainly a prohibitive impediment for most Indian students wishing to study abroad, as financial aid is rarely available for international applicants.

On the other hand, during my time at CMU, our programs, curriculum, faculty appointments and syllabi responded to the wants and needs of students from the Asia-Pacific region that were growing in number year by year. Our distinguished Chinese-American Professor of Costume Design, Susan Tsu, personally broadened the recruiting process to substantially increase the numbers of graduate students from China and South Korea, with smaller numbers from India, Thailand and the Philippines. What this shows is that appointing a faculty member with interests outside the home country can realise substantial dividends when it comes to diversifying the student body and the material studied and presented on stage.

When I first joined CMU in 2009 the syllabus was largely based on the Western canon. Over time, a forward-looking faculty and increased enrolment from black and Latino communities led to significant broadening of the repertoire studied and produced over a decade.

After the murder of George Floyd in 2020, the Black Lives

Matter and #MeToo movements demanded an end to racism and sexism in the US and diversity and inclusion have become central to the day-to-day activities and strategic planning within the School, and to many of our peers and affiliated professional companies, as well as across the theatrical field as a whole.

Indeed, opening up opportunities for artists long marginalised and excluded from positions of influence across the academy and the performing arts has brought about a revolution in a great deal of educational and professional drama practice in the US in recent years. This is both ongoing and appropriate, but in an unforeseen consequence, the increase in diversity and inclusion at home has often been gained at the expense of international geographic inclusion and outreach.

Looking forward

It is hard to capture or evaluate the impact of the interactions between Australia, India and the US I have been involved with, other than to say that I feel that my work with three leading drama schools has produced invaluable creative contacts, understanding of the richness of other cultures and a broadening of employment opportunities.

Over time I have found that interacting through creative practice is the most effective way of building sustained and advantageous relationships across the theatrical arts. One of the many challenges to a more fluid exchange between the countries in our region however is that the opportunity for individuals to travel and learn often sits within the control of those holding positions of influence in educational institutions and theatre companies. I have experienced changes in leadership at arts bodies in India, Australia and the USA that have led to thriving inter-institutional relationships being dropped as individual leaders pursue their own agendas. Years of personal outreach can evaporate in an instant when little thought is given to evaluating and perhaps grandfathering existing relationships when leaders change seats.

What is needed is an internationally recognised body focused on promoting our arts disciplines in order to build relationships and promote our creative practices throughout the Indo-Pacific region. Our flagship performing arts companies have the administrative personnel, prestige and clout to raise funds and support for international tours, but where is the support and exposure for small to middle-sized performing companies, experimental ensembles or student-led projects? Who is championing their activities? The challenges faced by these small to mid-sized groups with limited support from government and donors, especially post-COVID, puts these opportunities out of their reach.

Such a body would add to a more fluid exchange of ideas, personnel, students, faculty and cultural projects. A federally funded national body with local and international centres, similar to the Alliance Française or the Goethe-Institut, could become a centralised agency where students, individual artists and performing arts collectives could seek advice on festivals, internships, fellowships, scholarships and funding opportunities to participate with the creative communities of our region.

It is not the responsibility of artists to build bridges between governments. Just making the creative work can be taxing enough—and artists may well be at odds with government. When visiting the Kochi Biennale early this year, for example, I saw Richard Bell's powerful installation Embassy—'highlighting the discrimination and exploitation faced by Australia's First Nations people'.[4] The work needs to be seen. It attracted substantial press coverage and focused the attention of an international audience on current political and social issues in Australia that are of great moment. These complex conversations and interactions, that lead to deep mutual understanding between cultures, are soft diplomacy in action.

Establishing an international cultural agency will take focus, collegiality, philanthropy, clearly defined goals and considerable political support. But given that we sit at a moment in time when reinforcing relationships throughout the Indio-Pacific is a Government priority, it is clear that our arts training and cultural institutions have much to offer and we must seize this opportunity to become actively involved in furthering that goal.

Endnotes

---

1. Personal correspondence with Aubrey Mellor. 6 June 2023.
2. *Uniken*, The University of NSW, No.4 of 1980.
3. John Clark, *NIDA*, Focus Books 2003, p. 113.
4. IANS, 'Richard Bell's "Embassy" a hit at Kochi Biennale', *IndianLink*, vol. 30, no. 4. p. 23. issuu.com/indianlink/docs/2023-01_sydney.

Looking Outwards: The Need for an Australian International Cultural Agency

Dr Alison Carroll AM
Wurundjeri country

Eleven years ago, Carrillo Gantner and I wrote a Currency House Platform Paper, *Finding a Place on the Asian Stage*, which focused on Australia's cultural engagement with our region. Carrillo had been Chairman of Asialink when I was establishing the arts program there in 1990 and we had kept the fire burning since. Late last year, with the new Labor Government in power, we thought it was timely to reassess our international cultural strategy by inviting arts managers experienced in this area to a discussion in Melbourne under the banner of the Playking Foundation. Now Currency House has revisited the topic at their 2023 Convention.

Our focus now is on how to achieve enduring cultural

relationships between Australia and the Asia Pacific (and indeed globally) in the most effective way. One suggestion we made in 2012 was creating a new Australian international cultural agency, an 'Australian Goethe-Institut'. Our current discussion is still wrestling with this, but we can find no better solution. This Paper argues why.

***

Not much has changed for the better in Australia since 2012. We have an even less empowered capacity for international cultural engagement than we did then, that has certainly been greatly impacted by the lack of interest or support from recent governments.

Finding a Place on the Asian Stage analysed Australia's engagement with Asia, twenty years after the first Australia Council directive that 50% of its international funding was for Asia-Pacific projects.[1] Despite this early directive, a graph showed the decline in funding for activities in our region over the subsequent two decades (see page 262).

Since then, while governments have been static in this area, artists and organisations have just got on with it, knowing—or despite—the paucity of official policy and strategy. They have understood the energy and interest of contemporary cultural life in our region. They have taken advantage of being so close to Asia and the Asia-Pacific more generally. This has been aided by major changes since 2012 in communications and IT. How to engage is no longer a mystery. The internet is ubiquitous, with google-translate, information, contact details galore, and pictures so you can see what you may encounter.

But is this *laissez-faire* response optimum for us as individuals and a community? Now, with a new Government, we have a chance to rethink how we can best engage: you know, have some principles articulated, policies agreed, and strategies implemented. That way this activity can take place, not straightjacketed by government, but guided and enabled by a thoughtful, proactive, professional, experienced entity, with an overview of what might be most effective and rewarding for us and for our colleagues and audiences elsewhere.

Carrillo and I have since had further discussions about how to carry Australian international cultural engagement forward, but we cannot get past our original idea of a new cultural agency. Most of our peers have such an agency—countries like Britain, France, Germany, Italy, the Netherlands, Russia, India and Japan—and in almost every case it includes a physical cultural presence, i.e., buildings, like the Goethe-Institut in Singapore (figure 14). The only Australian-named cultural-engagement space overseas, as far as I know, is a very nice, but small, house in a village (figure 15) in the Japanese countryside. (The Australian Pavilion in the Venice gardens is for Australian 'display' use only, a different intention.)

The first reaction of the arts community to the idea of a new agency is to worry about more bureaucracy. However, the bureaucracy is already in place. The bigger question is whether what we have now is working well. We have an unfocused Australia Council and an impoverished (they say) Department of Foreign Affairs and Trade (DFAT) capacity. If we want to engage in an intelligent, effective and rewarding way, we need a rethink.

A lot of the ideas we proposed in the 2012 Paper still stand, including the need for a strategic overview, a focus on funding options, and the linkage of programs to national priorities.

Other parts however seem dated—like national profiling years, for example, in India one year and the UK the next, as well as Brand Australia.

I was conscious of this, in part, because of the discussion we had with a dozen arts managers with strong international backgrounds in November last year at the Playking Foundation, where we talked about core *principles* for international engagement. I thought there had been a notable shift of tone from past discussions, moving on from straight promoting Australia or touring or profiling (though this is still the mantra of the Federal Government), to a focus on the importance of dialogue and coming together through dialogue. It was informed by the Uluru Statement from the Heart—needless to say, such a wonderful document.

These are the priority principles for a new cultural strategy for international engagement summarised from that discussion:

- Understanding that arts engagement is a process, not a product or simple transaction, and will take time.
- Understanding that we are part of a wider whole, with creative engagement, communication and reciprocity driving our agendas.
- Understanding that international arts engagement relies on individual initiative and people-to-people relations, not just institutions.
- Being clear that what we do is with our own voice, independent of the expectations of others and capable of surprising.
- Being strong in our engagement with the cultures and communities of the Asia Pacific, expanding our presence

there, not just being visitors. As Tim Lindsey, a key writer in this, said, 'being present'.

- And last but certainly not least, recognising our cultural legacies, including First Nations, to represent our diversity to the world.

Expansive and open, curious and flexible. All can flow from this. If every proposed activity had these words run over it, I do believe there would be a profound shift in how we do things; how we think about engagement. This is very different from the program-driven, outcome-oriented funding focus that occurs now. Everyone in that discussion approved of this. Later in the day of our discussion we were joined by visitors who had not heard the earlier words and they immediately started to talk about money. It was very clear to me that was never the point. It still isn't.

Carrillo and I sent our model to Tony Burke's national cultural policy review late last year. You may have noticed 'international' barely rates a mention in that review published early this year.[2] There were some motherhood statements about the Asia Pacific and that was it. Contemporary music and literature are still part of the Australia Council but they now have new entities with an international remit. We will see how that works out, but I must say it's a strange response in this day of de-siloing art forms. But there it is.

So, the alternative almost all our peer countries enact is a relationship with their foreign ministries, in our case, DFAT. In Australia we have got used to the idea that domestic (in-country) *and* international (overseas) work take place under one institution: the Australia Council. This is almost never the case elsewhere, with ifa (Institut für Auslandsbeziehungen) *and* the Goethe-Institut in Germany; the Arts Council of Great Britain *and* the British Council in the UK; the Agency for Cultural Affairs *and* the Japan Foundation in Japan, and so on. *We* are the unusual entity.

DFAT has pros and cons. They are not arts people, hence the need for an arm's length agency run by arts people, but with a wider agenda that is understood by government more broadly. It would build a cohort of arts professionals with serious international experience and capacity who in turn would be able to engage across government. In this scenario culture is seen in its most inclusive form, as it is, for example, in most of Asia, the Pacific and indeed Indigenous Australia: being about the core of us. And if we respect this in, say, Pacific Island countries or Indigenous Australia, and work with dialogue, respect, and flexibility (all the principles I outlined) then we start to have relationships of meaning and worth. DFAT is about relationships. It says its bottom line is politics and economics, but in this context, those words are not the key ones.

The Goethe-Institut seems to have best worked this out. This is a précis from a colleague there:

> The Goethe-Institut is an independent registered non-profit association, founded in 1951. It is funded by the federal office of the German Foreign Ministry, with agreements negotiated between the GI and the federal office for a duration of four years. The parliament unlocks funding for the Institut every year. After a significant reform in 2009 the funding provided by the parliament is more or less stable (around 270m Euros per annum). On top of these grants, revenue is generated with language teaching. The profitability of language

classes is very uneven—very low in the US or Europe, very high in India or Mexico and many Asian countries.

The Institut has its head office in Munich. The head office serves as a controlling and service entity, but the budgets are in twelve global regions, which can operate with these budgets relatively independently.

In terms of its politics: as the GI is independent and autonomous, our main partners are not government organizations from the host countries, but representatives of civil society. This means, of course, artists and cultural producers, but also art initiatives, and collaborative and experimental projects. This is of great importance where there is no funding structure (like in India) and of less importance in a place like the US, where there is both state or federal government funding and private funding.

The GI does NOT follow political intentions or strategies of the respective government, but, of course, cannot be immune to political or societal currents. The focus on climate change or sustainability is a case in point. The tension between art as being instrumentalized in the context of 'soft power' or as an educational tool on one side, and as having 'a value in itself', is constantly there and needs constant negotiations and deliberations.[3]

The Goethe-Institut is open about its funding of around A$400 million per year, as is the British Council: around A$320 million per year. Others are harder to pin down but let us compare those two budgets to Australia. I made some calculations based on the Australia Council's International Engagement Strategy for a piece I wrote for *The Conversation* in 2022.[4] The average budget over the previous five years had been $2.7 million per year, which I believe still holds, while DFAT's Australian Cultural

Diplomacy Grants program had an allocation of $400,000. There are other programs here and there that loosely come under the cultural diplomacy tag, so let us average the national figure up to around $5 million. International comparisons are hard because each country defines cultural activity differently, but the contrast with Germany and Britain is stark: on these figures, they spend A$4–5 per capita on international cultural engagement and diplomacy, and we spend twenty cents.

When I ask my colleagues here to guess what we spend, they offer 'five cents'. This is part of the problem: we *expect* this and seem to accept it. Why? And when I talk about the Goethe-Institut, there seems to be an acceptance we cannot emulate this. I also don't understand why not.

Let me give some other practical examples of what others do and we do not. The Japan Foundation, celebrating 50 years of activity, recently published impressive figures for work from its 25 overseas offices as well as in Japan: 5,400 television programs made available to 170 countries, 1,500 books translated into 50 languages, 349 exhibitions organised in 87 countries, their Japanese language program utilised in 199 countries, and so on.[5] This year the French Institute in China produced a 110-page brochure for a three-month program of 255 high-quality cultural activities in that one, albeit large, country.[6] The French have four cultural centres in Indonesia, and we have *zero* cultural presence. We used to have a cultural counsellor at the Embassy in Jakarta: no more, though it is our biggest diplomatic post in the world.

In 2003 I advocated for an Australian Cultural Centre in Yogyakarta. At that time 'everyone' supported a physical cultural presence in Indonesia—a building, staffing and a budget for events. I wrote about it in 2005 and 2006 in *Art Monthly*.[7] I said

Britain, France, Germany, Italy, the Netherlands, Russia, India and Japan all ran cultural centres in Indonesia. Twenty years later, these countries continue to support active centres, with others like the Koreans more visibly 'present'. Twenty years ago, the two countries in this 'peer' list without a physical, stand-alone cultural space were Australia and America. Now, the overt change from that is the establishment by the US government of AtAmerica, a new expensive centre in Jakarta. Looming in the background are the Chinese with plans to build 50 China Cultural Centres around the world (figure 16). Still nothing for us.

Why would these countries create and fund such centres if they could see no need, purpose, or advantage? What is Australia missing? Is this because they are stupid and we are smart? Because we don't want or need to be 'present'? I won't reiterate the positive outcomes of engagement noted before: dialogue, reciprocity, wider cultural curiosity, relationships, and so on. They all exist, and indeed if they did not, we would not be even thinking about this, but they do exist alongside another set of pressures: the real-world triggers that have led other countries to be proactive in the past. For example, the British Council was founded as a direct response to Stalin's cultural diplomacy in the 1930s; the Goethe-Institut was established in the early 1950s to help Germany's international engagement post-war; and the Japan Foundation was set up in the 1970s when Japan had reestablished itself sufficiently, also post-war, to start to look outwards. And China currently... well, join the dots.

We also have reason to be proactive about engagement in this politically nuanced world. I used to say one reason to do so was tackling a confusing identity, often thought of as second-rate European. Maybe that issue is retreating, maybe not. I also used to say we needed to pay special attention because we were so far away physically—maybe also not so true nowadays vis-à-vis the focus on Asia and the Pacific. But the main reason has always been the perceived or real issue of inclusion or exclusion, based overtly or covertly on race, increasingly raw and articulated internationally today. We all know this. It is from the treatment of First Nations since 1788 to the reaction to Chinese goldminers in the nineteenth century; the very well-known White Australia Policy; the words of Pauline Hanson and John Howard seeping into the famous questions for intended immigrants about Don Bradman's batting average;[8] the treatment of asylum seekers of brown skin in comparison with, say, Ukrainians; AUKUS, the Anglo-phone pact; and now the Voice and the true despair if it fails. With this track record, we need all the help we can get to keep communications and engagement as open as possible. And beware if we do not.

So, what now? After our Playking group had put our proposal for an agency to the Federal Arts Department without any reaction, we approached DFAT, and included the idea of a feasibility study into a new agency, with some small funding from the Foundation. However, despite the arguments put, DFAT has referred us back to the Australia Council.

The Australia Council. Carrillo and I were saying how sad it makes us nowadays; we have both loved the Council in the past, and done a lot of work with it and within it. In my last days running Asialink Arts, I was told we received the highest amount of funding from them of any organisation outside the Major Performing Arts Board. And I always talked them up in Asia, to the general disbelief that I could so like working with my main government funders. I said: 'They back us, they understand us, they help when things go wrong, they want us to succeed.' What is it like now? It seems to have become fearful when it should be fearless; bureaucratic when it should let things soar; focused on brand rather than substance. It is increasingly difficult to get detailed information about their budgets or clarity on what they do. I hear that the seventh head of their international program in seven years has recently resigned, so maybe this is the case internally as well.

As I say, this scenario does not give us confidence. We need the Government to see the situation and act. The first step is an independent enquiry, taking on board the need for intelligent and swift action. We would like to see a feasibility study into a new agency. It is part of Australian folklore that Gough Whitlam formed the Australia Council. Now is the chance for an initiative of lasting worth from this new Government.

Endnotes

---

1. Carrillo Gantner was Chairman of the Performing Arts Board when the Australia Council passed a resolution that 50% of its international program funding must go to programs in the Asia Pacific within three years. He writes, 'For Performing Arts it happened immediately, for Literature, Community Arts and Aboriginal Arts it took a couple of years but every board got there with surprising speed... artists immediately applied for grants for projects in or with Asia.' Email from Carrillo Gantner to Harriet Parsons, September 6, 2023. See also *Australia Council for the Arts Annual Report*, 1993—1994, pp. 20-1.
2. *Revive: A Place for Every Story, A Story for Every Place, Australia's Cultural Policy for the next five years.* Commonwealth of Australia, 2023, pp, 93, 106. arts.gov.au/culturalpolicy.

3. Email to the author from a colleague in the Goethe-Institut, May 5, 2022.
4. Alison Carroll, '"Where have all you Australians gone?" Australia's shrinking role in cultural diplomacy'. *The Conversation*, May 18, 2022. theconversation.com/au.
5. The Japan Foundation, 50th Anniversary (website). jf50.jpf.go.jp/en/#index_base.
6. *Festival Croisements*, Institut Français, Embassy of France in China, April–July 2023.
7. Alison Carroll, 'Letter from Indonesia'. *Art Monthly Australia*, no. 183 (September 2005), pp. 3-5; Alison Carroll, 'Wish you were here: Australian Government funding for our art overseas'. Art Monthly Australia, no. 196, (December 2006), pp. 46-9.
8. ABC News, 'Don gets dropped from citizenship test'. Posted November 22, 2008. *ABC News*. abc.net.au/news.

Closing Discussion

The convention concluded with a general discussion. The opening remarks of Carrillo Gantner and final comments from David Pledger, who will be convening next year's meeting, are published in full, with a summary of comments from other delegates. This is an edited version of the transcript.

Carrillo Gantner

It's been a really fascinating morning, thank you. Alison's work I know well, but there were dimensions to Peter's talk that were new to me, and shouldn't be.

I believe we have a failure of leadership in Australia at the moment and that's at several levels. At a political level, because the new government has tried so hard not to be wedged on anything, particularly on national strategic issues, that they have allowed themselves to become swept up in what they think of as an AUKUS wave, and revert to a comforting mid-twentieth century anglosphere view of the world. In fact, of course, it is not going to be a gentle wave, it's going to be a dumper, and one that is potentially going to embroil us in conflict, even to the extent of an American war with China over Taiwan, which is not our issue. But we won't go down that track today.

We also have a failure of leadership in our arts organisations, both at a government level and in the companies who deliver the arts to the Australian people. Look at the leadership of the major companies. Generally, the larger the company, the less interest they have in where we live and what it means to be part of our region at the beginning of the twenty-first century. We have festival directors—major metropolitan arts festival directors—who have never been to Indonesia or India or China. We have company directors in the opera, ballet and large theatre companies, who know nothing of the region in which we live, let alone the repertoire and the different forms of performance that come from these areas.

Peter, I was very encouraged to hear about the NIDA faculty members' links with Asia, which happily were broader than I had realised, but I don't think any of the other professional theatre schools—certainly not the VCA, here in Melbourne, and not that I'm aware of, WAAPA, Griffith or any of the other professional schools around the country—have faculty members from Asia, or more than a token one or two. We certainly do not offer courses that are of particular interest to the Asian students we say we want to attract—largely for the wrong reasons, because we see them as piggy banks rather than valuable envoys of cultural diversity and exchange.

We do not have the leadership in our companies and our

schools to make the changes that Australia needs. So, where do we start? Well, I think we start with support for the little companies that, Peter, you mentioned: they are the ones who are actually out there doing the important work. They are the ones who are finding ways to scratch together tours and bring counterpart artists to work with them here in Australia. They are doing this with virtually no funding from federal or state agencies, and when there are small pockets of funding, they have to scrabble to get thrippence here and tuppence there, because we have siloed everything.

The bilateral councils—the Australia-India Institute, the National Foundation for Australia-China Relations, the ASEAN Council, the Indonesia Institute—are all focused on the bilateral relationship. They don't even engage with each other. So, if a company is organising a tour to Jakarta, they don't say , 'While you're there, why not go on to Singapore and Tokyo and maybe even further?' They don't deal with each other. There is no strategic overview of our international cultural engagement.

Now the new *Revive* national cultural policy has siloed the very limited international support that is available through the Australia Council. When you talk to them about what they are doing internationally, they say, well, our new music board (or whatever it is to be called), is going to have their *own* international program, as is the new literature board. So you say, okay, what about dance and theatre? And they say, well, we haven't actually got anything for that. As Alison said, the Council's last international director, Joe Mitchell, left recently in despair because they were doing nothing and a strategic plan he had put forward was rejected. That is seven international directors in seven years at the Australia Council.

The government has given us a cultural policy, and that is a very good thing, but the policy itself is a bit of a disappointment. I mean, they took the five pillars from *Creative Australia*, the Labour government's cultural policy from ten years ago, and said, well we want to get something out quickly, so we'll just take the same five things they did last time. They appointed a dozen people to flesh those areas out and invited submissions. The new policy has not actually come up with anything startling or original. It doesn't even acknowledge where we live. The one area where it has been strong, and where Australian culture itself is very strong at the moment, is the acknowledgment of, and focus on, the whole Indigenous cultural world that for most Australians has been not even a mystery, but more a blank wall.

The focus on Indigenous arts over the last 5–10 years has certainly been the one area where cultural policy has made Australia stronger, and that is reflected in *Revive*. But the same is not true of our place in the world, which is in the Asia Pacific. The word 'Asia' is not uttered, like other four-letter words.

In my view, one of the things that has disadvantaged us, and not only in the cultural sphere, has been the transformation of the Department of Foreign Affairs into the Department of Foreign Affairs *and Trade*. Since then, the trade people have risen to the top. Trade people sell things, and that looks good to government ministers who tell us the impressive financial statistics. The downside is that DFAT has become a transactional department and, in my observation, what we have lost are the great thinkers and analysts. Foreign Affairs used to be full of thinkers. You look at them now and these people are mostly dead or retired: people like John McCarthy and the senior and serious Australian diplomats, who reflected on relationships and understood the cultures of the countries with which they were dealing. Now they are told to go forth and sell things and that has been, I think, a source of national weakness. It might be good for the economy to have trade dominate our international relations, but it has not strengthened our understanding or appreciation of the countries around us or the world in which we must make our home.

We were told after our Platform Paper was published in 2012 that the Australia Council would lift its game and the Asia Pacific would come back onto the horizon. And it did, briefly, in their conversations, but certainly not in any significant way in practice. So we have not gone anywhere, except perhaps backwards. I think, Ali, you were very generous when you said, 'three steps forward and two steps back'. It feels—and perhaps I am just getting old and cynical—more like three steps forward and about seven back.

There is an enormous amount of goodwill towards a more comprehensive and strategic delivery of Australia's international cultural work, and people who want this to happen, but we have had a dead bat played back to us by both the Australia Council and DFAT. When you have this discussion, they point to each other and say, 'Well, it really is their responsibility'. No-one wants to do anything. There is no-one in government with the political will, by which I mean members of parliament who are behind the idea of an entity focused on Australian international cultural engagement, who are prepared to push the case for it. When we were young, we had Gough Whitlam who opened these cultural doors and there was a wild rush of blood to the head, and it was wonderful for a time. At the state levels, you also had leaders like Don Dunstan in South Australia and Rupert Hamer in Victoria, and probably others in other states, such as

Peter Beattie and Wayne Goss in Queensland. When you have had these politicians, with the political muscle and the cultural understanding, there have been these wonderful moments, but we never seem to be able to turn them into more permanent structural benefits for our artists.

I have always said that arts management is not an independent science: it exists only to make the work of artists and the creation of art possible. The very best work that we do in this country is the sort of fusion that happens when you bring different cultures and forms together. In my own career in the theatre, the two highlights for me were, first: directing an Australian play with the Shanghai People's Art Theatre in the mid-1980s and the extraordinary results that happened—I won't say I achieved—but they happen because of things you don't really understand, even while you're doing it. And second: inviting Suzuki Tadashi to direct with the Playbox Theatre Company. That was like the Heidelberg Under 11s asking Steve Smith to open the batting, but he did it. And he produced remarkable results, something new for Australia.

Suzuki said, 'I'll do it, but first, you must do certain things to make it possible. One is to send your artists to come and work with us in Japan. Two, you have to bring me out to do workshops for a wider group of actors in Australia. Only then, maybe, will we have a platform on which we can make a production in the third or fourth year.' And that is what we did. Of course, we were never like the Suzuki Company of Toga in terms of our ability, but, at least for me and for all of us who were involved in that production, this work with Suzuki opened up a whole new vocabulary of theatre that we had not even known existed.

I have seen the same things happen with Chinese traditional

art forms. Bringing the teachers from the Nanjing Acrobatic Troupe here in 1983–84 utterly changed acrobatics, circus and physical theatre in this country. And it led directly to the establishment of the National Institute of Circus Arts (NICA) at Swinburne University in Melbourne. Now I am furious that Swinburne is trying to kill off NICA, because, they say, it does not accord with their strategic vision. Frankly, I don't give a rat's whether it accords with Swinburne's vision. The important question is, 'Is it good for Australia?' And the obvious answer is a resounding 'Yes'.

So why are we not embracing NICA and celebrating it, and giving it the support it needs at every level? Why aren't we embracing and celebrating and supporting the rich opportunities that our own regional neighbourhood offers? That's what we need to do to make this a great country.

***

The comments of the other speakers focused on the need for greater cooperation, particularly between institutions, in education, government and the profession.

Peter Cooke

Peter Cooke began by talking about the importance of collegiality:

> I'm going to a respected school in Kerala soon, which is run by somebody who was at the National School in Delhi, and he reached out to various universities and said 'We've got Peter Cooke. Do you want him?' Three universities said, 'yes': I'm also going to Hyderabad

> and the University of Sanskrit. I can't imagine that ever happening here: that somebody might ring somebody else up and say, 'Hey, we've got this person, are you interested?' Australia's a small country with a very small pool of people in theatre education: they simply have to work together.

He also noted that in America the Goethe-Institut, the Japan Foundation and the Alliance Française, had all been very helpful, offering not just money and support for events, but also advice. An Australian institution, with a physical building, would be enormously valuable:

> All the students that I taught in America want to come to Australia. They love the acting, they love what they're seeing on film and television, and on Broadway. I love the idea of a place where every student in America could go and find out what's going on in the Australian scene.
>
> We have fantastic people flying the flag for us over there, and every time we have somebody nominated for an award, it's on the front page of every newspaper here, but there's no quid pro quo.

Institutional change, he argued, has to start with the boards: who they appoint, how they appoint them and what they bring to the institution. He noted that there was a dearth of practitioners and educators on the boards of major companies and teaching institutions, and this was affecting their priorities:

> I'm not sure that they ever ask, 'What is the most important thing we're doing?' It's about educating young people and getting them interested in the cultural arts of their country and the wider world.

Lisa Reihana

Lisa Reihana commented on the responsibility that artists take up on behalf of their communities, when they become the member of a board, and the importance of representing all generations. Echoing comments made by Rachael Maza last year, she emphasised the value of an extended and inclusive decision-making process. At Māori decision-making gatherings, *hui* or *hui rūnanga*, every individual in the meeting house has the right to speak, regardless of age or status. It's a long discussion, she said, but the richer for it and it leads to more complex, mutual understanding.

Margaret Leask

Picking up on Lisa Reihana's point, Margaret Leask emphasised the importance of meeting in person. She said:

> I'm going to sound like a dinosaur—what I remember from the seventies, setting up the Australian Youth Performing Arts Association is how exciting it was, to quote *Hamilton*, which has become my mantra, to be 'in the room where it happens'. I think we don't do enough of that anymore: people getting together to solve their problems. We get our information and social experiences digitally now, and our interactions with the world have got much smaller, and that concerns me.

David Pledger

I'm participating in this conversation as one of the bowlers of the Heidelberg Under 11s, so it's nice to be in the conversation alongside Carrillo, who is the captain and Alison, who is probably umpiring. I'm coming to you from the lands of the Bunurong people of the Kulin nation in Narm and I've been listening attentively to the conversation, which is very familiar to me.

I've had a company for 25 years and we do what Carrillo has said: scrabble around for lots of money so that we can work in Korea, Japan and, courtesy of Asialink, Shanghai. So, I know the story well, but I look at it through a slightly different prism to some of you, in that I have deliberately chosen to be an independent artist and curator. And I suppose my reading of what has been described today, in relation to the Asia Pacific, is what I would call the atomization of the Australian cultural sector over the last two decades. I would also say that the conditions are much worse than anybody's mapped out in this very polite conversation today.

Some of the asks are unlikely ever to be granted, and that's largely due to changing world conditions, but also the political dynamics. Margaret, I absolutely think you have to be in the room: if you're not in the room, you're not part of the conversation. I've also learned, as an activist, not to ask for what you think you can get: ask for what you need. One of the reasons conditions in the Australian arts sector are so bad today, is because advocates have asked for what they thought they could get instead of what they actually needed.

And never, ever, give up your seat at the table. Over the last decade artists have given up their seat at the table and often their places have been taken by advocates who have conservative alignments with funding agencies, and tell them what they can ask for and what they can advocate for; and they're advice is often not in the best interests of independent artists.

Activism is pretty much the core of my practice. I think to be an artist in the 21st century, you also have to be an activist, and that's the intention for the next Convention. It will be about the relationship between arts activism and climate change, which is one of the existential crises that face us today. It will be built around a mechanism called Assembly for the Future, which is a deliberative, propositional and generative process that takes place at the intersection between philosophy, policy, arts practice and the agency of every human being to be to make a change. It will be an in-person event—depending on funding, of course—but hopefully there will be about 150 people 'in the room'.

Contributors

LISA REIHANA CNZM works in film, sculpture, costume and body adornment, text and photography. Since the 1990s she has earned an outstanding reputation as an artist, producer and cultural interlocutor who explores the intersection between representations of identity and history with concepts of place and community. Her large-scale video installation *in Pursuit of Venus [infected]* (2015–17) reinterprets a nineteenth-century French wallpaper, *Les sauvages de la mer du Pacifique* to explore Captain Cook's encounters with the diplomatic envoy Tupaia in Tahiti and other First Nations peoples. The critically acclaimed work represented New Zealand at the Venice Biennale in 2017 and has since been shown around the world. She received the Arts Laureate Award from the Arts Foundation of New Zealand in 2014, the Te Tohu Toi Ke Te Waka Toi Māori Arts Innovation Award from Creative New Zealand in 2015, and was made a Companion of the New Zealand Order of Merit in 2022.

DR PETER COOKE AM is a theatre designer, consultant and teacher in Australia, India and South East Asia. He was the Deputy Director and Head of Design at NIDA for 22 years and Head of Carnegie Mellon University's School of Drama from 2009 to 2020. He has taught and lectured extensively throughout Southeast Asia, leading master classes in design and designing productions for the National School of Drama in New Delhi, India, where he has been a visiting professor for sixteen years. His Australian, Indian and American students have gone on to win accolades including Helpmann and Green Room Awards in Australia and Tony, Emmy and Academy Awards in the USA. He was awarded the Medal of the Order of Australia, AOM, in 2008 for 'Service to the performing arts through theatrical design education, research and administration' and was made a Member of the Order of Australia, AM, in 2017 for 'Substantial service to the performing arts as an administrator and academic, particularly to theatre and dance'.

Dr Alison Carroll am is a critic, writer, curator, administrator and senior lecturer at the Victorian College of the Arts, Melbourne University. She was the founding Director of the Arts Program at Asialink, Australia's most influential NGO in regional engagement, from 1990 to 2010. The exchange program she created between Asia and Australia encompasses the visual arts, performing arts, literature and arts management practice. In 1989 she curated the landmark exhibition, *Out of Asia*, which presented Australian representations of Asia by contemporary artists including Tony Clark, Susan Norrie and Fiona MacDonald, and in 1994 she was responsible for the first major inclusion of contemporary Asian art at the Adelaide Festival. She was awarded the Visual Arts Board of the Australia Council's Emeritus Medal in 2006 and was made a Member of the Order of Australia for her work with Asialink in 2010. That same year she published a major book on twentieth-century Asian art, *The Revolutionary Century: Art in Asia 1900–2000*. She is currently a senior research fellow at the Victorian College of the Arts, Melbourne University.

Carrillo Gantner ac has had a lifetime of involvement in the arts in Australia and Asia and held many positions in public life, both as a creative practitioner and advocate. In 2019 he was awarded a Companion of the Order of Australia for Service to the Community through professional involvement in, and philanthropic support for, the performing and visual arts, and to Australia-Asia cultural exchange and in He co-authored Platform Paper no. 31, *Finding a Place on the Asian Stage* with Alison Carroll in 2012.

Dr Margaret Leask was an arts administrator in Australia and England for many years. Since 2004, she has recorded and archived interviews as an oral historian for the National Library of Australia, the State Library of New South Wales, the Sydney Theatre Company, the National Film and Sound Archive and other organisations in Australia. She continues to work as a freelance researcher and theatre historian.

David Pledger is the Artistic Director of Not Yet It's Difficult. As an artist, curator, writer, activist and producer he operates at the intersection of the performing, visual and media arts. He often performs in these roles simultaneously and retrospectively, in highly collaborative, constructed fields. The dramaturgical practice he has developed engages artists in all art forms, and experts across the social, scientific and academic spectrum, situating artistic practice in a broader cultural frame. He creates artworks and public events of scale that have multiple intentions and outcomes in the pursuit of progressive social change. He has written numerous articles, particularly on the relationship between art and climate change.

Finding a Place on the Asian Stage

Alison Carroll

and

Carrillo Gantner

Reprinted from the original series

no. 31

April 2012

Acknowledgements

We wish to thank the many colleagues in Australia and Asia who over decades have enriched our work in this area. We express particular appreciation for their contribution to this Paper to Peter Eckersall, Barbara Hatley and Aubrey Mellor.

Introduction

> Meeting for their 'arts day' at PricewaterhouseCoopers, the suited, confident, articulate young hotshots of Asialink's annual Leadership Program look up from their chatter to evaluate the newcomer: a casually dressed man, mild of appearance, almost self-effacing of manner who has come to talk to them about his art. Quietly he starts, describing his experience as a drummer going to Korea to meet and study with the shaman musician, called in his country 'Intangible Asset Number 82'. Then the visitor turns on a small recording machine to let the group hear the results. His quietness enhances the sound of his music and the power of his story. The group is spellbound and silent, aware of the significance of such a cultural transformation to the musician, Simon Barker, and of their privilege in being brought into an understanding of it. They are moved by the human passion behind it all—a few even moved to tears.

This Paper looks at the last twenty years of Australian cultural engagement with Asia through the prism of the performing arts.[1] It reviews some modest achievements and important failures, and then suggests a forward path to maximise the opportunities that will benefit Australia through stronger cultural relations across the Asian region. In particular, we write about the roles and funding of the Australia Council and the Department of Foreign Affairs and Trade (DFAT) for international cultural engagement, and how the changing face of Australian Federal politics has had a significant influence on levels of funding for the Asian agenda.

Should we care about our cultural engagement with the Asian region? Does this question even need putting in 2012? We believe the answer to both questions is a decisive 'yes'. Today most thinking Australians who consider these things would almost certainly share our response to the first question. Sadly, on the evidence, it is clear that Australia has not yet answered the second.

The most cogent reason why we should care is that Asia is a treasure chest of cultural richness and diversity on our very doorstep. Since Asia is so far away from most other countries whose culture is largely based on Western traditions and values, this is Australia's special opportunity. We don't want to diminish our Western heritage but rather to enrich it, to embroider our multi-hued cloak with new colours and textures. The more prosaic reason is that it is in our economic and strategic self-interest to build a broader base for our relationship with the dynamic economies of Asia. Simply put, Australian jobs and security depend on the health of these relationships, a reality made even more apparent by the current Euro-American meltdown. Such relationships need to be built on more than the profit-driven transactional nature of commerce or the diplomatic balancing acts of political calculation, important as these are. It is the 'people-to-people' links that give a relationship resilience, depth and understanding, and allow it to weather the inevitable and usually unpredictable setbacks of business and politics.

Cultural engagement is at the heart of this.

To build strong cultural links with Asia we need to be proactive. It is not easy for people in Asia to access our arts by themselves: the distance to Australia is long and Australia itself is huge. Currently, with a strong Australian dollar, it is also more expensive. And what reason do people from Asia have to search out our arts when we can be perceived as having a largely derivative culture, when from a distance it appears that we are little more than a quarry or an unfenced zoo? We have to take the initiative, to invite and encourage, to knock on doors and 'be out there'. We are fortunate that we have the capacity to do so: a robust economy and a vibrant arts sector strongly supported by government. Yes, it is.

In considering these issues the two authors of this Paper bring different perspectives: Carrillo Gantner has had a long association with Asia, and especially with China and Japan, as an actor, theatre manager, diplomat and producer. Alison Carroll has had an equally rich experience of the region, largely in the visual arts. She was founding director of Asialink Arts 1991–2010, which included responsibility for developing the Asialink Residency Program. This began with the visual arts and expanded into the performing arts, literature and arts management. During her tenure, the Asialink Arts program included the initiation and management of more than seventy exhibitions, dance and other performance exchanges.

1

Why should we engage with Asian cultures?

The best answer to this lies in the richness and diversity of Asian performance, working with arts practitioners of another culture, and learning to understand their performance style and traditions, which in turn gives us an individual insight into how humans model and resolve their world. There is so much we can learn from Asia to enrich our own, largely Western derived, practices.

Some people argue that when we talk of exporting Australian arts to Asia, that we ought only to be talking of their role in 'soft-diplomacy'—that is, assisting Australia's political and economic agenda. The implication is that the arts in Asia should not be valued on their own terms and that Asia as an arts destination has no cogency. At its extreme, this attitude could be seen as racist. When such people want a project to go to Paris, do they say it is because of 'soft-diplomacy'? No, they want it there because French culture is valued per se. The word racist might be considered too tough; perhaps 'ignorant' is better. It is an ignorance that many Australians and, sadly, not least Australians working in the arts, commonly share. It is sobering for us to learn how few of those in leadership positions across the arts in Australia have any in-depth knowledge, let alone experience of the arts in Asia, let alone cultural fluency in any one Asian culture, let alone competency in any Asian language.

Let us consider what we have to learn from Asian cultures. Traditionally in the performance forms of most Asian countries the focus is on the refined movement of the performer, interpretation being the aspect for both audience and performer to anticipate, judge and enjoy. The key person is the actor who, after years of training of his (and it was always 'his' in the past) mind and body, initiates the action with few props and often no words. Time is not fixed, the ancient story is known and only part of it usually performed at one time. The audience can come and go.

The practice that comes closest to this in Australia is traditional Indigenous performance, with its respect for the learning of the elders, the part-performance of stories well known to the audience, the intensity of the gesture, the paucity of words and props, the merging of roles, and the important knowledge that these stories reflect.

If we let go of the Western narrative form, we can release ourselves into a metaphysical experience more akin to those of Asian cultures. We learn that the rational does not have to rule. Edward Said in his great work *Orientalism* describes how during the nineteenth and twentieth centuries, at the height of Western hegemony, the colonial impulse was to reinforce this emphasis on the rational and scorn the nuances of other levels of expression, thinking and performance.[2] We are still in the thrall of this attitude. Immersion in the arts of Asia leads us towards the discovery of new ways of thinking, new forms of performance and new perceptions of our own humanity.

Noh theatre works on a very distinctive level of thought and expression, slowly building layers of meaning beyond the verbal interchange intrinsic to Western drama. Sitting in the Noh theatre, the audience is given time to change their mode of breathing and thinking: a kind of meditation can take over. The deeper our knowledge and appreciation of the form, the deeper our emotional response.

Like time, space is not measured in the same way. Spaces between objects are as important as the objects themselves. In Japanese gardens, the spaces between rocks give significance to the rocks themselves. In North Asian painting, the artists leave spaces into which the viewer steps to add their own active contemplation, a process through which the viewer becomes intimately involved in the work. Asian theatrical space is also used differently and understanding this enhances our experience. Think of the empty Beijing Opera stage on which walking in a simple circle can describe a long journey; or one small table and chair a palace.

Styles of performance also differ from Western styles. Apart from opera, where many performance strands are woven together, Western performance has developed into separate traditions—spoken drama, classical dance, modern dance, puppetry and so on. Asian performing arts tend to blend these elements across such boundaries: live actors and shadow puppets together, with symbolic gesture, colour, costumes and properties; sung theatre forms with masks and stylised movement; and folk art blending many other forms. James R. Brandon writes that Western performance is driven by content, Asian by rhythm, tone, volume, mass, colour, intensity and speed.[3] Even in the use of the body, Asian performers work with a different intent: Indigenous dance forms for the most part push down towards the earth, keeping the upper body firm and controlled. In Western classical ballet, the body aims at lightness, stretching the arms upward, lifting the heels and extending the body's reach upward. An artist who experiences this difference within the body, adds a new dimension to their expressive vocabulary.

Asian music also offers difference: different scales and

rhythmic structures. Yet despite these differences, music is a natural bridge and is so far the most active form in the exchange of performing arts with Asia. This is, no doubt, because music is not language-based, it literally creates harmony, and can travel economically. For all these reasons, cross-cultural work in music can more readily be assayed than other forms. Peter Sculthorpe was a pioneer in this, blending instruments from the Balinese gamelan into his compositions; the Australian Art Orchestra is another, collaborating with Indian musicians. Asia is so close to us and so many elements of Asian performance are so enticingly different and interesting. Why then has it taken the mainstream of the Australian arts so long to recognise the creative opportunities that beckon here?

Aubrey Mellor, former director of Playbox, then of NIDA; now senior fellow, LaSalle College of the Arts Singapore, had this to say to the authors about our arts sector:

> On a recent return to Sydney, it depressed me to see no sign that we are in Asia, at least not in the performing arts. It worries me that Australia, in such a great position to access both traditional and contemporary Asian arts, is missing out on a giant palette of stimulus and innovation; and, in theatre, seems stuck with a repertoire that has not changed much since the days of the Old Tote. International leaders like Lepage, Mnouchkine and Robert Wilson have long been tapping Asia for inspiration, and this is enriching their work. It is sad that the rest of the world is falling over itself to access Asia, and yet our theatre leaders seem to know nothing of these extraordinary achievements. Unlike Europe and the United States, Australia has not yet seen a single professional production of any of the plays or adaptations by the many Asian Nobel Prize winners, including

> Kenzaburō Ōe, Gao Xingjian, Yasunari Kawabata, Rabindranath Tagore and their equals, Kunio Kishida, Cao Yu and Kōbō Abe. Despite his regular productions in London, we have never seen the work of acclaimed director Yukio Ninagawa and only rarely seen that of Suzuki Tadashi. We remain ignorant of the great theatre movements of Japan and classic writers such Zeami and Chikamatsu and the innovators from the 1980s onwards, including Yōji Sakate, Jūrō Kara, Ren Saitō, Hideki Noda and Keishi Nagatsuka. And equally ignorant of the inspiring aesthetics of Ōta Shōgo, Oriza Hirata, and Danny Yung of Zuni Icosahedron. Despite the wonderful work of Makoto Satō and Yoshio Wada, who have laboured hard and long to bring Australian plays to Japan in both readings and full productions, apart from Playbox we have never offered the courtesy of reciprocity. I am delighted that Meng Jinghui's production of *Rhinoceros in Love* was recently well received in three Australian cities, but that production is now almost twelve years old. We must make up for lost time, and should be collaborating regularly with a range of Asian companies and artists; not only seeking new horizons in art, but also helping to position our nation in other ways.

But Australians can and do offer reciprocity. Our own cultural diversity allows us to draw on the widest palette: Indigenous, South American, Eastern European and African cultural forms enrich the Western European base. And Australia's new mix of peoples and experiences has freed us from the constraints of some older cultures. History has its drawbacks. Milanese street engineers have a saying: 'How can we change the drains designed by Leonardo da Vinci?' Australians are not bound by the rigidities of such ancient traditions. This is a great liberating dimension of Australian culture. We see this again and again with expatriate Asian artists who say that they can experiment here as they could not have done in their home country. In China, the traditional learning method for artists is by repeated copying of the work of the masters. In Australia, artists are encouraged to find their own modes of expression, their signature 'voice'. Collaborating artists can find ways to combine these two approaches so that we achieve the best of both technique and originality.

Here are some outstanding examples of Australian-Asian co-production and exchange:

The Theft of Sita

Nigel Jamieson was director of this large-scale production which followed an episode in the Ramayana about the abduction of Sita, wife of Lord Rama, which also alludes to the stealing from the poor by the rich in Indonesia.

Jamieson chose to use as narrator a humorous bumpkin who is a familiar figure in Asian theatre. The main visual element was provided by a Balinese wayang master, with giant puppets of great contemporary relevance and invention. Central to the performance was the music by both Indonesian gamelan masters and the Australian Art Orchestra. It was a fantastical mix: big, loud, funny, human and full of contemporary meaning, taking the audience into its grasp and rolling them around in its huge hands. It was a great success at the Adelaide and Melbourne Arts Festivals and then toured internationally.

Grant Nundhirribala

Grant Nundhirribala is a leading musician from Yilila in Arnhem Land. He went to Flores in Nusa Tenggara Timur, Eastern Indonesia (NTT), to be part of an Asialink project with musicians there and worked with the local people exchanging musical knowledge and technique. The outcome was a fine CD of the music they composed in Flores, and performances at the 2008 Darwin Festival, where it was voted one of the best events of the year. For Grant, a senior Aboriginal artist, his time in Flores was particularly meaningful to him, in part, he said, because it was the first time, by working with people outside his own group, that he became a leader. Intercultural arts projects can open all sorts of opportunities.

Ria Soemardjo

Ria Soemardjo, who lives in Melbourne, is the daughter of a Javanese father whose ancestors were musicians at the courts of Central Java where the highest flowering of Javanese culture was to be found. She is a small and beautiful woman who sings the songs of her ancestors, unaccompanied, in Old Javanese. All who hear her are entranced by the sound, aware of being in the presence of something very special, offering access to ancient Javanese culture from someone who has direct familial links to it. Ria opened the 2008 Asialink Forum on Indonesian Culture with her songs, and her audience felt the importance and beauty of her ancient culture in a way that ten thousand words could not convey.

The Chronicle of Macbeth

In 1988 Japanese theatre director Suzuki Tadashi brought his Suzuki Company of Toga (SCOT) to Sydney with his version of Euripides' *The Trojan Women* as part of the Bicentennial celebrations. While here, Carrillo introduced SCOT to the Melbourne Festival to which they returned in 1990 with a production of *The Bacchae*. He also invited Suzuki to direct a production in Australia and he agreed to direct for Playbox on condition the actors were adequately prepared in his training techniques. These share similarities and rigours with training for the Kabuki theatre: physical strength is built up through a variety of 'stomping' exercises that connect the lower body to the earth, the source of power, channelled through the actor. The image often quoted is of a 747 in the moment before rolling down the runway, when the engines are at full thrust but the plane is not moving; but the responsibility for supplying 'meaning' belongs with the audience.

Several Australian actors had already discovered this work in Japan. A further group were sent to Toga to train with SCOT, and the following year Playbox brought these actors and several leading SCOT members to Melbourne for an extended workshop. From this coterie of actors Suzuki then cast his own adaptation of the Shakespearean classic, *The Chronicle of Macbeth*. After a rehearsal period that tested everyone beyond their physical and cultural comfort zones, the production opened at the 1992 Adelaide Festival. It then returned for a season at the Malthouse, Melbourne, and Theatre Royal, Hobart, and subsequently the Mitsui Festival in Tokyo. Demanding rehearsals continued on a daily basis during the tour, and, as the cast grew stronger and more confident, so did the production. Many of the actors went on to appear in the Playbox production of *King Lear*, the form of which owed much to Suzuki. This production also toured to Japan and then to Korea where it was well received. Some of the actors continued to adapt their Suzuki work into their performance technique or into the work of their own companies, including Not Yet It's Difficult in Melbourne and Frank in Brisbane.

2
People and partnership

We move now to give some recent history of Australia's engagement, but first a note on a key principle that underpins all that follows: the critical ingredients for international exchanges in the arts are people and partnership. Together these generate the creative product. If real partnership among the parties on both sides is built from the beginning of an exchange program, surprising results ensue. Partnerships are essential in this work so that everyone has a stake in the artistic outcome. Partnership means that new ideas and new works can be forged together, giving the greatest gift to all involved. Partnership also means that administration and costs can be shared, reducing one of the perceived barriers to engagement. Partnerships built on respect for each partner's creative and administrative contribution mean problems can be foreseen and overcome. In art as in life, this is the only way we can grow in a global world.

Partnerships are important everywhere. In Asia, where we experience cultural difference and where our expectations will be challenged, personal relationships are *even more* essential to building trust and a desire to move forward together.

The independent artist

Artists speak a common language of the heart and mind; they are motivated by their creative passions, rather than by profit or diplomatic niceties. Performing artists in particular are used to working closely with a team: they love to engage with other people and build strong relationships. Asialink's Residency Program lives on the spirit, energy and curiosity of individual Australian artists who are willing to open themselves to intercultural engagement with their peers in the region. Frequently these residencies have changed lives and artistic practice.

For many Australian artists of Asian background an involvement with the land of their ancestors is especially meaningful and rewarding. Kym Purling was the first Vietnamese orphan to come to Australia after the end of the Vietnam War. Years later he returned to the land of his birth as a jazz musician, and reported on a concert in Ho Chi Minh City where the army generals who might once have clapped his family in gaol, now clapped along to his music. Rendra Freestone, half Indonesian, returned to Sumatra to make new music which he then developed back in Australia. Chinese *sheng* player Wang Zheng-Ting came to Australia as a young man, completed his PhD in musicology, formed the Australian Chinese Music Ensemble to play in festivals around this country, and more recently returned to China to perform his own compositions on the *sheng* with major Chinese ensembles.

Many Australian performing artists have devoted much of their professional careers to involvement with the arts of Asia. Some artists of note in this vein include Matt Crosby, Yumi Umiumare, Tess de Quincey, Sally Sussman, Ian Pidd, Robert Draffin, Peter Wilson, David Pledger, Tony Yap and Andrish Saint-Claire. Others, like musician Paul Grabowsky and director Nigel Jamieson, have made it an important part of their professional lives. In recent years the Melbourne International Comedy Festival has sent its touring Roadshow to Singapore and Hong Kong and presented occasional Japanese and Chinese comic artists at their own festival. Many more Australian singers and dancers tour Asian cities regularly and some have developed a brand name in the region. Others have joined touring musical comedy or revue, without their national origins being recognised.

Presenters and managers like Rosemary Hinde, Marguerite Pepper, Barry Plews and Andrew Ross have been working in and with Asian companies over long periods, often in difficult times and difficult circumstances. The first to bring Indian classical music to Australia was Clifford Hocking (1932–2006), the entrepreneur who was also Playbox's partner in the early tours of Chinese performing troupes. Another outstanding Australian creative figure was Roger Rynd (1960–2010). He was born in Singapore, grew up in Australia and travelled the Pacific extensively. In Townsville he formed the REM theatre with his partner Catherine Pease and in 1997 settled in Seoul after receiving an Asialink residency. There he became in turn founding artistic director of the LATT children's theatre, wrote an important body of plays about the Pacific, and became the first foreign director of the Seoul Arts Festival. Before his death he was made an honorary Korean citizen for his services to the performing arts.

Performance companies

In the last two decades Australia has become known for its strength in various physical theatre forms. Enterprising small companies such as Strangefruit, Legs on the Wall and Stalker have toured to venues and festivals across Asia, but particularly to Hong Kong, Japan, Korea and more recently China. Of the major Australian performing arts companies the Australian Ballet has toured in Asia more than any. Sometimes it has been featured in the special country promotions that have attracted substantial federal government support. Australian symphony and chamber orchestras have also toured to major Asian cities over the last 20 years. They include the Tasmanian Symphony in the early 1990s to Indonesia, and in more recent years the Western Australian Symphony, the Melbourne Symphony and Sydney Symphony Orchestras to China. Graham Murphy and the Sydney Dance Company toured to China during his directorship and more recently he has choreographed a new work, *Mulan*, with a company of dancers in Shanghai.

Arts centres and festivals

In 2007 the Adelaide Festival Centre under CEO Douglas Gautier spearheaded an annual two-week Asian performing arts festival, OzAsia. Artists from India, China, Vietnam and Japan have been featured. What makes it successful is not only the variety of programming and art forms, but the whole-of-organisation support, which each year builds the level of government and private funding. To achieve this it closely involves the local Asian communities, supports education programs and seminars, and even offers menus from the represented regions in the Centre's food outlets. The OzAsia Festival stands alone now, but its ancestry includes Christopher Hunt's Asian-focused programming in his 1994 Adelaide Festival. It is a welcome sign of progress that the hostile reception it then received has today given way to greater understanding.

The Art Centre Melbourne has initiated the Kenneth Myer Asian Theatre Series as an important component of its programming. This brings high-quality performing arts companies from across Asia to Victoria and beyond, and leading individual artists from Asia to work with their Australian counterparts. Virginia Hyam, Head of Contemporary Culture at the Sydney Opera House until last year, included Asian material, some of it risky commissions in her adventurous non-genre based studio programs, and worked closely with local Asian communities. The Powerhouse in Brisbane under Andrew Ross has been an important pioneer in programming Indonesian performing arts, sometimes in special festivals that have brought Indonesian and other Asian performances to Brisbane audiences. Other Australian festival directors with an international outlook have included Asian product in their Festival programming. Robyn Archer, Jonathan Mills, Noel Staunton, Lindy Hume and Brett Sheehy come to mind, although most still seem more comfortable in the better-known corridors and green rooms of Europe and North America. Mills, now artistic director of the Edinburgh Festival, included extensive Asian programming in his 2011 Edinburgh Festival—a revelation for many of its audiences.

Major organisations, including the capital city arts centres and festivals, have enough public funding to support new projects and they should be the leaders in this field. It is a pity, therefore, that their record in the Asian arts is not better than it is. Under the leadership of CEO Sue Nattrass, Melbourne's Arts Centre initiated the Association of Asia Pacific Performing Arts Centres at a meeting in Melbourne in 1994. It would be fair to say, however, that since then the Australian arts centres have not capitalised on this by utilising the network to generate programming or build other exchange opportunities. In Singapore an Association of Asian Performing Arts Festivals was inaugurated in 2004 to promote exchange among major regional festivals. The first partners were from Shanghai, Jakarta, Singapore and Hong Kong. By June 2011 there were 19 full members of which the only Australian member was the Melbourne Festival, which joined this year. In addition, the OzAsia Festival and the University of South Australia's Arts Management Course are among the fourteen associate members. It is yet to be seen whether the Australian members will work these networks vigorously to increase the range of product from Asia, the number of co-productions with Asian counterparts, or the exchange of personnel for training.

Community groups

Organisations at the grassroots community level have made strong linkages with Asian immigrant groups. Multicultural Arts Victoria (MAV) and the Footscray Community Arts Centre are two shining examples. Occasionally these linkages shift gear into the mainstream, as with MAV's association with the ABC's *Music Deli* program and the Arts Centre's with Mix It Up. Most Asian communities in Australian capital cities are also involved in presenting festivals with performing arts programs supported by local government, sometimes with visiting artists and companies underwritten by governments in the countries of origin.

***

As indicated, over the last ten to fifteen years, significant parts of the performing arts sector in Australia have developed stronger and more mature links. Asian countries themselves have developed greatly improved arts infrastructure and increased their own interest in cultural exchange in their own region, which sometimes includes Australia. This represents an important change from their more Eurocentric focus of the earlier post-war period. Festivals across the Asian region now routinely include a high level of content from other Asian countries. Australia is not yet generally considered to be 'Asian' but has come to be thought of by some as an important regional player with a vibrant cultural scene.

But while there are successes, our record of active engagement with Asia is still very mixed. Many individuals and organisations have found creative stimulus in this field and through this work have built reputations for leadership, found new audiences and generated new sponsors. There are, however, many more for whom Asia still remains a complete blank. In this context, it is important to recognise that occasional performance tours by our leading companies and orchestras cannot be the way to maximise the benefits of exchange unless they program significant Australian repertoire and actively engage in local creative partnerships. Exchanges of artistic personnel and programs that reflect the strengths and creative expression of their place of origin have a much better chance of leaving a lasting impact than programs that are perceived to reflect a derivative European style or content, no matter how good the company's reputation at home. Such programs usually sink without trace in the crowded and star-studded calendar of major Asian capitals, though they may provide bragging rights back in Australia.

Some of the lessons drawn from those who do work with Asia are clear: the importance of reciprocity in enhancing opportunities and benefits; the commitment to developing real partnerships; the exciting and often unpredictable outcomes of shared creative inputs across cultural difference; the virtue of playing to national strengths and unique characteristics; and the value of long-term commitments in order to build real legacies.

Carrillo Gantner writes:

> From the late 1970s through the early 1990s, we at Playbox engaged very successfully with Asia: at the time we were virtually alone in this focus. With Clifford Hocking and other partners we toured major Asian companies around Australia—from China the Nanjing Acrobatic Troupe, Jiangsu Peking Opera Company, and Fujian and Hunan puppet companies; from Japan the Kanze Noh Theatre and Suzuki Company of Toga and the Yakshagana Puppet Theatre from India. We exchanged directors and plays with China: Jack Hibberd's *A Stretch of The Imagination* with Sha Yexin's *The Imposter*; and whole productions with Japan: John Romeril's *The Floating World* with Tanaka Chikao's *The Head Of Mary.* We toured our productions to China, Japan, Korea and Malaysia: Daniel Keene's puppet play *Cho Cho San, The Chronicle of Macbeth* and *King Lear.* We undertook significant work partnering with Suzuki Tadashi sending our actors to train with his company in Japan and bringing him to Australia to direct for Playbox.

We ran an annual Asian playwriting competition for Anglo-Australian and Asian-Australian writers, and we produced many plays by Australians on Asian themes: *Yamashita, Madame Mao, The Emperor Regrets, General Macarthur In Australia, Sex Diary Of An Infidel.* We helped other playwrights whose work we had premiered to have their plays translated and produced in Asia: Hannie Rayson's *Hotel Sorrento* in Japan, Joanna Murray-Smith's *Love Child* in Korea. We brought Chinese acrobatic teachers to work with young Australians on the disciplines and skills of their art. This 1983 Nanjing Project has had a profound influence on the development of acrobatics, physical theatre and circus arts in Australia.

We achieved these things with a clear sense of purpose and whole-of-organisation focus: by building networks in Asia and partnerships in Australia, by promoting reciprocity, making bold choices and taking huge risks: 'making the improbable inevitable', as our brochure proclaimed. If the little Playbox Theatre Company with its modest resources but unlimited ambition could do these things so many years ago, why are most Australian arts centres, festivals and other performing arts managements so timid now?

3
The Australia Council

Now it is time to look at the public record and see what some real numbers can teach us. How have government agencies managed our cultural policy on Asia since the Keating Government took the initiative in 1991? The authors of this Paper have lived through these changes and experienced on the ground how Australia has responded to the Asian agenda in the performing arts. We are not aware of any previous attempt to analyse the financial information that might give an indication of the level of performing arts engagement with Asia and, in particular, there has been no public analysis of the Australia Council, the Federal Government's funding and policy body in the arts.

The numbers in the graph below tell a tale, not just for those like ourselves who have had an active involvement in this work and have observed the field and the trends, but for the wider arts community. The raw numbers do not tell the whole tale but reveal enough of it for some truths to be uncovered, trends to be discerned, and conclusions drawn that might confirm the views of some and raise alarm for others. They are enough to give us some background from which to steer a way forward.

The Australia Council is the key organisation for anyone working in the arts in Australia. It is so familiar we tend to take it for granted and, like a member of the extended family, we feel we have a right to tell it to behave in our own image and we take pride in its many achievements. If you work in Asia you begin to appreciate this even more. Some of the arts agencies in Asia remain in the stranglehold of a bureaucracy uninterested and untrained in any arts practice. Others are internally focused and distant from the sector for which they have responsibility. The idea of peer evaluation, or even a grant for an individual artist, is a long way from their mind. There are exceptions, of course. We have worked happily with the Japan Foundation and with the Ministry of Culture in China, for example, and the Singapore National Arts Council is a model of focus, efficiency and knowledge. But it is worth sitting outside a dusty office in the Indian subcontinent, waiting for an audience and knowing you are just paper-shuffling, to really appreciate an organisation like the Australia Council.

The Council figures are focused on Australian performing artists and projects supported through the Council's programs for international work through the performing arts boards in their various forms, but mostly Dance, Music and Drama (or Theatre), and through the changing über-programs of Arts Development and the variously named Audience and Market Development (AMD) portfolio.[4] We can only do this, of course, because by and large the figures are available through the Australia Council's annual reports, a commendable characteristic of open government. The figures do not include the Major Performing Arts Board because it is not possible to dissect what was spent through their programs on overseas work. Our observation and involvement in this work tells us, however, that only a small percentage goes to international touring and, of this percentage, an even smaller percentage would have been directed towards Asia. We have included spending in places specifically named, but we have excluded named visual arts and literature programs. Sometimes the figures just say 'overseas' and the dollars relating to these have also not been included. Immediately you will see that the total is not exact.

Within the limitations noted above, the major focus of our attention is on the percentage of funds spent across two decades for performing arts projects to or in Asian destinations, as compared to expenditure directed towards the 'Rest of the World'. ROW (as DFAT sometimes calls it) is mostly Western Europe, including the United Kingdom, and North America, with only a tiny sum spent in other places like South America and Eastern Europe.

The first thing that strikes us about these figures is that broad policy decisions can have very specific outcomes. Following the Australia Council's decision in 1990–91 (twenty years ago) to apply at least 50% of their international funding towards Asia, this is what actually happened. Indeed for most of the early 1990s it was well above that.

The following statement comes from the Council's *Annual Report of 1993–94*:

> Since the Australia Council announced a shift in its international cultural relations policy three years ago, in recognition of Australia's place in the Asia Pacific region, there has been a 250% increase in funding for projects focused on the region.
>
> The Council is aiming to spend 50% of international funds in this region in the future; in 1993–4 the proportion passed 35%. Council's international policy fulfils one of its major statutory duties, 'to promote the knowledge and appreciation of Australian arts in other countries'.[5]

Note that the 35% plus quoted above for 1993–94 represented expenditure from all boards of the Australia Council, not just the performing arts. In fact, the figures above show that the trend in the performing arts was well above this percentage, probably because of the entrepreneurial and international interests of this sector, and because grants to performing arts touring tended to be larger than those for other boards.

Prime Minister Keating announced the major cultural policy document *Creative Nation* in 1995, reconfirming the 50% of international funding allocated to Asia. He left office in

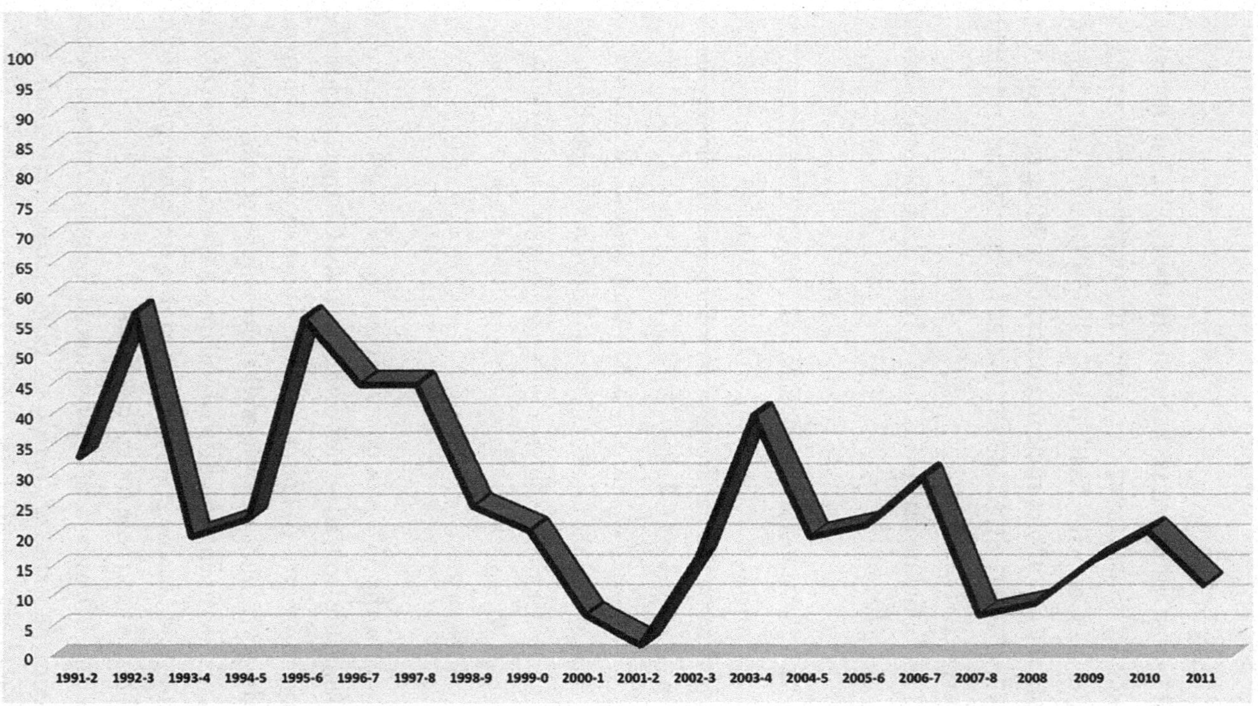

Chart 1: Australia Council funding in Performing Arts following named destinations in Asia from Board and Arts Development, AMD Programs as a percentage of International Funds, from 1992–2011

March 1996, however, and in the eleven years of the Coalition Government that followed Prime Minister Howard loosened the ties with Asia and reprioritised Australia's relations with the United States. How has the Council managed this engagement since it took the initiative in 1991? In the decades since, the proportion of funds 'for Asia' sank to and has remained at 10–20% of the Council's total international expenditure.

Notes on the totals in Chart 1

1990–91 The Australia Council's Report provided for 1% of performing arts funding for overseas projects, but this figure is not broken down by geographic focus.

1991–92 The international funding of 1% remains but is broken down geographically. In the areas we tracked, we see a high amount of funding for Asia: 3%. Indonesia stands out with some $60,000 spent in that country, Korea $35,000 and Japan $42,000. This expenditure almost certainly reflected preparation for the Australian Promotion year in Indonesia in 1993. These country-specific promotional years have become an important stimulus for geographic focus and expenditure.

1992–93 A high year for Asia at 5%, though the figures themselves are small: $166,000 for Asia against $55,000 spent in Europe and $70,000 for everywhere else. Japan received the most with $80,000, Vietnam $27,500 and Indonesia was again funded.

1993–94	'Asia' was allotted only $66,500 of $344,000 (20%).
1994–95	A new Performing Arts 'International Fund' was instituted as a channel for major funding. Asia received 23%.
1995–96	This was the year of Keating's *Creative Nation* agenda which confirmed the policy of 50% of international touring money to go to Asia, a challenge which the Australia Council met. It introduced a new Audience Development and Advocacy program set outside the range of peer assessment and able to be proactive in broader areas. Asia was well treated by ADA, which spent almost all its funding, or $674,000, on projects there and only $67,000 on other places. Together with the Performing Arts International Fund, around $1 million was spent on projects in Asia, compared with $465,000 in Europe and $272,000 in North America.

It is worth looking at which countries these increased funds covered. In the country-focus promotional program, India received $490,000. The new Australia Centre in Manila was also of note, gaining $99,500 while Japan received $84,500. The performing arts stood out here: figures in this period for the visual arts to Asia show that they never made it above 35%. Other areas of Council were even less likely to be focused on Asia, specifically Community Cultural Development and the Aboriginal and Torres Strait Islander Board. The Literature

Board should be looked at in more detail, but spot-checks suggest their Asia agenda has been very low. So across the full spectrum of the Australia Council's international expenditure, at 57% this year was the high-water mark:

1996–97 The figure shrank a little to 45%. India was there again with $88,000, and there was modest expenditure for South America and New Zealand.

1997–98 Funding held at 45%. Major organisations undertook a lot of international travel, with touring in Asia above 50%.

1998–99 Only 25% to Asia this year.

1999–2000 Down to 21%: a year with a major Australian promotion in London.

2000–01 A continued decline, down to 7%, with a major promotion in Brooklyn, USA. Of those Asian countries that were included, the more financially attractive destinations—Singapore, Taiwan and Korea—began what became a regular inclusion. China also appeared on the list more overtly.

2001–02 The lowest point in the twenty years at just 2.5%: $36,500 for Asia compared with $814,000 for Europe and $788,000 for North America (again including the Australian promotion in Brooklyn).

2002–03 Slightly up to 16.5%, with Japan taking the largest amount, $80,000, again because of the Australian promotion year there. China, Singapore, Taiwan and Hong Kong were dominant—again the more financially attractive destinations. There was also a showcase in Berlin.

2003–04 Up to 40% to Asia with the Japan promotion continuing to attract funding: a hefty $461,500; and again Singapore, Korea, Hong Kong and China.

2004–05 Down again to 20% after the Japan promotion. Asialink showed up with $235,000 as part of this promotion, and the Singapore Performing Arts Market received $23,500. The big event this year was *Undergrowth*, the major Australian arts promotion in the UK with funding of $336,000.

2005–06 *Undergrowth* funding increased to $695,000, and there was $220,000 for New York. Asia-focused grants totalled 22% or $534,000, of which $337,000 was for Asialink. Japan was the major recipient and other countries received only minor amounts. Many smaller Asian countries did not appear at all. The other trend starting to show is a retreat from international expenditure by the Council boards, leaving this to the big-spending ADA. Board funds were mostly for small and individually initiated projects.

2006–07 30% for Asia, of which Asialink again got the lion's share, $330,000 out of a total of $493,000. Japan received most of the remainder with $80,000.

2007–08 A mere 7% here to Asia, but Asialink was not included. As the Australia Council's financial year was being switched to the calendar year, we believe the actual funds expended for Asialink were allocated in a different time frame. The annual figures from now on are for calendar years from the Council website: *https://online.australiacouncil.gov.au/Grantlist*

2008 We see 9% for Asia, and only in Arts Development, Japan getting the largest part of this with $87,000. However, if 2007–8 and 2008 are combined, Korea starts to lead with $148,000.

2009 A big international year: for Asia the total rose to 16%, or $570,000. Korea is the standout with $256,000, then Japan, Taiwan, China and Singapore. India is there, and a rare allocation for Indonesia ($7,000), and for Thailand ($4,000).

2010 Up again to 21%, with $494,000 for Asia of which $306,000 was for Korea. Japan fades.

2011 Six months to June: 12% with a total of $215,000 of which $98,000 was again for Korea.

This analysis shows the general trend of funding to Asia versus funding to the rest of the world and which areas of Asia caught the Australia Council's attention. Again we note that these figures are from certain parts of the Council's grant figures and are to be regarded only as a guide to trends.

Some conclusions

The Australia Council's own policies and, more broadly, the Federal Government's stated and unstated priorities, have had a direct bearing on the Council's commitment to Asia.

Funding for the countries of South East Asia have fallen away over the last ten years with the exception of Singapore, which has coasted along in a small way through the two decades.

The countries of North Asia have almost always received the lion's share of funding, with Japan the standout over the two decades, topped by the *Ancient Future* Australian promotion year in 1993. Support has declined in the last few years as spending in Korea has risen.

South Asia has been an area of activity only during the New Horizons promotion in India in 1995–96. All the funding for South Asia has been for India with the exception of one grant of $6,000 for Pakistan in the early 1990s.

Expenditure on China has been fairly constant but low. Taiwan and Hong Kong are also constant but low, but for different reasons: they are smaller societies than their giant neighbour and they tend to work on a more commercial model. Hong Kong's Cantonese-speaking population represents a narrower market opportunity, and Taiwan's political overshadowing by the mainland has meant it was not in the mindset of Australian artists and arts organisations.

So what might these conclusions mean?

Public funding has clearly leant towards those countries that might offer at least a partial box office return: Singapore, Korea, Japan, Taiwan and Hong Kong. This has become particularly clear since the Audience and Market Development division of the Australia Council came into being. Underlying this concentration on the more 'Western' market orientation in these countries has been their sophisticated, State-supported arts infrastructure: performing arts complexes, focused arts bureaucracies, festivals and colleagues familiar with a global stage with whom it has been easier to share understanding and build long-term relationships.

In the early 1990s, in keeping with a rising enthusiasm to engage with Asia, the objectives and the spread of activity were much broader. We see more activity in the 'non-commercial' countries such as Indonesia or India where they had very little expectation of commercial return. Separate arrangements were made for government-supported projects, compared to fully commercial projects. Jennifer Lindsay spelt out the reality in 1994, in her ground-breaking publication *Cultural Organisation in Southeast Asia*, namely that your venture was either government-supported and therefore a 'propaganda' exercise giving away tickets, or an entirely commercial event like a pop concert.[6] There was no middle way. Even today it is difficult to put together a financial package to send a project to these countries. The physical and management infrastructure is less likely to be there, their organisations are often run and supported by individuals without institutional backing, and festivals and other special events are dependent on fleeting support. As the tougher commercial criteria were brought in under Audience and Market Development policies, funding for projects with the 'non-commercial' countries fell away and the Board programs did not pick up the deficit. Today it is still the case that much of Asia is omitted from Australian funding models which require viable budgets based on significant but, in reality, non-existent support from the receiving country.

This has meant that, as the period under review proceeds, to see an Australian program in India, once the 1996 promotion was over, or in the Philippines, Indonesia or Vietnam, is to be surprised. We note that expenditure on the Asialink Residency Program under which many performing artists have worked, is not itemised country by country. Many of the artists on Asialink residencies to these countries have returned to Australia with plans for projects and reciprocal exchanges that have arisen out of their experience but have then found it almost impossible to raise the funds to bring such projects into being.

When looking at the figures, it is interesting to note the significant activity with Singapore. In recent decades Singapore has invested huge sums to make itself a cultural destination and so it punches well above its weight for a tiny island state. It supports a performing arts centre (Esplanade), a regional performing arts market, an important international festival, a range of producing and presenting managements, and various attractive and well-managed venues. Korea is also interesting. Some five or six years ago we started to see more Korean arts officials coming to Australia, and usually armed with money. They were being proactive, positive and inviting. A lot of Australians were invited to arts markets, festivals and events. Both Korean and Australian arts practitioners have benefitted from these invitations and, in return, Australian arts organisations have invited Koreans here. Pro-activity works. The Australia Council figures show how this has led to an increasing number of programs in Korea. Importantly they have been backed by goodwill and good organisation on the ground in Korea. In the meantime we have seen the 'retreat' of Japan. What has happened there? One element has been the general reduction in funding and programs, including the closure of the Japan Foundation's specialist 'Asia Centre' in Tokyo. Another has been the rise of China, which has attracted increasing attention from all sectors of society, including artists.

***

While a focus on financial viability may be inevitable in choosing where to tour and perform, it comes at a cost, especially the loss of access to, and creative engagement with, many dynamic and exciting cultures of Asia, including India and Indonesia. Both of these countries are of high strategic importance to Australia, both have wonderfully rich and diverse cultures, so it is certainly Australia's loss to pull back from cultural engagement with them. The 1996 Australian promotion in India was the best we have seen to date, because of the high quality of the selected work and because the engagement with local artists was so successful. Alison Carroll was in the audience and watched as the world-weary citizens of Delhi, forced by good manners to attend a performance by the Australian Art Orchestra, thawed as the excited audience in the hall rose to applaud this wild collaboration with Indian artists. Real money was spent on our side, and real effort put into a high-quality wide-ranging program. Commercial viability and ticket sales were not the priority: the goodwill generated has been ongoing and should be intrinsic to the planning of all promotions of this kind.

The promotions in Indonesia, first in early 1990s and then more recently, have suffered in two ways: neither had the level of support given to the Indian promotion and the relations developed in Indonesia were, and remain, based on individual enthusiasm. The income and funding streams so important in AMD criteria do not exist in the Indonesian archipelago.

Interestingly, the 2010–11 Year of Australian Culture in China was felt to be a rather lacklustre affair focused predominantly on the visual arts. Despite the huge revenues some Australian businesses are earning from China, and despite active lobbying by the Australian Ambassador, negligible support came from the Australian corporate sector. In addition, those engaged in the delivery of the programs, while hardworking, often lacked the appropriate skills, experience and networks, illustrating the loss, during the Howard years, of specialist and experienced cultural counsellors. To compound matters and needlessly put offside highly competent Australian arts managements, DFAT even gave the management of Australia's Cultural program in the 2010 Shanghai Expo to an American agency.

The case of Indonesia

Indonesia is an exciting and culturally rich country but it has received very little funding support for engagement through the Australia Council. Why this is so is partly explained by it not being seen as commercially viable. But there are other issues as well. Since 2001 Indonesia has had the misfortune to be judged as unsafe for Australians due to the perceived threat of terrorism.

Negative 'travel advisories' have been constant, and, given the proximity of our nearest neighbour, when trouble arises the media paints a frightening picture. This has deterred many visitors and business people, and with them artists, teachers, students and public servants, eligible to travel under various programs. Indonesia also does not always have the infrastructure that makes for easy touring. You have to want to go there and you have to want to engage. But, if you do, the results can be extraordinary.

One of the best examples of international engagement we have seen is the Japanese-initiated and supported festival *Kita! Japanese Artists meet Indonesia*, which in 2008 played throughout the archipelago. They engaged, they collaborated, they used the streets and the public spaces just as the Indonesians do. And it looked wonderful: so exciting, so new, so dynamic, so funny, so political, so young, so great. The Japanese invested in people and time, and, as the Japanese can do, they produced the best promotional material we have ever seen. The graphics reflected the energy and youthful zest of the whole engagement. They got it right.

As Indonesia for these reasons is currently off the Australia Council's radar, any government funding for cultural engagement is left to the DFAT bilateral council, the Australia Indonesia Institute (AII). The AII has kindly provided figures of recent applications for funding. In 2010–11 they received 29 Arts and Culture applications for $588,000, of which fifteen applications were approved for $153,000. This means applications for $435,000 were left unsupported. That's a lot of unsatisfied 'desire to engage'. In 2011–12 (to midyear 2011), the AII had received seventeen applications requesting $304,000. Four applications were approved for $52,000.

4
The politics

The years 1991 to 1997–98 were the high-water mark for Australia Council funding in the performing arts to Asia. This was followed by a severe decrease to 2000–02 and then fluctuations as low at 7% and high as 40%, but mostly in the 10–30% range. We are not aware of any instruction from Canberra nor of any formal change in policy from the Council's own 1990–91 decision for 50% of their international funding to go to Asia, yet its own numbers clearly indicate how the signals from Canberra influenced outcomes.

Paul Keating was Prime Minister when the Australia Council seized the Asian initiative. The Liberal-National Coalition Government won election in 1996 and its new priorities quickly percolated throughout government agencies, including our national arts funding body. Perhaps in part this is explained by the different nature of the Government's appointments to Council membership, which gave much greater representation to business and other non-artist members. Since the Labor Government took office in 2007, there has been a modest rebalancing towards Asia.

We do not believe that any Australian government of the last two decades has been 'anti-Asia'. On the contrary, in this period our growing economic dependence on the region has highlighted Asia in Australia's consciousness. We think it fair to say, however, that our governments have generally failed to appreciate the benefits of the kind of wider and deeper engagement that comes from cultural and broad people-to-people links. When talking about Asia, governments think and talk in strategic and, even more, in economic terms. In a similar way, Australian business thinking tends to be transactional and short-term. There is pitifully little recognition of the long-term strategic or even financial benefits of building broadly based relationships through culture, education and other value-based programs if an immediate dollar value is not on the table.

Outgoing Australian-based BBC correspondent, Nick Bryant, spoke of Australian politics being 'increasingly provincial and parochial', as Prime Minister, Julia Gillard had famously said, on her first official overseas visit, that she was not interested in Foreign Affairs; and Opposition Leader, Tony Abbott, was quoted in the *Wall Street Journal* as saying he didn't give interviews to foreign correspondents because it made him appear 'up' himself. Everything looked terrific about Australia, said Bryant, except for its politics.[7]

***

In the end, the key point of this Paper is that leadership really matters. After Keating there has been no political leadership endorsing broad cultural links with Asia, and government agencies, as well as the majority of people in the cultural and educational sector, have responded accordingly. The attitude in the arts would seem to be that 'the dollars are not there, so why should we be?' The authors of this Paper would like to think it was time for the sector itself to promote change and generate leadership in this field. All of us in the sector have failed in allowing the programs and policies that Keating supported to be seriously diminished or ignored.

***

In the Howard years, Asia went off the map in the minds of those in charge of the Australia Council. A graphic example was the announcement in June 1999 of the Government's International Initiatives 1999–2001 with funding of $10 million, of which the Australia Council highlighted 'several significant Australian arts events overseas'. These included the work of the painter Howard Arkley at the Venice Biennale, the stage adaptation of Tim Winton's *Cloudstreet* in Europe, Australia Week in London, our part in the Hannover World Expo in 2000. The lone non-European event was the Festival of Pacific Arts in Noumea in late 2000. The media release for this program of 'international initiatives' lists *Cloudstreet* again, the rock group Yothu Yindi in Amsterdam, two gigs in London, and Howard Arkley. The Pacific Arts Festival is not mentioned in the media release, though as the sole non-European inclusion, it might have been expected. The general description of the Festival, however, opens with the following: 'New Caledonia is part of mainland France and therefore opens up the opportunity for Australia to promote the Aboriginal and Torres Strait Islander cultures in an appropriate context in Europe.'[8] What? To justify the funding the writer felt obliged to deprive the festival of its real context and attach its importance to cultural links with Europe. Need more be said?

***

Since then the political focus on our arts engagement with Asia has remained low. Various arts ministers have come and gone, none with any particular interest in Asia. The strongest supporter was Alexander Downer when he was Minister for Foreign Affairs. Near the end of the Coalition's eleven-year incumbency, in response to sustained lobbying and in partnership with the Arts Minister Rod Kemp, they announced new support of $20 million over four years to take Australia's arts to the world and especially Asia. However, the incoming Labor Government then imposed a 2% 'efficiency dividend' on all federal departments. What was among the first money that DFAT surrendered? This hard-won funding for the arts. Why? Probably because it was too closely identified with Downer. DFAT had never placed a high value on cultural exchange, and perhaps it thought that, as a new program, no-one would notice its untimely demise.

Both authors of this Paper have had meetings with arts ministers of both sides, in the attempt to further the Asia cause, but with little success, apart from the short life of Downer's $20 million, of which we believe less than $500,000 had been committed before the program was axed. It cannot be that government ministers are unaware of the dynamic growth and change across the region. Why then is it so difficult to imagine how engaging with Asian cultural markets might also inject a beneficial new dynamism into the Australian cultural sector? Is it such a low priority because politicians think there are no votes in the arts, let alone in artistic engagement with Asia? Or is it because the arts community itself is too uninterested to use their potentially powerful voice to tell them otherwise? Does working in Asia simply sound like a junket? Anyone who has tried to build an overseas project that transcends cultural difference—to raise funding, generate partnerships, profile and audiences—knows that the idea of it being a junket is laughable.

Now, under Arts Minister Simon Crean, we have the promise of a new national cultural policy, the first in sixteen years. Interestingly, his national cultural policy discussion paper, circulated in 2011 to provoke the arts industry's response, did not mention 'Asia' once in connection with the arts. We hope that when the policy is released it will rectify this omission. Addressing the Ten Point Plan of action outlined at the end of this Paper would be a good starting point. It would also be productive to link this enriched cultural policy into this same government's White Paper on Australia's broad engagement with the Asian region.

Leading into the recent G20 meeting in Cannes, on 2 November 2011, the British *Guardian* newspaper published a graph of the economic situation of the G20 members. This is the most powerful politico-economic world group to which Australia now belongs, and includes most of Europe, USA, UK and the 'rich' countries of Asia including Japan. Who had the highest Human Development Index (that is, the quality of life index measured in economic terms)? Australia. Our figure was .94. Who had the second highest GDP per capita—tellingly after Singapore? Australia. We can afford to do better.

5

Other government funding bodies

Department of Foreign Affairs and Trade (DFAT)

After the Australia Council, DFAT is the major Commonwealth player involved in taking Australian arts abroad. Not surprisingly they are very different in their focus: the differences in the role of a ministry of foreign affairs and one of the arts is something that often causes strain in countries around the world. Foreign

Ministries want to use the arts to promote an agenda of political and economic advantage for their country; arts ministries usually believe their role is to support artists to be as creative and interesting as possible. Asialink used to say that 10% could always be found at each end of DFAT's and the Australia Council's agendas that was unacceptable to the other (the Council wouldn't fund a politically-pleasing golf exhibition and DFAT wasn't comfortable with sex) but everyone could work well with the 80% in the middle.

DFAT has many outstanding officers who are experts on the politics and economies of particular regions, and not least on Asia, but it is not an arts organisation nor is it staffed by arts professionals. Looking to the political security and economic agenda (core business for DFAT) is not always productive for the arts. DFAT does have a Cultural Relations Branch specifically for its 'soft diplomacy' possibilities but its status in the Department is moot. Where DFAT does sit up and focus on the arts is when an Australian artist presents in another country what DFAT believes to be a negative image of Australia. And occasionally, tension can flare the other way when a diplomat or politician inappropriately exploits an art piece for political ends. But DFAT is a good partner. It knows the international situation. In our experience the locally-engaged arts officers in Australian diplomatic posts abroad are usually well-informed about the local cultural and current conditions in a way that we cannot emulate from Australia. On the other hand they know little of the complexities of the field in Australia itself. A supportive Ambassador can make a huge difference to the conduct of our cultural engagement, even when the Embassy's direct budget for such work is painfully small.

In the 1980s Australia went through a period when DFAT appointed specialist arts people as cultural counsellors to major posts in Asia. Carrillo had that experience in Beijing 1985–87 following his eight years at Playbox where he was actively engaged with China. Others are the cultural writers Jennifer Lindsay in Jakarta, Alison Broinowski in Tokyo; and, succeeding Gantner, Nicholas Jose in Beijing. Soon after his appointment as Foreign Minister, Alexander Downer cancelled these positions on the grounds of cost savings. It is understood that it costs around $500,000 to keep an Australian-based officer in the field.[9] DFAT's budget saved costs, but what we lost were people on the ground with active and informed cultural fluency and networks in both countries. They had status and 'clout' with government and cultural circles in the host country that their locally engaged replacements could never enjoy. They had authority to negotiate exchange programs, and, frankly, were able on occasion to bypass the Department in Canberra to facilitate links more speedily.

We believe there is more that DFAT could do even within existing resources to enhance Australia's broad relationships with regional countries. Placing a higher value on the role of culture only enhances other dimensions of any bilateral relationship. Many Australians still think that culture is what you do on Saturday night. Across Asia, culture has a much broader meaning, encompassing language, history, philosophy, food, arts and much else. In countries like China where culture and ideology are intimate bedfellows, an understanding of the intricacies of the culture becomes doubly important.

DFAT bilateral councils

The DFAT-funded bilateral councils, like the Australia-Indonesia Institute (AII), the Australia-China Council (ACC), the Australia-Korea Foundation (AKF) and the Australia-Japan Foundation (AJF) each receive dismal funding: the AKF, for instance, receives $750,000 per annum to distribute across the entire range of culture, media, education, science and technology, Australian studies programs and any other people-to-people exchange areas. The councils all make some valuable and productive grants across diverse areas but, in most cases, current funding is less than they received when they were established 20 to 30 years ago. They also have high overhead costs relative to their grant-making capacity and they each keep to their own territory. It seems to us worth proposing a wider discussion of their role. While we can understand that no Australian government has wanted to be seen downgrading relations with these countries, it is surely worth examining whether other models might serve our national interest better. Would putting the funding for all the councils into one collective 'pot' provide a more strategic and coordinated approach to our relations with the region?

The Australian International Cultural Council

For the several Australian Focus Country promotions in Asia over the last two decades, the Australian International Cultural Council (AICC), funded by DFAT and chaired by the Minister for Foreign Affairs, has been the lead agency. Their website states:

> The AICC mounts country-specific cultural programs which aim to strengthen and deepen ties with the countries through

integrated events and activities in the performing arts, visual arts, literature and film.

So far it has undertaken focus-country or focus-region promotions in:

2001	United States
2002	Germany and China
2003	Germany and Japan
2004	South East Asia
2005	Singapore, United Kingdom and India
2006	United Kingdom and India
2007	France and Malaysia
2008	Indonesia
2009	United States
2010	China
2011	Republic of Korea
2012	India

The figures for international funding from the Australia Council have usually reflected the engagement of Australian artists in these promotions.

For the successful Japan and India promotions, Australia had specialist arts people on the ground in each place. These people in turn brought in various arts institutional partners, especially Australian, that were keen to work in the host country. Many of these partners brought a lot of their own resources and often they had existing connections with the country on which they were keen to build. But there has been little support to follow up the initiatives already taken so the goodwill and potential built has been allowed to fade. Governments by their nature deal in tangibles: they count the media space achieved and the audience numbers, then move on. The train had moved to another station.

The model for these major promotions seems to work well if:

- They are driven by specialist arts people who understand how to make the most of the available resources;
- The resources of all parties are combined;
- A long lead-time is available to make the relationships productive;
- The artists and companies included in the program already have a commitment to the host country and already have relationships there. This is especially important if there is a collaborative element to the work presented;
- There is support to continue to build on the events in the promotion in the years that follow. Often this is critical to any real legacy.

Would these promotions not work even more effectively every time if there were better advance coordination between a single agency charged with the delivery of Australian culture abroad and if they were led by an experienced arts manager? In this way there would be one pool of money for artists and companies, and one management to deal with them instead of being shunted off to scrounge funds from a variety of sources. We discuss this in the options for the future at the end of this Paper.

AusAID

AusAID, which sits within DFAT, plays a very important role in the delivery of Australian international aid programs, not least in Asia. It currently funds little in the arts, focusing on 'capacity building' which in their framework sits uneasily with arts activities. There are some 'capacity-building' arenas, especially in a place like Indonesia, where cultural programs of skills and management training could be beneficial—Australia has excellent institutions and programs for the professional training of artists and arts managers, and our arts infrastructure is very strong. Bringing students into these programs would enhance a country's capacity to strengthen its own cultural assets and create future partners for cultural exchange. One of Asialink's many projects has been the production of three popular 'how-to' booklets in the Indonesian language on Event Management, Exhibition Touring and Community Cultural Development for use in that country. Australia could do much more in this field.

Australian cultural centres

In the past, some Australian posts have included spaces and program support for cultural events within the diplomatic compound. Manila had a very successful Australia Centre in the early 1990s, and Jakarta, Kuala Lumpur and Singapore were among posts that had active programs on site. The threat of terrorism put paid to these, but also time has moved on. The arts have become more sensitive to the overt role of Government hovering over them, and an arms-length relationship is both cheaper and more credible.

Our advocacy is for Australian cultural centres, located at arm's length from Government, including a physical presence separate from the Australian diplomatic post in that country. Some six years ago the Australia Indonesia Institute investigated the cost of setting up an Australian Cultural Centre in Yogyakarta. The cost of rent for suitable premises, one Australian locally engaged director, three or four local staff, and some core running costs totalled around $200,000 per annum. In countries like Indonesia or India where local infrastructure is tricky, this makes good cultural and financial sense.

A similar facility in China would be a more expensive proposition today. Major city rents are rising as the country moves to a market economy. But many other countries have made the jump and opened important cultural centres in Beijing: the Japanese, French, German and Spanish all have facilities there and regard them as central to their efforts to keep their national profiles high on the Chinese agenda. In Beijing, Australia only manages one locally engaged officer working in the cultural field and reporting to the public affairs counsellor whose focus is on gaining local media attention, most often for visiting Australian ministers.

The states' agencies

We mention almost in passing the state government arts agencies involved in international relations as our experience inevitably focuses on Victoria and its agency Arts Victoria. Mainly through Asialink, however, we have had some experience of the arts agencies of other states. State agencies are important supporters of Asian programs through their grant systems and also through their support of key arts organisations. Queensland has made a big point of supporting Asian initiatives such as the Asia Pacific Triennial. Western Australia had a policy of supporting Indian Ocean programs for a time, but this seems to have faded.

Victoria has a good record as a supporter of international activity. This support is based on the state's policy document *Victoria and the Arts 21 Strategy* which was published by the Kennett Government in 1996 and has had bipartisan support from successive Victorian governments.[10] Arts 21 established a stand-alone International Program with specialist staff and policies. These staff could work across art forms, appropriate in the international context. The policy has been flexible and responsive, accepting proposals from the sector as well as initiating new programs itself. Arts Victoria has been happy to work with the Australia Council and DFAT, and has been willing to amend programs to meet their different criteria. Their funding for their international work, however, has diminished from around $800,000 in 1999 to $620,000 today, although this does not include any special allocation. In 2011 this added another $150,000.

New South Wales is notorious for leaving its state-based international activity to the Australia Council. It has always claimed to have very meagre funding for Asialink programs (though the NSW arts staff have tried hard to make things happen). Apart from Victoria, none of the other states has stand-alone programs. From Asialink's experience, a good relationship with Asia has existed naturally in the Northern Territory, though their budgets have decreased in recent years. Arts NT has always been interested in programs which include their artists working in Asia (projects in the Philippines and in Eastern Indonesia come to mind), and which take advantage of their proximity and expertise.

Arts Victoria has taken Asia seriously. It has a memorandum of understanding with the Singapore National Arts Council and a whole-of-government relationship with China and Japan through Sister-State links with Jiangsu and Aichi. These include the arts. For state governments, trading partnerships are always in mind, but Arts Victoria insists that the opportunities are for artists in their own right. In assessing Asia-related projects, Arts Victoria looks for opportunities, creative engagement, some financial return and—of particular relevance for the performing arts—an extension of the original season to expand the employment of artists. It's an excellent model and its reach and effectiveness would be enhanced with greater funding.

6
Arts training

A key part of the Asia agenda ought to be what we learn about Asian culture, especially as part of our secondary and tertiary education, and in particular, in specialist arts areas. Knowledge, it is said, is power. The introduction to the Federal Government's discussion paper on a new *National Cultural Policy 2011* notes the importance of training in the arts, and how much money is expended by the Government on the Australian Youth Orchestra, the Australian Ballet School, the Australian National Academy of Music, the National Institute of Dramatic Art (NIDA) and so on. It runs to nearly $20 million per annum. This figure does not include the major state tertiary training providers for the sector, particularly the Victorian College of the Arts (VCA), the Western Australia Academy of Performing Arts (WAAPA), Queensland University of Technology (QUT) or consider the many music conservatoria and other institutions.

This sector, of course, feeds all our performing arts practice.

If Asia is both culturally interesting and nationally important, it is surely worth contemplating how much focus our arts training institutions place on teaching their students about Asia and Asian cultural practice. Little has changed since the early 1990s. What Alison Carroll wrote for an Asia Education Foundation Conference in 1994 holds true today: 'People don't want to teach about Asia because they don't feel they have the background—there is nervousness to address the huge cultural issues and agendas under-riding much of Asia's cultural work.'[11]

Then, eleven years ago, in 2000, in a paper for the Asian Studies Association of Australia Conference, she argued for 10% of the international curriculum in our tertiary arts education sector being focused on studies of Asia 'by 2005'.[12] This very modest target seems today almost unattainable. The paper quoted Peter Eckersall, an expert in Japanese theatre, who:

> believes there is a decrease in the amount of material on Asia in curricula because of perceived economic forces on graduates... recently more conventional training institutions for mainstream theatre practice have retreated from anything except EuroAmerica. We are seeing a narrowing of outcomes, determined by a supposed notion of what the industry is.

Alison did an audit of what was happening in the tertiary training sector at that time, and found almost no change since the early 1990s in the formal core curricula of the institutions in which these staff and students taught or studied.

The research in 2000 saw Queensland University of Technology as the most proactive institution in the area of Asian cultural literacy, with courses including Dance and Theatre of Asia, Asian Identities and Visual Arts of Asia among their offerings. These changes arose from QUT's internationalisation policy articulated in the mid-1990s, access to wider expertise across the whole university, the appointment of key people like dancer Cheryl Stock, who had had long experience of working in Vietnam, to head dance in the Creative Industries Department at QUT, and many exchanges of staff and students.

There was, however, a significant increase in personal exchanges among staff and students ('lots of travel, lots of residencies, lots of guest lecturers'). These short sharp residency and guest projects are, of course, very welcome. In the early 2000s, Lindy Davies, then head of the School of Drama at the VCA, spoke of the residency of Indonesian dance master Sardono Kusumo: 'You had an immense impact upon the students. Your ability to interface your own traditional training and your experience of Western art was inspiring.'[13]

Some of the training schools have benefitted from the importation of Asian experts and a range of independent artists have had a continuing influence on the development of technical skills and work disciplines in the fields of acrobatics, circus and physical theatre across generations and geography. Lu Guang Rong, today the head of teaching at the National Institute of Circus Arts in Melbourne, itself a direct outcome of the Nanjing Project, was one of seven visiting teachers in 1983. Twenty years ago, Dr Chandrabanu led the professional Bharatham Indian Dance Company in Melbourne, but has long since returned to Malaysia to pursue his art and teaching.

***

So what is the situation in arts education in 2012? How things are presented is important and indicative of an issue's sensitivity. In this light, the VCA's promotional brochure for its 2012 programs is notable for not including one student profile or general photography of a person of Asian background—though the student cohort includes many. Under the course offerings, any reference to Asia is slight and fleeting (for example, only one among 15 of the 'leading figures' from the industry coming as guest lecturers is of Asian background, while nine are from Europe and the UK). Musicology/Ethnomusicology refers to the French Revolution, Stravinsky and Wagner, and even Latin America, but there is no mention of Asia at all.

Besides the professional training programs at the VCA, WAAPA and NIDA, there are many more general performing arts programs at QUT, Ballarat, Deakin, Monash, Flinders, UNSW and Wollongong that can and do include small elements on Asian performing arts in their programs, but in none is it core curriculum. Queensland again seems to be in the forefront with the Conservatorium of Music in Brisbane including a three-year program built around Indonesian performing arts. At a time when the Australian university funding model has pushed our tertiary institutions to chase high-fee paying students from Asia to sustain their core operations, is it not extraordinary and depressing that no Australian tertiary institution providing professional arts training, or more general performing arts studies, has made any serious effort to develop core curricula offerings around the arts of Asia?

For tertiary institutions focused on getting their students jobs in the future, understanding the way the arts of Asia work must be a key component for enabling them to work in our own neighbourhood. It is about the performing arts representing the world that in itself is cross-cultural. Knowing about Kabuki, Beijing Opera or the wayang forms may not seem essential for a young Australian actor wanting to appear on television, but an appreciation of such different forms can only expand an artist's expressive vocabulary and enrich their experience.

Of course, the education sector is itself self-reflexive. If there are not the right skills in the mix, the students who might one day teach are not taught. In the last year, agreement among the states has been reached for the first time to include in the new national curriculum of the secondary school sector an underlying theme of understanding Asia, so perhaps in some years' time we might begin to see wider change: information on Asia at school should, we assume, lead in due course to changes at the tertiary level and beyond. Such things ought to be self-evident to more people, not least those in positions of leadership. Sadly, however, even the relevance of the proposed theme has been challenged by some in the Federal Opposition.

7
Towards a better future: a ten point plan

As we have outlined, there are serious problems in the field of Australia's cultural engagement with Asia. The authors have talked and written about these matters for 25 years and yet so little has changed. We want to see more. We need action— action backed with sticks and carrots—or we shall continue to lose out in so many ways detrimental to our collective and creative interests.

We therefore put forward a Ten Point Plan to redress the focus over the next ten years. We need specific policy, specific money allocated against targets, and a specific body to realise this agenda. Here is the Plan:

1. Funding quotas

Funding is crucial. So is its intelligent application. Of the Australia Council's and DFAT's Cultural Relations budget we advocate 60% of international funding be allocated for Asian engagement over the next ten years. Today the Australia Council's international funding for Asia is around 20%. We need to raise the bar.

It is always controversial to put percentage quotas on funding figures. You can always make a case against quotas 'for Asia': 'Artists want to go to London, Berlin, Florence or New York, not Beijing, Delhi, Tokyo or Jakarta.' Arguing for Asia is harder. The focus on Asia is in our national interest. Logically that means it needs more resources and attention, not less.

2. Spread of focus

As a broad guideline that reflects relevance and opportunity, we propose expending this 60% as follows:

China (including Hong Kong and Taiwan)	20–30%
Japan and Korea	20–25%
India	15–20%
Indonesia	15–20%
Balance of SE Asia	15–20%
Total	**85–115%**

3. The Middle Way

By the Middle Way we mean that open stage between individual engagement (e.g. residencies) and the big tours by major companies. This is where the creative collaborations between Australian artists and colleagues in the region are supported to develop new projects and present them to audiences in the participating countries and beyond. This should be established as a new program with new funding, a minimum of $3 million per annum to be administered by a new Australian International Cultural Agency (AICA)(see Point 8).

4. In-country Australian cultural centres

In-country Australian cultural centres should be established in key places, especially in priority countries and where existing local infrastructure is minimal. Start with India and Indonesia. The new centres should be established as independent NGOs at arm's length from government but with advance funding commitment on a rolling triennial basis for their ongoing operation and programs.

5. Arts management capacity building in Asia

A program of support from AusAID should be established to bring arts managers and students to Australia from developing countries to participate in the arts management programs which already exist at tertiary level in most states. An evaluation should also be made of the potential to deliver short-term arts management programs and materials in the region.

6. Cultural directors in key embassies

Australian-based cultural directors drawn from the ranks of professional arts and cultural managers should be reappointed to key Australian diplomatic posts. The directors of established in-country centres might also fill this role. Otherwise the cultural directors should be employed by the new agency, the AICA, but be attached to the Australian diplomatic mission. Priority missions are those in Beijing and Tokyo along with Jakarta and New Delhi until such time as Australian cultural centres can be established in the latter two. We would also want to see cultural directors posted to our missions in Seoul, Bangkok and Singapore at the earliest opportunity.

7. Major events

Major events can have various manifestations but the currently favoured model is the year-long Australian cultural promotion program in another country. We have noted previously how these can be run effectively. The funding can be co-ordinated through one agency (see Point 8). It is our view that the very big companies such as the Australian Ballet and the symphony orchestras should only be included in these promotional years when and if they have already built real, long-term creative relationships in the host country, and if they are touring a repertoire that is distinctively Australian. Otherwise, taking a hundred Australian musicians to give concerts of Mahler and Mozart in Shanghai is largely a waste of money and effort.

8. A new Australian International Cultural Agency

Within three years, all related Federal Government funding should be brought together into one new body, provisionally named here as the Australian International Cultural Agency (AICA), although following the Goethe-Institut's example, the name of an Australian cultural icon might equally be used. The AICA should have government representation but operate at arm's length from government. Its functions would include:

- Strategic overview;
- Linkage of programs to national priorities and national interest;
- Establishment of funding priorities;
- Program development;

- Funding of major national profiling years;
- Promotion of a positive international image for Australia (Brand Australia) and especially in Asia, through many channels including programs that nurture rich cultural exchange, wide people-to-people diplomacy, and the development of Australian Studies abroad;
- Recruitment of the cultural directors to be posted to the major Australian diplomatic missions (see Point 6).

What is the appropriate level of funding for the AICA? If we started by putting in one pot the funding currently spent by the Australia Council's international programs, DFAT's Cultural Relations budget and the cultural budgets of DFAT bilateral councils and the Australian International Cultural Council, we would have a strong starting point. More could obviously be achieved with more, but it is not just new resources that are needed but new resources well applied through a strategic framework and coordinated program delivery.

The common arguments against such a body are these:

- Cost. But surely the virtues of a clear strategy, co-ordination of resources and forward planning is as valid here as in any other area of activity? Surely it might even save some ineffective expenditure?
- Our small population. It is said that the other countries that have such bodies, like the British, French, Germans, Japanese, Italians, Koreans, Chinese, Dutch, Swiss and Scandinavians have a much bigger population and GDP than Australia. In many cases this patently untrue. Taking Britain as an example—a country with three times our

population—we would be much better resourced than we are now if we could allocate a third of the British Council's budget to AICA.

- Unnecessary change. People and organisations always defend their patch. It's natural. So the most commonly used argument against change is that it won't be the same. Exactly.

Frankly, even if you accepted the points against change, we would argue that we need such a body more than the other countries. Apart from our geographic proximity to, and our economic dependence on, Asia, we are huge within our own borders and difficult to access externally and internally. We are 'confusing' to people in Asia because of our Indigenous/British/immigrant/transitional culture. As a nation we aren't easy to understand, which often tells against us, as do our regular political swings and roundabouts. And then, we criticise ourselves too much. We are not good natural promoters of ourselves. A new body would work to counter these negatives more effectively.

9. Tertiary education

As a prerequisite for funding, all tertiary education programs for arts practitioners must include at least 20% Asian content in their core curricula, including Asian histories, cultures and art forms, as well as practical sessions with visiting Asian artists and teachers, and collaborative projects with Asian creative colleagues. This matter should be monitored and coordinated by each education provider's Academic Board.

10. A major review

A first step towards establishing a new Australian International Cultural Agency is for the Government to initiate a major review/ inquiry into the delivery of our overseas cultural engagement and especially with Asia, by appointing a small, senior review panel backed by staff and resources. The panel's terms of reference should include a review of the current situation, a comparative examination of how other countries conduct and resource their cultural engagement programs, and recommendations to government on how things could be improved for Australia's benefit.

As Mao Zedong said, we learn from the past to serve the future. Let us learn and act.

Endnotes

---

1. We have used terms like 'Asia' and 'cultural engagement' as usually accepted in practice in Australia: that the geographic region includes the region east of Pakistan, and 'North Asia' includes the various Chinas, Japan and Korea, 'South East Asia' the countries of ASEAN and the old Indo-China and 'South Asia' the Indian subcontinent, including Pakistan. Cultural engagement is a broad term; for this Paper we take it to mean the space where people who work or take part in the arts (as creators, administrators, audiences, discussants), and who come from different backgrounds, get together to exchange ideas or work or to do whatever is meaningful.
2. Edward Said, *Orientalism*. Vintage Books, 1979.
3. James R. Brandon, *The Cambridge Guide to Asian Theatre*. Cambridge University Press, 1997, p.10.
4. Australia Council, *Annual Report*, 1993–94, pp. 20-1.

5. The Australia Council figures are meant as trends. They are taken from the following sections of the Council's program areas:

   Dance: Touring; Presentation and Promotion; Development; Skills and Development; Partnerships and International Ties; Market Development.

   Music: Touring; Presentation and Promotion; Development; International Pathways; Skills and Development; International; Skills.

   Theatre/Drama: Touring; Presentation and Promotion; Development; Playing the World; Skills and Development.

   Performing Arts: International Audience Development and Advocacy; International Marketing and Promotions; International Activities; International Market Development and Promotion; International Export and Market Development; Arts Export; 2002 Showcases; Performing Arts Markets; International Market Development and Promotions.

   Arts Development: Community Partnerships and Market Development; International Market Development; Strategic Market Development.

6. Jennifer Lindsay, *Cultural Organisation in Southeast Asia: a guide for artists, performers and cultural workers*. Australia Council, Department of Foreign Affairs and Trade and Myer Foundation, 1994.
7. Nick Bryant, interview with Geraldine Doogue on *Saturday Extra*, ABC Radio National, September 3, 2011.
8. Australia Council promotional folder, June 1999.
9. This figure was quoted for a senior member of staff in Tokyo. No doubt other cities would be cheaper. There are two usual lines of employment at Australia's over-seas posts: 'Australia-based' or shorthand 'A-based', meaning the person is sent from Australia and their employment includes salary, living and travel costs for them and their family, school fees and so on; and the second is 'locally-engaged', where the person lives locally and just has their salary paid. The second is obviously cheaper.
10. *Arts Victoria and the Arts 21 Strategy: Maintaining the State for the Arts.*

Auditor General's Special Report 41 ordered under Section 16 of the Audit Act 1994, Victorian Government Printer, 1996.

11. 'Asia and Arts Teaching'. Asia Education Foundation Conference, October 10–11, 1994.

12. '10% for Asia'. Asian Studies Association of Australia, Annual Conference, Melbourne, July, 2000.

13. 35,000 days in Asia. Asialink Residency Program, 2004, p. 56.

List of Platform Papers

Platform Papers

First published July 2004

PP1 *'Our ABC'—A Dying Culture?* Martin Harrison

PP2 *Survival of the Fittest: The artist versus the corporate world*, Christopher Latham

2005

PP3 *Trapped by the Past: Why our theatre is facing paralysis*, Julian Meyrick

PP4 *The Myth of the Mainstream: Politics and the performing arts in Australia today*, Robyn Archer

PP5 *Shooting Through: Australian film and the brain drain*, Storry Walton

PP6 *Art in a Cold Climate: Rethinking the Australia Council*, Keith Gallasch

2006

PP7 *Does Australia Need a Cultural Policy?* David Throsby

PP8 *Body for Hire? The state of dance in Australia*, Amanda Card

PP9 *What Price a Creative Economy?* Stuart Cunningham

PP10 *Satire—or Sedition? The threat to national insecurity*, Jonathan Biggins

2007

PP11 *A Regional State of Mind: Making art outside metropolitan Australia*, Lyndon Terracini

PP12 *Film in the Age of Digital Distribution: The challenge for Australian content*, Richard Harris

PP13 *Cross-racial Casting: Changing the face of Australian theatre*, Lee Lewis

PP14 *Who Profits from the Arts? Taking the measure of culture*, Kay Ferres and David Adair

2008

PP15 *A Sustainable Arts Sector: What will it take?* Cathy Hunt and Phyllida Shaw

PP16 *The Permanent Underground: Australian contemporary jazz in the new Millennium*, Peter Rechniewski

PP17 *What is an Australian Play? Have we failed our ethnic writers?* Chris Mead

PP18 *Getting Heard: Achieving an effective arts advocacy*, Chris Puplick

2009

PP19 *'Your Genre is Black': Indigenous performing arts and policy*, Hilary Glow and Katya Johanson

PP20 *Beethoven or Britney: The great divide in music education*, Robert Walker

PP21 *Television: What will rate in the new tomorrow?* Ian David

PP22 *Copyright, Collaboration and the Future of Dramatic Authorship*, Brent Salter

2010 (one paper cancelled)

PP23 *Whatever Happened to the STC Actors Company?* James Waites

PP24 *The Digital Playing Fields: New rulz for film art and performance*, Shilo McClean

PP25 *Moving Across Disciplines: Dance in the twenty-first century*, Erin Brannigan

2011

PP26 *Not Just an Audience: Young people transforming our theatre*, Lenine Bourke and Mary Ann Hunter

PP27 *Hello, World! Promoting the arts on the web*, Robert Reid

PP28 *The Fall and Rise of the VCA*, Richard Murphet

PP29 *Democracy versus Creativity in Australian Classical Music*, Nicole Canham

2012

PP30 *Indig-curious: Who can play Aboriginal roles?* Jane Harrison

PP31 *Finding a Place on the Asian Stage*, Alison Carroll and Carrillo Gantner

PP32 *History is Made at Night: Live music in Australia*, Clinton Walker

PP33 *Changing Times at NIDA*, Chris Puplick

2013

PP34 *It's Culture, Stupid! Reflections of an arts bureaucrat*, Leigh Tabrett

PP35 *The Music of Place: Reclaiming the practice*, Jon Rose

PP 36 *Re-valuing the Artist in the New World Order*, David Pledger

PP37 *Not at a Cinema Near You: Australia's film distribution problem*, Lauren Carroll Harris

2014

PP38 *Enlightenment or Entitlement? Rethinking tertiary music education*, Peter Tregear

PP39 *The Retreat of our National Drama*, Julian Meyrick

PP40 *Take Me to Your Leader: The dilemma of cultural leadership*, Wesley Enoch

PP41 *Education and the Arts: Creativity in the promised new order*, Meg Upton with Naomi Edwards

2015

PP42 *The Time Is Ripe for the Great Australian Musical*, John Senczuk

PP43 *The Arts and the Common Good*, Katharine Brisbane

PP44 *Cultural Precincts: Art or commodity?* Justin Macdonnell

PP45 *Paying the Piper: There has to be another way*, Cathy Hunt

2016

PP46 *The Designer: Decorator or dramaturg?* Stephen Curtis

PP47 *Why We Need a Cultural Economy*, Justin O'Connor

PP48 *When the Goal Posts Move*, Ben Eltham

PP49 *The Lighting Designer: What is 'good' lighting?* Nigel Levings

2017

PP50 *Restless Giant: Changing cultural values in regional Australia*, Lindy Hume

PP51 *Missing in Action: The ABC and Australia's screen culture*, Kim Dalton

PP52 *Putting Words in their Mouths: The playwright and screenwriter at work*, Andrew Bovell

PP53 *The Jobbing Actor: Rules of engagement*, Lex Marinos

2018

PP54 *Young People and the Arts: An agenda for change*, Sue Giles

PP55 *Art, Politics, Money: Revisiting Australia's cultural policy*, David Throsby

PP56 *Falling Through the Gaps: Our artists' health and welfare*, Mark RW Williams

PP57 *Cultural Justice and the Right to Thrive*, Scott Rankin

2019

PP58 *The Changing Landscape of Australian Documentary*, Tom Zubrycki

PP59 *Ngarra-Burria: New music and the search for an Australian sound*, Christopher Sainsbury

PP60 *Capturing the Vanishing: A choreographer and film*, Sue Healey

PP61 *Criticism, Performance and the Need for Conversation*, Alison Croggon

2020

PP62 *Performing Arts Markets and their Conundrums*, Justin Macdonnell

2021

PP63 *On the Lessons of History*, Katharine Brisbane

The New Platform Papers

2021

Vol. 1 *What Future for the Arts in a post-Pandemic World?*

Foreword by Julian Meyrick

Season's Greetings from Katharine Brisbane

No. 1 *Imagininaton in the Arts and Economics: papers from the inaugural Platform Papers Authors Convention*

'Introduction: A Snail May Put His Horns Out', Harriet Parsons

'Models, Uncertainty and Imagination in Economics', Richard Bronk

'What's Wrong with Cannibalism?' Jonathan Biggins and John Quggin,

'The Fable of the Bees' (1714), Bernard Mandeville

'A Modest Proposal' (1729), Jonathan Swift

'You Can Sing (Averagely)!', Astrid Jorgensen

PP63 *On the Lessons of History,* Katharine Brisbane (2021 reprint)

2022

Vol. 2 *From the Heart: The Voice, the Arts and Australian Identity*

Foreword by Julian Meyrick

Season's Greetings from Katharine Brisbane

No. 2 *Arts, Culture and Country*, Josephine Caust

'The Trouble with this Canoe', Tyson Yunkaporta

'*J'accuse*: Australia's great crim against the jobless', Noel Pearson.

No. 3 *From the Heart: the imperative for the arts~the sector responds: papers from the second Platform Papers Authors Convention*

'The Meaningful Expression of Indigenous Sovereignty through the Uluru Statement From the Heart', Eddie Synot

'Art, Culture and Voice', Sally Scales

'Re-RIGHT-ing the Narrative', Rachael Maza

PP40 *Take Me to Your Leader: The dilemma of cultural leadership,* Wesley Enoch (2014 reprint)

CURRENCY HOUSE INC.

Currency House is a not-for-profit organisation devoted to promoting wider understanding of the work of artists and creative practitioners and how it contributes to Australia's social and political life.

currencyhouse.org.au

ISBN: 978-1-922762-55-9
ISSN: 2653-3308

Correspondence should be addressed to:
The Editor
The New Platform Papers
P. O. Box 2270
Strawberry Hills NSW 2012 Australia
Email: editor@currencyhouse.org.au

Typeset in Garamond.
Printed in Australia by Ligare Book Printers, Riverwood.
The paper used to produce this book comes from wood grown in sustainable forests.